PH6
250

THE DESIGN
OF
SUBURBIA

a critical study in environmental history

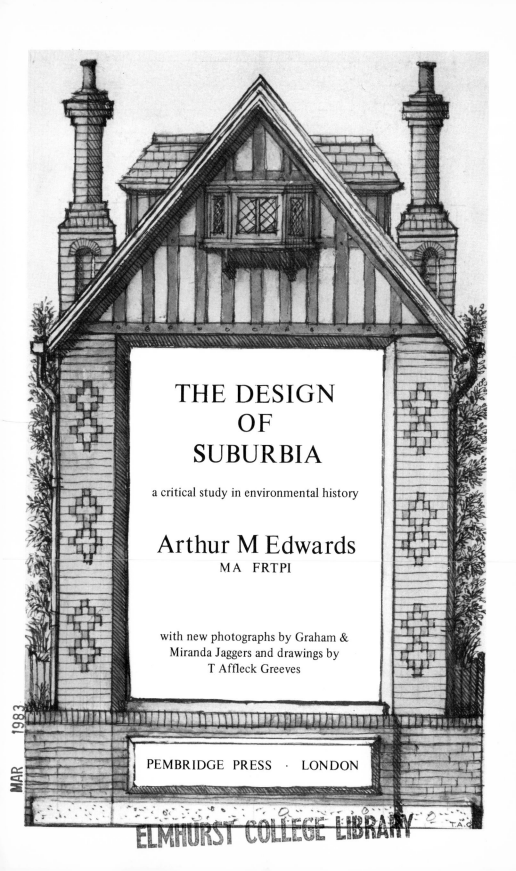

THE DESIGN OF SUBURBIA

a critical study in environmental history

Arthur M Edwards
MA FRTPI

with new photographs by Graham &
Miranda Jaggers and drawings by
T Affleck Greeves

PEMBRIDGE PRESS · LONDON

FIRST PUBLISHED 1981 BY PEMBRIDGE PRESS LTD
16 PEMBRIDGE ROAD LONDON W11 UK
SET IN 11 ON 12 POINT BASKERVILLE BY ALLSET
AND PRINTED AND BOUND IN THE UK BY
REDWOOD BURN LTD OF TROWBRIDGE AND ESHER
ISBN: 0-86206-002-8

To My Wife and Daughters:
Christine, Jennifer, Alison, Miranda

CONTENTS

ACKNOWLEDGEMENTS

This book has been written intermittently over a period of twenty-five years. I have, in consequence, lost touch with some of those who helped me in the earlier stages. I hope that anyone whose name has been omitted from the following paragraphs will accept my apologies. I have tried to keep the list short. A long list of names is tedious reading unless one happens to be directly involved. I must however thank:

First, my wife Christine, for putting up with me, and with the book, so joyously and for so long.

Second, my daughter and son-in-law, Miranda and Graham Jaggers, for taking and processing all but a few of the ground-level photographs, as well as some of those which come from published sources. Theirs was a long and often tedious task. The reader can judge how admirably it has been performed.

Third, my friend Thomas Greeves, for his page decorations. Ability such as his is, by definition, rare.

Fourth, my colleagues at the Polytechnic of Central London; Denis Broodbank and Professor Wilfred Ashworth.

Fifth, my typists Gina Lee, Marian Meads and Anita King, not only for typing the text, but even more for the diligence with which they interpreted my all but illegible handwriting.

Sixth, Richard Anderson and Gina Dionisotti for their bibliographical assistance. I know that theirs was a frustrating job. I suspect that it was often tedious also.

Seventh, Robert Meadows, Donald Barron, John Palmer, Ralph Rookwood, Leath Waide, Robert Thorne, Gillian Darley, Alan Jackson, Donald Greaves, Russell Craig, Mervyn Miller, Richard Lyons, Alan Jago and Carole James for reading parts of the text and making most helpful comments upon it. I need hardly add that what appears is my responsibility, not theirs.

Eighth, the staff of all the libraries where I have worked; in particular, those of the School of the Environment at the Polytechnic of Central London, and three of the specialist sections of the British Library (The Map Library and the Official Publications Library) and the British Architectural Library, formerly the library of the RIBA, for their courtesy and help in steering me through the jungles of their cataloguing systems.

Lastly, my colleagues in the School of Town Planning, the Regent Street Polytechnic, who, desperately overworked themselves, gladly agreed that I should have a term's study-leave so that I might be able to prepare the penultimate draft.

ILLUSTRATIONS: Apart from a few diagrams, the illustrations in this book fall into two categories: photographs taken by my daughter and son-in-law, Miranda and Graham Jaggers (together with a very few taken by myself), and photographs taken by others. The first category may be subdivided into two groups: on the one hand, illustrations of street-views and details of buildings, and, on the other, photographs of drawings, engravings, etc.

I have already expressed, in the list of acknowledgements, my gratitude to Miranda and Graham. I should like to reiterate my thanks, adding that the photographs which were chosen for inclusion are less than half of those which they took and processed. I must also thank those who gave permission either for their material to be photographed or for their own pictures to be reproduced. The illustrations in each group are numbered as follows:

1 Photographs taken by Miranda and Graham Jaggers

(a) Street-views and details of buildings: 1, 2, 4, 8, 11, 12, 14, 15, 17, 18, 20, 21, 24, 25, 28, 29, 38, 39, 41, 42, 43, 44, 45, 47, 48, 50, 51, 57, 58, 60, 61, 62, 64, 66, 72, 73, 75, 76, 82, 84, 86, 89, 90, 92, 93, 95, 97, 98, 100, 101, 102, 104, 105, 107, 109, 117, 119, 121, 124, 125, 131.

(b) Photographs of drawings, engravings etc with their sources: 3 Members' Library, Greater London Council; 5 Bedford Estate Archives; 9 The RIBA's British Architectural Library; 22 Guildford District Council; 34 Library of the Victoria and Albert Museum; 52, 53, 87a to 87j The British Library, Newspaper Library Colindale; 81 Garden exhibition, Victoria and Albert Museum (held in 1979); 126, 127 The Essex Design Guide.

2 Photographs taken by others: 7, 36, 49, 59, 70, 71, 74, 77, 80, 85, 88, 91, 96, 99, 103, 106, 108, 112, 116, 121, 122, 123 Aerofilms and Aero Pictures Ltd; 10, 40, 46, 54, 65, 67, 69 The RIBA's British Architectural Library; 23, 26, 27, 30, 31, 32, 33, 37, 68 The British Library Reference Division, including the Map Library and Official Publications Library; 110, 111, 113, 114, 115 Richard Lyons; 128, 129 County Council of Essex; 79, 83 Alan A Jackson; 13, 16, 19 A F Kersting; 6 The Public Records Office; 35 Gillian Darley; 63 The Hulton Picture Library; 78 The London Transport Executive; 94 The Architectural Review; 118, 120 County Council of Cheshire; 130 Sam Lambert.

INTRODUCTION

SUBURBIA is a dirty word. This is natural enough for, with rare exceptions, the appearance of Britain's suburbia is at best dull, and at worst hideous; but it is unfortunate that suburbia has no synonym. The word 'suburbia' is both too precise and too general. It is precise in a geographical sense, and general in the atmosphere which it describes, but is without geographical significance —a village housing-estate in a remote rural area can be an example of suburbia, though it can hardly be called a suburb.

This book is about suburbia, but the reader should try to clear his mind of the word's derogatory implications. For our purposes suburbia is a neutral world. It describes an area of houses. Shops, industrial estates and large blocks of flats are excluded. It is, furthermore, an area of houses which exists as the result of the activities of an estate-developer. The developer may be a city council, a new-town corporation, a speculative builder, or perhaps a farmer who finds that bungalows are a more profitable crop than corn. Thus a village street is not suburbia, since it does not normally derive from the estate-developer's activities, but the nearby council-estate may be.

1: Suburbia in a rural context—a view from the North Downs.

Finally, and most important, suburbia is a hybrid. It possesses something both of the countryside and of the city. It has trees, grass, hedges and flowers, but it also has buildings, streets and pavements. It is a place whose inhabitants are of a broadly similar social class, where the breadwinner sleeps but does not work, where houses are set in gardens, but where the streets have kerbs.

The appearance of suburbia depends on the manner in which houses, streets, fences and planting are related to each other, even more than upon the design of the houses themselves, while its character is the result of the social and economic circumstances of the people for whom it was built.

1

A discussion of suburbia must therefore consider not only the architectural style of the houses and the forms which they took, but also the social habits of their occupants, the shape and character of any gardens, the manner in which the streets were laid out, and how the houses related to them, the ways in which trees were planted and the type of tree employed, the effects of transport and of legislation on housing-layout and, perhaps most important of all, how much the inhabitants of suburbia could afford to spend on their homes.

This book is a history, and, like any history, it is a selective account of past events and situations. The basis of selection is the belief that suburbia will be built in the future as in the past, and that we cannot expect to do better than our forbears if we do not understand the influences which led them to build as they did. This is therefore a purposive as well as a descriptive book; and, because any attempt to build better in the future must be based on an assessment of present circumstances, it takes the story up to the time of writing: the summer of 1980.

The central assumption, that it is possible to make valid critical judgements about the aesthetics of architecture and townscape, is implicit in the opening phrases of this introduction—'With rare exception the appearance of Britain's suburbia is at best dull and at worst hideous'. The assumption is one which few students of these arts would dispute, though I have little doubt that many of them would question the validity of each other's expressed opinions. As to this I can only declare my belief, first that the assumption is correct, and secondly that the judgements which I make can be justified—though like other critics of the art I do not attempt to argue their justification. To do so would involve prefacing this essay with a dissertation on the philosophy of aesthetics, and I doubt whether any of my readers would wish to see that done.

The foregoing paragraphs are an attempt to define the subject of this study precisely and to establish its terms of reference. They are unsatisfactory insofar as suburbia eludes exact definition. The location of an estate does not make it an example of suburbia, nor does suburbia depend entirely upon such matters as housing-density, the way in which an estate grew up, the social class of its inhabitants, or the arrangement of its gardens. Suburbia is, as we have already implied, a matter of atmosphere. This atmosphere is common to Wimbledon, Park Village, Edgbaston, the earlier new towns, Wythenshawe, Peacehaven, the Kingston bypass and St John's Wood. It is with places such as these that this book is concerned.

1 ORIGINS, STYLES AND
INGREDIENTS

1 *The English tradition of housing:* The city dwellers of Britain live by tradition, if not by recent administrative fiat, in houses. Their counterparts on the continent of Europe occupy flats. This book is concerned with the history of suburbia, but before we investigate this phenomenon it may be worth considering why it exists; why, for the most part, the Londoner lives in a house and why he does not occupy a flat like the Parisian.

Many events and situations have produced this result. Other writers have discussed the subject,[1] but the most important reason is also the simplest. Britain is an island. Unlike the countries of the continent, she has not, since the eleventh century, suffered foreign invasion. During the Renaissance the cities of England never had to guard themselves against siege. They were, in consequence, free to grow untrammelled by the needs of defence. The continental city, on the other hand, was constantly in danger of war. It protected itself against this peril by an elaborate system of ravelins, curtain-walls, bastions and redoubts. Building beyond the fortifications was discouraged, if not actually forbidden. Outlying settlements could not be defended and might provide cover for an advancing enemy. When at last the continental city could not grow further, a new set of fortifications was built, the old ones were razed and their site turned into a park or boulevard. The area between the old walls and the new provided a space upon which the town could grow. Usually the walls were kept short (a long perimeter was expensive to build and difficult to defend). In consequence, housing within the city had to be densely concentrated. It usually took the form of flats, and thus, to a Parisian or a Viennese, the flat became the normal form of city-dwelling. In England it was different. The channel provided the fortification, the navy the defence. Cities could spread and the house remained, as it had been during the Middle Ages, the accepted, inevitable home for the Englishman.

The continental city grew like a crab, casting its shell at intervals and forming a new one. The English city grew like lichen, in an irregular formless manner, spreading along roads, engulfing villages and leaving here and there pockets of countryside to form parks. Since the Middle Ages the only effective limits upon the growth of the English city have been its system of transport and the readiness (or ability) of landowners on its periphery to sell for building. It was not until the 1950s that green belts and the redevelopment of our inner-cities led the Englishman to adopt flat-life.

2 *Georgian estate-development:* During the eighteenth century, public transport within the city did not exist.[2] A man going to work, to church or to visit his friends had to walk, ride or travel in his coach. This scarcity of transport, combined with the Englishman's preference for a house, caused the builders of the time to devise a kind of dwelling which could be arranged to provide the maximum number of houses with the minimum of road frontage. They developed the Georgian terrace: a row of contiguous houses formed like towers. The better-class houses were twenty-two to thirty feet

2: *Area steps, Bedford Square, London WC1.*

wide, with a staircase on one side and two rooms (one at the front and one at the rear) on the other. The principal rooms were on the first floor. The servants worked in the basement and slept in the attic. The area with its steps provided a convenient and unobtrusive tradesman's entrance, fuel was stored under the pavement, and the coach, its horses and its driver were accommodated in a mews nearby.

The character of these houses was influenced by local legislation. London's statute was the Building Act of 1774. This was, in the words of Sir John Summerson, 'A milestone in the history of London improvement'.[3] It was a consolidating measure, which tied up the loose ends of many earlier provisions. Its main purposes were to ensure fire-protection and to prevent the jerry-building of party walls. To this end it defined, *inter alia*, four 'rates' of house-building. The first rate included houses which occupied not less than 900 square feet of area, were not less than four storeys high and were valued at over £850. The second rate dropped a storey and had a maximum value of £850. This process continued until the fourth rate was reached. These houses were two storeys high, were valued at a maximum of £150 and occupied less than 350 square feet. Each rate had its own code of structural requirements, but, as Summerson remarks (p126), 'The real importance of the system was not so much that it facilitated the enforcement of a structural code, but that it confirmed a degree of standardisation in speculative building. This was inevitable; for the limitations of size and value set out in the rating tended to create optimum types from which there was no escape and within which very little variation was possible. Especially did the second,

6

third and fourth rates of houses tend to become stereotyped. This was in many ways an excellent thing: it gave some degree of order and dignity to the later suburbs, and incidentally laid down minimum standards of urban housing which would have been decent had they been accompanied by legislation against overcrowding.'

But if the terrace-housing which resulted from the Act possessed a certain order and dignity, it also tended to be monotonous. Over a large area this would have been quite intolerable. One need only imagine an unlimited proliferation of Harley Streets. To avoid such monotony the developers of the time incorporated squares in the layout of their estates. Originally these squares were tree-less. An engraving of St James's Square dated 1749[4] shows

3: St James's Square 1749. Engraving by Sutton Nicholls (first state).

that at that time its centre consisted of a circular pool surrounded by paving and enclosed by an octagonal fence. Other squares had formal gardens of lawns and paved paths, but wide piazzas of this kind were out of keeping with the picturesque movement, and after a few decades they ceased to be fashionable. The taste of the early nineteenth century demanded trees, and soon Humphry Repton laid out the centre of Russell Square, Bloomsbury, in the fashion of the time.[5] Thus a new type of townscape arose; the formal, man-made buildings were contrasted with the picturesque gardens in the

7

centres of the squares. Drama was eschewed. Interest was achieved by antithesis. The streets with their narrow houses, even parapets, rhythmical front doors, wrought-iron railings and tall well-proportioned windows were a foil to the spreading plane trees across the way. There were no front gardens or tree-lined avenues to lessen the impact of this contrast.

4: Bedford Square, London WC1.

Occasionally an ingenious architect devised a variant on the typical georgian estate. Thus at Kensington Park, near Notting Hill Gate, Thomas Allom reversed the georgian pattern and placed the communal open spaces behind the houses instead of setting them in the centres of the squares. This arrangement made it possible for certain of the houses to possess gardens from which their owners could have access to what was, in effect, a small semi-private park situated in the middle of the street block. The system possessed a number of advantages. The communal garden provided an area adjoining the house where children could play in safety and where adults could stroll among the rhododendrons, while the open space in the centre of the block was large enough for tall trees to grow without difficulty. But what the householder gained the public lost. The trees of Kensington Park are hidden behind the houses, and the estate therefore lacks that contrast of building and planting which gives the georgian squares their charm.

The georgian formula produced a pattern of urban scenery which has never been equalled in this country, and has seldom been bettered elsewhere. It was made up of three components: road-layouts, trees and houses. The road-layouts were the work of the surveyors to the great estates of the time. The trees were the work of Repton and his followers. The houses were the work of speculative builders. In London the development was carried out in the following manner:

A nobleman who owned land on the then fringe of the city would instruct his surveyor to lay out a pattern of streets and sell the building-plots on ninety-nine year leases. He preferred the ground-rent to a lump sum in cash, and he knew that after a century or so the estate would return to his descendants. He therefore possessed an interest in its quality. In order to ensure that this was preserved, the surveyor incorporated squares in his street-layouts and controls over design in his building-agreements, (a system which derived from that which had been used for controlling the building of Inigo Jones' Covent Garden Piazza, and which had been developed further by the Earl of Southampton at Bloomsbury Square[6]).

One might have expected that, whatever else they contained, the agreements would always have defined the 'rate' of the houses under the Building Act, but this, though it often formed part of the agreement, was not invariably included; perhaps it was thought to be enough to state the dimensions of the plot and the number of houses to be built, since these together would determine the rate. In addition, the quality of the materials might be specified, the level of the parapets might be fixed so that all the houses in a street formed a uniform row, standard dimensions might be designated for the several storeys of the houses in a particular street (a device which helped to ensure similarity of scale in the elevations), window-levels might be defined, together with the dimensions of the area and the height of its railings. Standards of maintenance might be specified, and the articles of agreement might include a drawing showing the elevation of the proposed building. In the

5: *Part of one side of Hampstead Road, London NW1. A drawing forming part of a building agreement between a developer and the Bedford Estate.*

more important streets and squares even greater care was taken. In such places the estate and the builders might decide to follow the example of the John Woods (the father and son who designed much of Bath) and develop a square or one side of a street as a single architectural unit.[7]

Such agreements could ensure appropriate standards of design and construction, but they were insufficient to ensure a permanently satisfactory environment. The gardens in the centres of the squares not only had to be laid out, they also had to be maintained. Finance and some form of administrative mechanism were required for this purpose. Furthermore, the public might have to be deprived of their established right of access to the central part of the square. To achieve these ends legislation was needed. Thus the Russell Square Act of 1800[8] provided for the enclosure of the central part of the square, so that it could be 'planted and laid out with walks, and properly ornamented and embellished and made into a Pleasure Ground' for the benefit of the Duke of Bedford (the ground-landlord) and the occupiers of the houses in the square. To achieve this objective the Act arranged for commissioners to be appointed to carry it into effect and empowered them to levy rates for the purpose upon the square's residents.

Acts such as these were, however, only required in those cases in which the estate was already built before the planted square became fashionable. New development did not need such an elaborate device. All that was necessary in such cases was a clause in the lease requiring the payment of a small 'key-rent' to the ground-landlord. He looked after the garden in the centre of the square and the lessees had access to it. Sometimes, however, the ground-landlord did not want this rather tiresome responsibility and different arrangements were made. Ladbroke Square (one of the few real squares in the Kensington Park Estate) is an example of such a circumstance. The area seems originally to have been developed as a leasehold estate of the ordinary kind, but in 1864 the then owner sold his interest in Ladbroke Square's garden to a private company which was formed to maintain the garden and its appurtenancies. The company had 100 shareholders, who were presumably local residents, and from them a committee was chosen to collect rents and look after the grounds. In the process of time most, if not all, the residents have acquired the freehold of their properties, but the company still exists, providing an example of freehold tenure, combined with the shared maintenance of communal open space.[9]

Such an arrangement was, however, comparatively rare. Until the late nineteenth century, leasehold-tenure was, at least in London,[10] the normal system under which estate-development was carried out. It had, as we have seen, several advantages; it provided a means by which open spaces could be maintained, and a way in which the landowner could make certain that his estate would be well-managed in the long term. In addition, it ensured that the houses of the estate would possess a certain consistency of design, even though they were not all erected under the control of a single architect.

The houses which make up the georgian estates were, in fact, built by many different people, usually builders or building tradesmen—'small men' who would buy the leases of two or three plots, erect the houses and, if they did not go bankrupt first, sell them at a profit.[11] Sometimes, however, the job was done by a bigger and more successful speculator. The greatest of these was Thomas Cubitt, who not only developed much of northern Bloomsbury, parts of Stoke Newington and Camden Town and the greater part of Clapham, but was also responsible for Belgravia and Pimlico as well as building Osborne for Queen Victoria. The professions of architect and speculative developer were not distinct as they became. The two John Woods, father and son, who designed much of Bath, built Queen Square, the Circus, the

10

Royal Crescent and the adjoining streets as a speculative enterprise,[12] while Robert Adam and his brothers James and William were both the architects and the developers of the Adelphi.[13] The greatest of such projects were the various developments at Bath and the New Town of Edinburgh. The most grandiose was the scheme backed by the Prince Regent, and carried out by John Nash, for the layout and construction of Carlton House Terrace, Regent Street, Regent's Park and its surrounding buildings. For our purposes, however, the most important part of Nash's scheme is not the sweep of the Quadrant, nor the silhouette of All Souls, Langham Place, but rather his proposal for what is now Regent's Park; for Nash's concept was a true piece of suburbia as defined in the introduction to this book.

3 *Regent's Park and Park Village, the impact of the picturesque:* Nash was an official architect. He held, at the time, the unexpected post of Surveyor to the Office of Woods and Forests. He and another architect, Thomas Leverton, of the Office of Land Revenue, were each instructed to prepare a scheme for the development of Marylebone Park, an area of virgin land on the fringe of London, which had recently reverted to the Crown. The southern part of Leverton's scheme was essentially a continuation northwards of georgian Marylebone, its northern part was an assembly of detached and semi-detached villas set in a rectilinear grid of streets. Nash, on the other hand, 'saw the problem more humanly and set down on paper a truly remarkable conception of what we might today call a garden-city—the park landscaped on Reptonian lines with over fifty villas half hid in groves of trees,

6: *A detail from John Nash's panorama illustrating his project for the development of Marylebone Park.*

and belted by terraces all of which had full enjoyment of the park; a decorative lake, a pleasure palace for the Prince, a new Marylebone Church and even a National Valhalla'.[14]

Nash's scheme was accepted—he was, after all, the protégé of the Prince Regent—but happily for Londoners, the 'garden city' which was to occupy the greater part of the park was scotched in 1826. In addition, the northern

7: Park Village West from the air.

8: Park Village West showing the street, centre left, which leads off the main road.

12

terraces and the National Valhalla were excised by the Treasury, while the idea of the Prince's Summer Palace was extinguished on George IV's death. However, the other terraces were kept, the lake is there, a few villas were erected in the neighbourhood of the inner circle, the park remains, a superb addition to London's open spaces, and the final development included a small unobtrusive corner known as Park Village. This, from our standpoint, was the most important part of the executed scheme, for Park Village was the first piece of suburbia to be built.

Park Village was in two parts: Park Village East and Park Village West. Only half of Park Village East has survived. The houses on one side of the road have been demolished to form a railway-cutting. But Park Village West is still there for us to study. In its layout it is the antithesis of georgian civic planning. The plan of its road is horse-shoe shaped instead of being straight or gently curved. Its houses are wide, irregular, equipped with eaves and (with the exception of one short terrace) detached and set in well-planted gardens, instead of being narrow, parapetted, tall, and arranged in blocks. Road, houses, gardens, trees and fences are combined to make an informal picture instead of being separated into the opposites of street and open space. Its very name is rural. It is a group of country houses situated in the town.

Park Village was pastoral in its inspiration, and romantic in its intent. It is a product of the picturesque movement, and its building was the first occasion upon which this aspect of the arts was introduced into the layout of an English city. Architecture had taken to the picturesque after that movement had become the accepted basis of landscape design.[15] The contrived informality of Capability Brown's landscapes, together with the associations of mystery and horror implicit in ruined castles and hermit's grottoes, were the starting point of a new way of thinking about architecture. Design ceased to be a matter of rules. To be a man of taste, it was no longer enough to obey the principles of Vitruvius, to follow Palladio. Instead the picturesque became all the rage. Houses no longer needed to have a portico in the middle, wings on each side and a classical rectitude of proportion. They were allowed towers, gothic windows, and a rambling silhouette. It was this romantic, irregular approach to design which Nash and his assistant Pennethorne adopted at Park Village.

4 *The architectural styles of victorian and edwardian villa-residences:* The idea caught on. Park Village was built in 1824. In 1827 Decimus Burton, the architect of the Athaeneum, built at Tunbridge Wells for a certain Mr John Ward a whole estate of detached and semi-detached villas. In the 30s and 40s the Eyre Estate, St John's Wood, began to sprout, with Tudor gables and classic pediments.[16]

As the century progressed, more and more of these 'villa-residences' sprang up all over the country. Their variety of architectural character is astonishing. A pattern-book of the period, Richard Brown's *Domestic architecture* published in 1842, shows illustrations of houses and pavilions in an

9: *Early-victorian villa-residences—a project for development at Hove, by Decimus Burton.*

10: *A house in the 'Plantagenet Castle, style of Edward III' manner from Richard Brown's* Domestic architecture, 1842. *The* nouveau-riche *of the northern industrial cities were particularly attracted by fantasies of such a kind.*

14

extraordinary medley of styles, including among others the 'burmese', the 'egyptian', the 'venetian', the 'moriso-spanish' and the 'Plantagenet Castle, Edward III' styles. One of the most attractive styles was the italianate, with stuccoed walls, low-pitched slate roofs, arcaded windows, wide-spreading eaves, an irregular silhouette and a prominent square turret. Tudor was common also, but there was little half-timbering. It was the tudor of Audley End rather than that of Little Moreton Hall. Gothic flourished, for gothic was not only the most obviously picturesque of all architectural styles, it was shown by Pugin and the luminaries of the Cambridge Camden Society to be not merely picturesque but christian.[17] Being christian it was necessarily good, while the classical mode derived from Greece and Rome was pagan and consequently bad.

The regency and earlier victorian villas were normally stuccoed externally and painted, but as time went on fashion changed. Nash's painted plaster was found to be an unsuitable material in the grimy atmosphere of the industrial revolution, and in the cheaper 'third rate' developments it gradually gave place to stock bricks, remaining here and there to frame a window or form a portico. In the less conventional houses bands and diaper patterns of red and blue bricks would appear, roofs became steeper and might occasionally be crowned with wrought-iron ornaments in distant recollection of some French chateau. Barge-boards were cut in bold and striking curves, and a curious raised arch with straight sides leading down to the impost became a

11: A mid-victorian villa-residence in Teddington, Middlesex.

15

favourite motive of the suburban builders of London. These men were enthusiastic searchers for 'character'. In seeking this indefinable quality they coarsened their details, mixed their styles and elaborated their silhouettes until they produced that architectural curiosity, the mid-victorian 'villa-residence'.[18]

In the fifties and early sixties, a new and less ornate type of house began to be built, more suited to the small suburban plot than the rambling fancies of earlier times. This too was gothic in inspiration but was cheaper and more functional in character than the earlier gothic villas. Its principal exponent in the London area was George Truefitt, an architect who built chiefly in Tufnell Park, to which estate he was surveyor for twenty years. This manner of building was followed about fifteen years later by yet another style, known for some reason as the 'Queen Anne', though it would never have been recognized by that monarch.[19] This was characterised by white-painted woodwork, square-headed windows, eaves-cornices, tile-hanging and rubbed-brick ornaments.

At the same time, Richard Norman Shaw, the only real genius among the English domestic architects of the late 19th century, was experimenting with

12: *The house in the Queen Anne style, Rosslyn Hill, Hampstead referred to in note 19.*

16

13: Cragside, Northumberland, by Richard Norman Shaw.

half-timber in some of the huge mansions which he built for the millionaires of the period.[20]   In this Shaw seems to have followed the example of the shopkeepers of Chester who, as early as 1840, had begun to reface the Rows in the local idiom of black and white half-timbering. This fashion was adopted for part of the Royal Jubilee Exhibition which was held at Manchester in the year 1887. One of the features of the exhibition was a reconstruction of 'Old Manchester and Salford'. This model village included a group of shops ingeniously contrived to represent part of a sixteenth-century street.   It included girls dressed in period costume and buildings with diamond-paned windows, cantilevered gables and walls constructed in elaborate patterns of white plaster and black stud-work. A few years later a number of local architects (Douglas and Fordham, Grayson and Ould, W S Owen, J J Talbot and J Lomax-Simpson) adopted the style for some of the houses which W H Lever (later Lord Leverhulme) built for his workers in the model village of Port Sunlight nearby in the Wirral peninsula.   These tudor houses form only a small minority of the buildings of Port Sunlight, but they are its most striking, most memorable and most frequently illustrated monuments.   From here, and from Shaw's office, half-timbering spread over the face of Britain.

17

14: Tudor houses at Port Sunlight.

(An excellent account of housing in Port Sunlight appears in the catalogue of the 1980 exhibition devoted to Lord Leverhulme at the Royal Academy in London.)

Port Sunlight was started in 1887. At about the same time, Shaw changed his style. He gave up his search for the picturesque, eschewed Queen Anne tile-hanging, tudor half-timber and Ipswich bay-windows, and built in South Kensington two houses (the Bolney House, Ennismore Gardens, and no 170 Queen's Gate) whose style constituted a return to the classical traditions of the late seventeenth century. In this Shaw followed after his ex-partner William Nesfield who, some years earlier, had built at Kinmel Park, Abergele, a house whose style is described by Pevsner as a 'mixture of William-and-Mary with Louis XIII motives'. Abergele however was remote, Nesfield was less well known than Shaw and the building was not immediately imitated. 170 Queens Gate seems to derive from the Bolney House, but the neo-georgian mode derived from 170 Queen's Gate.[21] This too had its imitators: houses became symmetrical once more, and were equipped with the appropriate paraphernalia of multi-paned sash windows and classical details. Many Edwardian and inter-war architects designed in this manner, and every town has a bank and often one or two neat little georgian houses in red brick or cream rendering whose lineage can be traced back to Shaw's work in Kensington.

Shaw was a friend of William Morris, and he, Nesfield, E W Godwin, and Philip Webb (who built the Red House at Bexley for William Morris in 1859) were all allied to the Arts and Crafts Movement. Their followers, Voysey, Baillie Scott and Edgar Wood, carried the logic of the movement beyond the free functional gothic of the Red House, or Godwin's Queen Anne villas, and sought to build middle-class houses in the manner of the sixteenth-century

18

15: *A neo-georgian house in Welwyn Garden City.*

16: *The origins of the 'mièvre' style—'The Orchard', Chorley Wood, Hertfordshire by C F A Voysey.*

farm-workers cottage. Voysey brought into domestic architecture a quality for which H S Goodhart Rendel could only find one exact word and that a French one: ' "mièverie", which can perhaps be loosely rendered as "only-little-me-ish-ness" '.[22] Voysey's houses have roofs to first-floor level, walls of stone or roughcast, huge chimneys and small-paned windows, glazed here and there with bottle-glass. The influence of this school persisted until recently, though less in housing than in the tearoom. Here one might see rush-seated ladder-back chairs, blue linen tablemats and a light-fitting made up of electric candles fixed to the wheel of some long-disused hay-wain.

While the avant-garde architects, the more adventurous speculators and the philanthropic industrialists were building in the manner first of Shaw, and later of Voysey, the speculative builders who supplied the lower end of the market were more conservative in their approach to design. Their small terraced or semi-detached houses were usually built in red-brick with slate roofs, bay-windows, stone-dressings and cement ornaments. Their entrance-porches were recessed or set between projecting bays. The style of their details was mixed: massive mullions might be decked with capitals of plants and leaves, motives which derived ultimately from the gothic fantasies of Lincoln Cathedral or Southwell Minster; square-headed stone lintels might be raised from their bearings as the arches of the mid-victorian villa-residence were raised from the impost; roofs of purplish Welsh slates might be crowned with ornamental ridge-tiles of red terracotta. We shall discuss these 'bye-law' houses more fully in the next chapter; for the moment it is enough to note their existence and attempt to define their architectural character.

With the turn of the century these speculators began to change the style of their products. They substituted a debilitated Queen Anne style for the ponderous lintels, gothic ornaments and slate-roofs of the bye-law house. They imitated the white-painted woodwork, red roof-tiles, casement windows

17: Bye-law houses in Kensal Rise, London.

20

18: An example of the debilitated Queen Anne style.

and projecting gables of the Queen Anne, but omitted, presumably in the interests of economy, its eaves-cornices and rubbed-brick ornaments. Tile-hanging was maintained between bay-windows on different floors, but elsewhere pebble-dash took its place. Mass-produced casements were substituted for carefully-detailed windows, and the half-timbering which sometimes embellished their gables was an applied decoration, not a structural feature.

Thus, at the end of the edwardian era, there were four architectural styles in current use for domestic purposes, all of which derived, in their details, from the work of Norman Shaw and his school: tudor, neo-georgian, what we may perhaps call 'mièvre' (the adjective from which the noun, mièverie is derived) and Queen Anne—this last occasionally in its original, more often in its cheapened, debilitated form.

5 *The disappearance of machinery for controlling the design of new developments:* The extraordinary shapes of the victorian villa-residences and the assortment of styles which were available to the architects of the time made it more than ever necessary for a ground-landlord who wanted to maintain the quality of his development to impose some discipline upon its developers. We have seen that during the greater part of the nineteenth century, and in the London area, leasehold-tenure provided a means by which this might be achieved.

Such discipline did not, however, accord with the moral, political and aesthetic ideologies of the time. As early as 1834 the editor of the *Architectural magazine* rebuked for his reactionary views a correspondent who had proposed

21

that controls be imposed to ensure uniformity of elevation in new streets in London. The editor held (vol 1, p116) that 'restraining the taste of individuals . . . would assuredly lead to monotony' and monotony was the bête noire to be avoided at all costs. 'The fear and loathing of monotony is a predominant and recurring feature of Victorian architectural criticism', wrote Olsen in *The growth of victorian London* (p224).

Variety, on the other hand, was sought as an end in itself; Olsen declares (p68) that 'the identity and separateness of every building from every other . . . were jealously preserved and vehemently emphasized . . . the freedom of each architect, each householder to express himself as he saw fit had moral and political as well as aesthetic significance. The facade was to represent the special creative vision of the designer, just as the house represented the independence and identity of the family it contained.' Developers might continue to build on lease, but the design of the houses which they built was a matter for their individual judgment, not for the directive of the ground-landlord.

Furthermore, towards the end of the century, leasehold-tenure began to fall into disuse. The reasons for the change are obscure, but it seems to have had two causes: an increase in opportunities for investment, and an ideological dislike of the system itself.

The suburban expansions of the victorian era were fuelled by the investment capital which accrued as a result of the prosperity of the time. Olsen declares (p158) that there was an 'abundance of investors, virtually forcing their money on the builders', and goes on to explain that 'the opportunities for investment open to the thrifty victorian were far more limited than those of his twentieth-century descendant. Anyone who wished to earn a greater return for his savings than he could from Consols without undue risk was almost forced to invest in mortgages, ground-rents and improved ground-rents.'[23] This situation discouraged development for freehold sale. An early-victorian landowner who sold his land freehold found himself the possessor of cash which could only be invested in Consols, deposited in the bank or used to buy rented property elsewhere. He did better to lease the land, pocket the ground-rents and look to an ultimate unearned increment. As time went on, however, circumstances changed. Stocks and bonds came to provide a reasonably lucrative and, if carefully chosen, a sufficiently secure form of investment,[24] and the landowner lost the incentive to lease his property rather than sell the freehold.

Furthermore, leasehold-tenure itself began to obtain a bad name towards the end of the century. It was thought to encourage jerry-building (there was no benefit to a developer in erecting a substantial house which would outlast the term of the lease, and the prevalence of many cheap poorly-built houses was held to be due to the short leases upon which land was sold). It was considered that by severing occupation from attaining ownership it prevented the working-classes from the 'politically and socially advantageous'[25] circumstance of freehold-tenure; it was believed that leasehold houses were less well maintained than those held in freehold, and it was thought that the system enabled the landowner to rob the lessee. Such ideas were encouraged by radical journalists who declared ground-landlords to be heartless monopolists exploiting their unhappy tenants to their own personal advantage.[26] Leasehold enfranchisement became a political issue, and in 1886 a select committee was appointed (The Committee on Town Holdings) whose terms of reference included 'the expediency of giving to leaseholders facilities for the purchase of the fee simple of their property'. Shortly afterwards, in 1887 and 1888, two private members' bills were introduced—the Leasehold Enfranchisement (by Purchase or Rent charge) Bill and the Leaseholder's (Purchase of Fee Simple) Bill—both of which sought to grant the lessee power to acquire the freehold of his land.

The select committee reported against leasehold-enfranchisement, and the idea was dropped; but although they failed to achieve their objective, the opponents of the leasehold system gained a certain negative success. Their propaganda, combined with alternative opportunities for investment, seems to have caused landowners to think twice before engaging in leasehold development, and by the end of the edwardian era, housing-estates were no longer being developed on lease.

The abandonment of leasehold-tenure caused the landowner to lose interest in maintaining either the quality of his housing or the appearance of its open spaces. If his building-plots were to be sold separately, he might sometimes seek to raise their value by including restrictive covenants among the terms of sale, but such covenants were not particularly effective, and in any case they only controlled the purchasers of individual house-plots. The speculator, building houses for sale, was left untouched. Furthermore, neither the landlord nor the speculator gained by making arrangements designed to ensure a decent standard in the layout of new estates, and in the maintenance of their communal open spaces.

Leasehold-tenure did not, however, constitute the only means by which estate-development was controlled during the first part of the nineteenth century. The other devices which performed this function were provided by the building societies of the time. Present-day building societies are hardly societies concerned with building. They are more akin to a specialised form of bank, accepting money from investors on deposit account, and lending that money to others on the security of real estate. Originally, however, the building societies were what their name implies: associations formed for the purpose of building houses. They were known as 'terminating benefit societies' because they were formed for the benefit of their members and when the houses were built their task was over and they were dissolved. The system as it operated in the late eighteenth century is described by Seymour Price[27] in the following terms:

'These early societies existed for one purpose only, to provide each and every member, and no-one else, with a house erected by the society and paid for out of its funds . . . These pioneer societies consisted of a number of

23

people, usually not more than twenty, who joined together to do collectively what they could not afford to do individually. They paid fortnightly or monthly sums which accumulated at interest. When sufficient money was available, land was acquired either by the purchase of freehold or the acceptance of a lease and the members then proceeded to build. Membership was limited to the number of houses proposed to be erected, and lots were drawn to decide the order of their allocation. Every member, whatever his fortune or misfortune in the ballot, had to continue his fortnightly or monthly payments until all members had been provided with a house, the liabilities of the society discharged and the society formally terminated.'

This system of development had considerable advantages from standpoint of townscape. It was in the interest of all the members of a terminating society that the estate which they were developing should reach a certain standard of design, and the society was therefore able to impose conditions on its members to ensure that this was achieved. Thus the statutes of the Oakdale Society required that no buildings other than houses, churches and chapels should be erected, that each plot should contain only one detached or semi-detached house, that the houses should be at least two storeys high and above a fixed minimum in value, that all walls other than those facing the road should be built in stone to a minimum height of five feet, and that all plans should be inspected by the society's surveyor who also prepared the road-layout. In addition, materials were specified in detail, and much attention was paid to boundary walls and the screening of outbuildings.[28]

The effect of such regulations may be seen at Kenwood Park, Sheffield, an estate of wealthy houses set in their own grounds, which was developed in the eighteen-fifties. Kenwood Park possesses a peculiar charm. Its plots are large and so well treed that in summer the houses are scarcely visible. The boundary walls are of a consistent height, the roads are laid out in sweeping curves and the buildings, in a rather dour northern version of the contemporary gothic, are all built of the local stone.

Kenwood Park is a mid-victorian upper-class suburb. It bears an obvious affinity to Park Village West, but while Park Village is an essay in the picturesque, Kenwood Park is an example of arcadia. At Park Village the houses are an important part of the design, at Kenwood Park they are dominated by the planting. At Park Village there is contrast; the winding road and the tree-encumbered gardens are set against the severe architecture of Albany Street. At Kenwood Park, on the other hand, there is little variety, and no surprise. It is less a housing-estate than a stretch of woodland intersected by walled roads. Roger Gill sums up the arcadian suburb in a single sentence (p26): 'It is a natural treescape in which the houses are but incidents, and the gardens small clearings in the forest'. It was achieved by very low density, generous planting, and strict control of design.

Such control was, of course, dependent upon the building societies acting as their name implies. As time went on, however, they gradually changed their function and became building societies as we know them now. It seems that they had certain disadvantages from a financial standpoint. They were small, often inefficiently run, and they frequently failed. Officers of the more successful enterprises sometimes founded them in series, starting a new society every two or three years, while some people lent money to a society as an investment, rather than as a means of obtaining a house. Gradually the terminating societies became permanent and gradually they ceased to be building societies, and became the mortgaging associations which they are today. This trend was given legal form in 1874 when an Act was passed to regulate their activities. One of the clauses of this Act prohibited them from owning or purchasing or leasing property other than that needed for the conduct of their own business.[29] Building societies no longer built, and because they did not build they became interested less in the architectural quality of their houses than in the value of these houses as security for a loan.

6 *Victorian pseudo-arcadia: the estate of detached houses:* The disappearance of design-controls was a grave disaster, but its effect would have been less noticeable if suburbia had been exclusively arcadian. Had this occurred, the irregularity of the buildings would have been masked by the forest in which they lay, but arcadia, with its big houses and plots of half an acre or more, was a pattern of development which could only be used in the wealthiest estates. The wealthy, however, are a small minority in society, and there were others, less prosperous than they, who also wanted detached, individually-designed houses set in their own grounds. These people, though reasonably well-off, could not afford the extensive pleasances of arcadia. They required cheaper plots in which there was less space for planting.

This demand had existed from the first (there were detached houses on their own plots in the Leverton's scheme for Marylebone Park), but as the century progressed the demand for such houses increased, while those who wanted them had less to spend. Landlords were ready to supply this need, and soon estates of small, individual plots began to be laid out. Their roads were usually straight (a rectangular road-pattern is more economical in land than the sinuous curves of arcadia), their plot-frontages were narrow (narrow frontages enable more houses to be accommodated on a given length of road), their trees were small. The pattern of design which resulted from these requirements was a pseudo-arcadia in which no single feature, trees, houses or roads, was dominant over the others, whose silhouette was jagged and irregular, and where no effort was made to fuse the parts into a new coherent whole. In those cases where consistency of design existed, it was due less to the desires of the ground-landlord than to the activities of speculative architects. These men used to buy adjoining plots along a street, and sell them for building on condition that they were appointed to execute the designs. When this was done (as seems to have occurred in parts of North Oxford[30]), the scale of the buildings and the harmony of the architecture does something to redeem the weakness of the layout, but as time went on architects ceased to speculate in this way and these small benefits were lost. The abandonment

25

19: Houses at Norham Gardens, Oxford.

of design-controls, and the disappearance of the speculative architect caused a loss of consistency, while the growing demand for small detached houses led to a diminution in scale.

7 *Spatial design:* The detached form and irregular design of the victorian villa-residence were, of course, a reaction against the simple repetitiveness of the georgian terrace-house. The victorians, as Olsen declares in *The growth of victorian London* (p55) 'hated the London that their regency parents and eighteenth-century grandparents had bequeathed to them'. It seems that they were unable or unwilling to appreciate the quality of the georgian estate: to them the eighteenth-century street was no more than a pair of plain brick walls with holes in them, dingy and monotonous.

In 1857 a leading article in *Building news* (vol 3, p1) declared that 'till within the last 25 or 30 years nothing answering to the name of street "architecture" was to be found in the capital of the world. Dowdiness, blankness and sulkiness seem then to have been considered quite *comme il faut* and the order of the day.' As for the squares, they wasted space which could have been more usefully and agreeably devoted to individual gardens.

In 1858 a letter to the same journal (vol 4, p606) objected vehemently to the 'rage which now prevails among builders for the formation of "squares" in the suburbs! In the densely-crowded streets and alleys of London we are but too happy to find, here and there, an opening sufficiently expanded to allow a short glance at the sky or a compassionate look at some blackened trees; but after travelling five miles from the Bank we begin to grow impatient of gardens desecrated to semi-public use, and to demand a plot, however small, for the special delectation of our own family. Surely at places like Highbury, Camberwell, Brompton or Bayswater, removed so far from either the Strand or Cornhill, we may be spared the infliction of "rows" of brick and mortar walls even in squares, and may be excused for spurning the offer of a common parade-ground where no plot is left to the private dwelling except the compulsory 10 feet by 10 at the back . . . What is it that makes St John's Wood the most pleasant-looking to the eye of all the suburbs of London but the circumstances of nearly every house having a good piece of garden about it! Many of the roads are quite rural-looking and many of the dwellings also.'

The authors of such notes did not realize that, despite its superficial monotony, the georgian estate possessed a rare combination of refinement of detail, contrast of scale, unity of floorscape and variety of space—qualities which were absent in the villa-suburbia which they admired. They did not appreciate the manner in which the treeless streets of Bloomsbury provided both a foil to, and a contrast of scale with, the spreading planes in the squares nearby. Agreeable as they were, the bosky gardens of St John's Wood were seldom large enough to accommodate such planting. The victorians did not understand that, for all their blankness and sulkiness, the rows of brick and mortar walls defined the spaces which they enclosed in a manner which the developer of a street of detached or semi-detached houses could hardly achieve; nor did they realize that while the houses of suburbia were (initially at least) diversified, the scale of the suburban estate was uniform and its floorscape fragmented, while its close mixture of building and planting created an even, and so an ultimately boring, texture of scenery.

In the georgian estate the buildings were repetitious, but the scene as a whole possessed variety. In victorian villa-suburbia the buildings were varied but the scene as a whole was repetitious. The victorians rejected the London of their forebears because they failed to perceive what is now held as the fundamental canon of urban-design; that the quality of a scene, whether in a village, a city centre or a suburb is less a matter of the forms of its buildings than of the scale of its constituents, the nature of its floorscape and above all the characteristics of its spaces.

8 *Privacy and boredom:* The even texture and varied constituents of victorian suburbia were physical expressions of the victorian system of values, a system in which the home occupied the central place. It was during the reign of George IV that J B Papworth, discussing one of the villas in Regent's Park, described the Englishman's attachment to his home in the following words: 'The desire to congregate about him in his dwelling and domain all the means of domestic comfort is a prominent feature of the character of an Englishman,

27

and there he lays up his chief resources against the cares of life. His home is the depository of his most interesting pleasures, the anticipated enjoyment of which gives energy to his mind and cheers his exertion towards the accomplishment of his undertakings: he eagerly embraces its pleasures and repose during the intervals which he can spare for recreation, and flies to it as a welcome retreat from the bustle and the toils of life, when desirous and prepared to transfer them to more youthful energies. Thus the suitableness of this dwelling becomes, as it were, the measure of the Englishman's enjoyment.'[31]

A century or so later, Sir James Richards expressed the same idea in the opening paragraph of his highly perceptive study of the suburban ideal, first published in 1946. 'Ewbank'd inside and Atco'd out, the English suburban residence and the garden which is an integral part of it stand trim and lovingly cared-for in the mild sunshine. Everything is in its place. The abruptness, the barbarities of the world are far away. There is not much sound except perhaps the musical whirr and clack of a mowing-machine being pushed back and forth over a neighbouring lawn and the clink of cups and saucers and a soft footfall as tea is got ready indoors. There is not much movement either: a wire-haired terrier lazily trotting around the garden in a not very hopeful search for something new to smell and the pages of a newspaper being turned and refolded by some leisurely individual in a deck chair.'[32]

The Englishman's *lares et penates*, so accurately described by Papworth and lovingly evoked by Richards, required for their full development a high degree of privacy. To achieve such a privacy the gardens of victorian villa-suburbia were surrounded by separating walls—we have already noted their existence at Kenwood Park, Sheffield—but the pleasing seclusion of a walled suburban garden might, however, mean a disagreeable isolation for the garden's occupants. The isolation of suburbia was not, perhaps, too serious a matter for the husband; indeed for him it was often a welcome relief from the gregariousness of his working-life, but for his spouse suburbia's isolation could easily become inordinately tedious. Sir Walter Besant, quoted by Olsen in *The growth of victorian London*, considered that the inhabitants of suburbia endured 'as dull a life as man ever tolerated'.[33] He described it as follows:

'The men went into town every morning and returned every evening; they had dinner; they talked a little; they went to bed . . . The case of the women was worse; they lost all the London life—the shops, the animation of the streets, their old circle of friends; in its place they found all the exclusiveness and class feeling of London with none of the advantages of a country town . . . in the new suburbs of Stockwell there were no interests (in common); the wife of the wholesale merchant would not call on the wife of the retail dealer; the wife of the barrister would not call on either; there was no society and so for fifty years the massive dullness of the London suburb continued.' (Olsen, p210-211.)

Dullness, however, was what the victorians wanted. Olsen points out (p25) that the ideal environment for individual and familial privacy was the single-class villa-suburb. 'There bourgeois respectability could best flourish. . . The suburbs that proved the most successful were the most suburban, that is to say the most dull, the most uniform, with the fewest cultural or social institutions, since they thereby offered the fewest counter-attractions to those of the home or the hearth.'/ He goes on to quote a correspondent of *The builder* (vol 14, p145) in 1856: 'And it is better morally and physically for the Londoner when he has done his day's work to go to the country or the suburbs, where he escapes the noise and crowds and impure air of the town; and it is no small advantage to a man to have his family removed from the immediate neighbourhood of casinos, dancing-saloons and hells upon the earth which I will not name.'

The variety of villa-suburbia's dwellings concealed a more profound uniformity of behaviour in their residents. Olsen continues (p25), 'In the 1840s one escaped into a villa miraculously transported from the Lago di Como to Surrey; in the 1870s into a seventeenth century Dutch farmhouse, by the nineties into an overgrown tudor country-cottage: each of them individual yet standardized, one's own, yet inconspicuous. Boredom was the price willingly paid for a respite from urban tensions. Social segregation simplified problems of behaviour, expenditure and beliefs; one simply did what the neighbours were doing.'

9 *Social segregation and snobbery:* The social segregation to which Olsen refers was a characteristic of the victorian but not of the georgian estate. The latter was a balanced community which excluded only the very poor and industrial nuisances on principle: 'Segregation, social and functional, took place between street and street, not between estate and estate' (p23). Thus Samuel Pepys Cockerell, who prepared in 1790 the first plan for the Foundling Estate, recommended that it should 'comprise all classes of building from the first class down to houses of twenty-five pounds per annum', but arranged so as to 'prevent the lower classes interfering with and diminishing the character of those above them'[34] while Tyburnia included mews and second and third-class houses as well as the very grand first-class houses of Hyde Park Gate. 'Even Mayfair had its mean streets and narrow courts as well as a variety of services from markets to mews to benefit the residents of the principal streets and squares.'[35]

This need to provide local services derived from the lack of public transport at the time. The tradesman, the wheelwright or the joiner had to live near his workplace, and his workplace had to be close to the gentry whom he served. However, as the nineteenth century progressed, commuting, first by horse-bus and later by rail, provided a means by which the rich were enabled to escape from the proximity of the poor. Olsen declares (p234) that 'from the 1830s onwards . . . any suburb beyond walking distance of Central London became . . . safe from working-class contamination'.

The street-by-street segregation of the georgian estate did not satisfy the residents, and still less the builders of new developments. The speculators who erected them found it both easier and more profitable to construct an estate whose houses were all of similar size and accommodation, rather than to vary them in order to achieve a mixture of social groups. The following account describes how this occurred in the case of Eton College's Chalcot estate, located between Swiss Cottage and Chalk Farm.

'The landlord's agent to some extent, but the speculative builders above all, were insistent on the desirability of building one single type of house on the estate . . . The builders having created a supply of a particular kind of house, the district was peopled by social groups suited to that type by their means, way of living and aspirations. From the side of housing demand there was a very powerful urge for people of like condition to want to live in the same neighbourhood with their kind, to decline to be mixed up with their inferiors or at the very least to keep away from noxious, unhealthy or otherwise unpleasant areas. These were strong tides making for segregation.'[36]

'To decline to be mixed up with their inferiors.' The phrase epitomises the snobbery which has always permeated the mind of the suburban. This snobbery was, and indeed is, always ridiculous, occasionally harmless, sometimes outrageous. In 1871 it led the tenants of Adamson Road, Swiss Cottage, to object to the establishment of a church school nearby, a project which had been suggested 'so that the poor on the estate may receive a religious education'.[37] In 1894 it provided George and Weedon Grossmith with the material for that admirable lampoon *The diary of a nobody*; it caused Charles Snell (the author of *Modern suburban homes*) to regard a view of the garden and a southern aspect for the reception rooms as a matter of less importance than the placing of these rooms on the street frontage;[38] it caused the suburban builders to give the name 'Park' to many of their estates, as if Park Village, Kenwood Park, Sheffield, and Tufnell Park could, by being so named, possess the trees, the lake and the greensward of a landscape by Humphry Repton or Capability Brown; during the georgian era it caused the Duke of Bedford to build gates at the approaches to his Bloomsbury Estate so as to ensure that people who had no business within it were not admitted;[39] a century later it caused the developer of Victoria Park, Manchester, to erect similar gatehouses there and to charge the public a toll for permission to enter his refined precinct;[40] during the late nineteenth century it caused a merchant of Beckenham to declare it as the view of the estate in which he lived '(if a neuter thing like an estate can have a view) that houses for the class of people that we have been speaking about [the lower orders] and houses for the class of people to which, if you will allow me to say so, I belong, should be kept very widely apart';[41] and in the 1930s it caused the inhabitants of a speculative estate in Oxford to build two large brick walls across their estate roads to separate them from the council-housing beyond.[42]

The snobbery of its inhabitants helped to establish suburbia's stratification into three distinct types: the individualistic suburbia of separate houses built on their own plots to suit the owner's particular requirements, the speculative suburbia of the development companies, and the municipal suburbia of

30

council-housing. In later chapters we shall study these three varieties of suburbia in detail, considering how their forms derive partly from historical influences and partly from the problems which their builders set out to solve.
But first we must glance quickly at victorian middle-class speculative suburbia
in order to define the ingredients which it contained.

10 *Victorian speculative suburbia:* So far we have discussed the stylistic
development of the detached 'villa-residence' and the estate of individual
houses set in their own grounds, but in the early nineteenth century such
buildings were the prerogative of the wealthy. Only a small proportion of the
population could afford homes of this kind. The great majority of housing
took the form of speculative building.

Speculative builders are, by nature, conservative men. They build what
will sell. Richard Brown's Plantagenet Castle was all very well for the man
who built for himself, but, as a commercial venture, it was too chancy.
Stuccoed terraces in the Nash manner were a far safer investment.[43] In consequence, much victorian speculative building is georgian in character. The
streets and squares of Kensington and Tyburnia are coarser in detail than
those of Bloomsbury or Bath, but their street layouts are similar, their houses
are similar in plan, and their classic or italianate style derives directly from
georgian prototypes. The more venturesome speculators might occasionally
take a chance on a gothic or tudor scheme,[44] but such fancies were rare and
in 1857 the Mildmay Estate, Stoke Newington,[45] was being built in a standard georgian idiom with stock bricks and plaster detailing.

By this time, the more serious-minded architects were thoroughly imbued
with mid-victorian eclecticism, or the pious strivings of the Cambridge Camden society. In either case they had little use for the 'bread-and-butter' work
of the speculative builder. The architectural profession gradually drifted
away from estate-development, and after 1850 it is rare to find an architect
of any reputation meddling with work of this kind.[46] Thus in 1858 *The
builder* declared (vol 21, p630) that 'what is really the architectural talent of
the day has nothing to do with what becomes the character of London's
architecture', and went on to say that 'houses are built even without drawings
. . . the utmost the builder gets in the way of architectural skill is comprised
in the assistance of one of his own order who is able to draw a rough plan
and an elevation that will allow any kind of ornament he has on hand to be
used, and without regard to proportions and congruity.'

The ornament which the speculator had on hand might be either classical
or gothic. It might consist of ionic porches (the bane of *Building news*),[47] or
of pseudo-venetian capitals (the 'Frankenstein monsters' which impelled
Ruskin to move house).[48] In either case the plan kept its eighteenth-century
form and the vernacular architecture of the time consisted of a georgian
structure surfaced with a victorian veneer.

The georgian terrace consisted, as we have seen, of a row of contiguous
houses, all of a similar plan. Indeed, though their sizes varied, the houses of

20: Ionic porches in Queen's Gate, Kensington.

eighteenth-century London were all built to the same pattern. This uniformity was maintained by the victorian speculative builder. In 1883 *Building news* complained (vol 45, p399) that suburban houses are 'planned generally without the slightest regard to the different requirements of tenants; they are cast in the same mould and stereotyped in feature. Every suburb of the metropolis is overrun with these ready-made houses. The needy tenant has no choice—he is obliged to take the stereotyped dwelling.' It was, indeed, the speculative builder, producing his houses by the hundred, whether as detached villas, semi-detached pairs or terraced rows, who made the towns and cities of victorian England.

11 *The semi-detached house, the narrow house, the front garden and the avenue:* The great advantage of the terrace was its economy, both of land and of structure. The terrace is, however, by its nature a wall along the street. A terrace-house cannot readily give access from the roadway to a private garden at the rear.

At first this did not matter—the eighteenth-century town garden seems to have been a place of vegetables and herbs rather than a pleasance[49]—but as the picturesque movement began to invade the town, the public demanded pleasances with their homes. To meet this need the terrace had to be modified. The problem was solved in 1794 when a firm of auctioneers by the

32

21: Raised lintels and Ruskinian details in a terrace in Steeles Road, Hampstead.

name of Spurrier & Phipps published a project for the development of the Eyre Estate, St John's Wood.[50] This scheme was made up entirely of semi-detached houses. It was the first suburban layout, as Park Village was the first piece of suburbia actually built. Spurrier & Phipps' plan never went beyond the paper stage (Sir John Summerson suggests that the war with France put an end to the original project), but the suburban idea survived and the Eyre Estate was developed in the 1830s and 40s with detached and semi-detached villas in the current fashion of painted stucco and slate roofs.

The semi-detached plan was not a new idea.[51] Houses and cottages of this type had been built previously. The most notable example occurred in Dorset, where Capability Brown erected a planned village at Milton Abbas to take the place of an earlier settlement which had been demolished in order to perfect the setting of the local great house.[52] These, however, were cottages built for farm-labourers. The houses in Park Village and the Eyre Estate were for the middle and upper classes.

The regency and early-victorian semi-detached houses consisted essentially of pairs of georgian terrace-houses mirrored about the party wall. The architects of these buildings used the semi-detached plan to give access to the

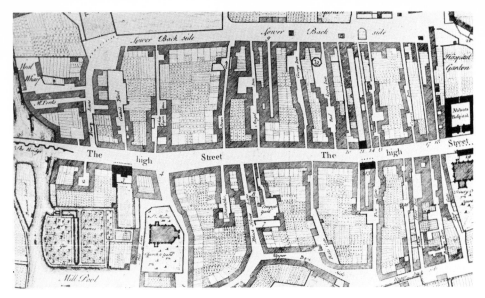

22: *Detail of a map of Guildford, 1739, showing the arrangement of gardens.*

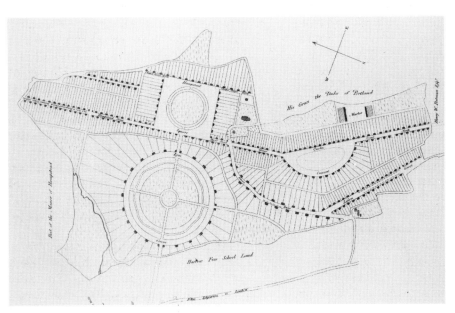

23: *Spurrier and Phipps' plan for the development of the Eyre Estate, St John's Wood.*

garden, but they stopped there. They seldom exploited the possibilities of this type of house. They kept the basement-kitchen (which had originated in georgian times as a means of providing an unobtrusive tradesmen's entrance on the street-frontage) and they preferred not to place the back door in the

24: Part of the Eyre Estate, St John's Wood.

empty flank wall, its most simple and economical position.

The arrangement of rooms deriving from the georgian terrace-house was adopted so generally that it has come to be known as the 'universal plan'.[53] It survives today in a modified two-storied form as the standard pattern of municipal and speculative housing. It is convenient, cheap to build, and because of its narrow frontage is economical in the use of land. Houses of this type are built in terrace or semi-detached formation, and also (alas!) as detached units. The detached house built to the universal plan (we may call it the 'narrow house' for short) deserves special mention because it is the commonest, the ugliest and the most economical of detached houses. It also seems to have originated in the Eyre Estate, for there are narrow houses in Clifton Hill and Blenheim Road. (Two examples are illustrated in Summerson's *Georgian London*, p176.) Early in this century Charles Snell included an exceptionally hideous specimen in his book *Modern suburban homes*, published in 1903, and since 1918 they have proliferated everywhere (I have counted eleven in a single Hertfordshire village).

The earlier examples, such as those in Clifton Hill, possess a certain grace. Their classic or tudor detail is attractive, and the fact that they are often three-storied buildings gives them some decency of proportion. The more recent specimens of the type lack these redeeming qualities. The typical narrow house of the twentieth century is a hideous building. It has a facade just higher than it is wide, a pyramidal roof, an arch over the front door and chimneys growing like tulip stalks from the eaves. When provided with a garage it supplies the Englishman's every housing need. There seems little reason to suppose that it will not be built in the future as extensively as in the past.

From the standpoint of layout (as against the design of the houses

35

25: *A narrow house in Blenheim Road, St John's Wood.*
Modern suburban homes *by Charles Snell.*   26: *A narrow house from*

themselves), the most important changes which took place in the design of early nineteenth-century middle-class speculative estates were the introductions of avenue planting and of the front garden. The avenue had been a feature of landscape-design for many years, but in Britain it was kept out of the towns. The trees of Park Village are in the gardens, not on the roadside, and when Repton introduced trees into Bloomsbury he planted them in the centre of Russell Square, not along the street (a policy which was changed by the Borough Council of Camden during the 1970s). Avenue-planting in housing-estates seems to have started (at least in London) in 1851[54] when an antiquarian, explorer, architect, eccentric and local speculative builder by the name of Dr John Samuel Phené included an avenue in his development of Margaretta Terrace, Chelsea. The project caught the attention of the Prince Consort, and he and the Queen went to visit it. The Prince met Phené, discussed street-planting with him, and became an enthusiastic supporter of the idea.[55] With such encouragement other developers also began to plant avenues, though it was some time before every new estate was so adorned. The five-feet-to-the-mile Ordnance maps of the 1860s show that few of the new developments of that time were provided with avenues. At the outset, avenue-planting seemed to be a good idea. Trees were picturesque, squares were wasteful of land. Why should trees not be planted along the street? Unfortunately, as the trees grew their branches spread. They cut out light from the windows of nearby houses. They obstructed traffic. The branches had to be lopped. The trees lost their lovely widely-spreading limbs and instead became ugly trunks with stubby branches ending in callouses of bark from which grew a bunch of long whippy stems. Every city has trees which have been butchered in this manner. Phené and (perhaps) the Prince Consort have much to answer for.

Front gardens were introduced earlier than avenues. They did not exist during the eighteenth century. Even Spurrier and Phipps' plan, for all the originality of its semi-detached villas, shows the houses abutting directly on to the road as if they formed part of a Bloomsbury terrace. But front gardens were a feature of the Eyre Estate when it was finally built, and Nash provided them to go with his semi-detached houses in Park Village East.

With the front garden came the dwarf wall and the boundary hedge, so that by the eighteen-fifties all the ingredients used by the twentieth-century speculative builder were in existence: the narrow economical plot, the semi-detached house, the avenue of trees later to be lopped to avoid interference with traffic, the shallow front garden planted with a few depressing evergreens, the pairs of houses following each other along the roadside like identical beads upon a thread.

Though these features existed at this time they were not always used together on the same estate. Adelaide Road between Swiss Cottage and Chalk Farm, which was built in the early fifties,[56] had semi-detached houses and front gardens, but was not lined with trees. Semi-detached houses also appear, interspersed with terraces, in the fine georgian layout of the Camden New Town Estate, while in Douglas Road, Canonbury, water, front garden trees and a curving road made a charming vista of semi-detached villas.

The pattern of semi-detached housing which originated in Spurrier & Phipps' scheme for the Eyre Estate, and was the basis of the layout of Adelaide Road, gradually hardened into the accepted, inevitable form of speculative suburbia. The pair slowly took the place of the terrace as the typical unit of speculative housing. This change was the first of a series of innovations in housing layout which, though innocent and often desirable in themselves, had deplorable effects upon townscape. The silhouette of a row of semi-detached houses possesses a jagged monotony. It is like a scratched gramophone-record which repeats interminably the same fragment of tune. This restlessness is bad enough; it is made worse by the intrinsic difficulty of designing an attractive pair of identical houses mirrored about the party wall.

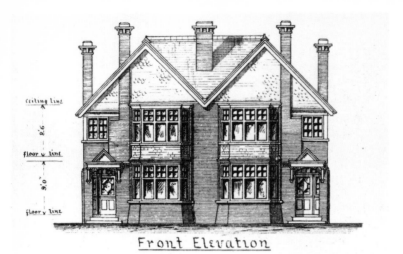

ceiling line

9'.0

floor v line

9'.0

floor v line

Front Elevation

27: A pair of semi-detached houses from Charles Snell's Modern suburban homes.

Such a building suffers unavoidably from the fault in design known to architects as duality: an uneasy balance between two competing parts. The most skilful architect can do no more than mitigate this fault, which is the natural consequence of the semi-detached plan—a symmetrical arrangement with no central unifying feature.[57] Furthermore, the spaces in a semi-detached estate are, as we have seen, uncontrolled. They dribble out between the pairs of houses. This fact is forcibly illustrated by the example of Milton Abbas. Brown's original scheme achieved spatial enclosure by the placing of large horse-chestnut trees in such a way as to fill the gaps between the semi-detached cottages. A forest tree is, however, an inconvenient object to have beside one's house and in recent years their overhanging branches caused the cottages to become dark and damp.[58] The chestnuts were felled, leaving gaps through which the space leaks out between the buildings; and today the scene has lost much of its original charm.

This combination of restlessness, duality and leaking space makes the estate of semi-detached houses the most intractable of all architectural problems. In the eighteen-thirties it can hardly have seemed so difficult as it does now. The pair of houses was the exception rather than the rule, and the speculators of the time were still imbued with georgian traditions. They possessed a natural instinct for fine detail and good proportion and the middle-class houses of the period were large and costly enough to possess a certain scale and dignity. As time went on the problem grew more difficult. Houses became smaller, styles changed, developers lost their innate architectural skill, verges were introduced between carriageway and pavement, and new fashions in planting began to be employed. At the same time suburbia spread ever more widely. These changes, and the vast extension of suburbia which accompanied them, were seldom sought directly. They were rather the

MILTON ABBAS 1820

28: A nineteenth-century drawing of Milton Abbas.

29: A recent photograph of Milton Abbas, after the removal of the chestnut trees.

secondary consequences of the solution of other problems. They came about as the result of population-growth, changes of taste, alterations to the pattern of land-tenure, the activities of philanthropic industrialists and of plant-explorers, new sanitary legislation, improvements in the technology of transport, the desire of the voteless to obtain a parliamentary franchise, the writings of social reformers, and a definition of the architect's professional code.

REFERENCES

1 See among others: Steen Eiler Rasmussen: *London the unique city*, Jonathan Cape, revised edition 1937, p33. 'The Valley Section, Patrick Geddes' World Image', (a set of extracts from lectures by Patrick Geddes, edited by Jaqueline Tyrwhitt) *Journal of the Town Planning Institute*, volume 37, no 3, January 1951, pp64, 65. Lewis Mumford: *The city in history*, Secker and Warburg, 1961, pp358-359. Donald J Olsen: *The growth of victorian London*, Penguin Books, 1979, pp114-120. J N Tarn: 'French flats for the English in 19th century London', in Anthony Sutcliffe, editor, *Multistorey living*, Croom Helm, 1974, pp19-39.

2 The first public vehicles appeared in London in 1829. See Gordon E Cherry: *Urban change and planning*, G T Foulis 1972, p59.

3 John Summerson: *Georgian London*, Penguin Books 1962, p125.

4 Reproduced in *The history of the squares of London*, E Beresford Chancellor, 1907, facing page 91.

5 Edward Hyams: *Capability Brown and Humphry Repton*, J M Dent, 1971, p183.

6 See *Survey of London, vol XXXVI, The Parish of St Paul, Covent Garden*, Athlone Press, University of London 1970, pp27-31, 64 and 78. Also Summerson, op cit, pp40 and 41.

7 Donald J Olsen: *Town planning in London: the eighteenth and nineteenth centuries*, Yale University Press, 1964, pp17-37, 78; and Melville Poole: *The Portman Estate*, unpublished thesis in the Marylebone Public Library, pp18-23. For the system as it operated in Bath see C W Chalklin: *The provincial towns of georgian England*, Edward Arnold, 1974, p78.

8 Local and Personal Acts, 39 and 40, Geo 3, 1800, vol 1, chapter 50.

9 See Florence M Gladstone: *Notting Hill Gate in bygone days*, Anne Bingley, 1969, pp128-129. I have also to thank my friend Mr Barrie Needham, once a resident of Ladbroke Square, for information about these arrangements.

10 Leasehold tenure was not universal throughout the country. The system was established in London, and in certain other areas, particularly in Wales. On the other hand, it was unknown in many provincial cities. Industrial Lancashire was developed on long leases, (ie, from 100 to 999 years). See *Report of the Select Committee on Town Holdings*, Reports from Committees, 1887, Vol XIII, Appendix 2, map facing p816.

11 This is a gross simplification of a highly complex and frequently long-delayed system. For detailed descriptions of the machinery of georgian estate-development see Summerson, op cit, pp77-79, and Olsen: *Town planning in London, pp29-96*.

12 See Chalklin, op cit, pp74, 75 and 80.

13 See Summerson, op cit, pp138-139.

14 John Summerson: *Architecture in Britain 1530-1830*, Pelican History of Art Series, Penguin Books, 1953, p298. Sir John suggests that Nash's conception was inspired by C N Ledoux's ideal city, illustrated in his *L'architecture considerée sous le rapport de l'art, des moeurs et de la legislation*, 1789-1804. See also the same author's *John Nash. Architect to King George IV*, George Allen & Unwin, 1935, pp112-114, and his 'The beginnings of Regents Park, *Architectural history*, Journal of the Society of Architectural Historians of Great Britain, vol 20, 1977, pp56-62. Engravings of Nash's and Leverton's schemes, together with a third, devised by John White, Surveyor to the Duke of Portland's estate, are in the Crace Collection, (Map Library, British Library Reference Division).

15 John Summerson: *Architecture in Britain 1530-1830*, p291.

16 See F M L Thompson: *Hampstead, building a borough*, Routledge and Kegan Paul, 1974, p247.

17 See Kenneth Clark: *The gothic revival*, Constable, 1928, pp184 and 221.

18 'To call it a quest for "character" is merely to provide a name which still requires and eludes definition. What the mid-Victorians meant by "character" may be apprehended equally by studying the anthromorphic dogs of Landseer or by reading Samuel Smiles.

The determination of common factors must be left to others.' John Summerson, 'The London suburban villa', *Architectural review*, vol 104, 1948, pp63-72.

19 'Further on, on the opposite side, a corner site is occupied by a small villa of some merit in the Queen Anne, or, we should rather prefer to call it, "Old English" cottage style.' *Building news*, vol 31, 1876, p409.

20 Eg, Leyswood, Sussex; and Cragside, Northumberland. Shaw also participated in the development of the Queen Anne style. For an account of this see Mark Girouard: *Sweetness and light. The 'Queen Anne' movement, 1860-1900*, Clarendon Press, 1977, pp25-32.

21 For an account of the origins of neo-georgian, see Andrew Saint: *Richard Norman Shaw*, Yale UP, 1976, p245; and Pevsner's essay on Shaw in *Victorian architecture*, edited by Peter Ferriday, Jonathan Cape, 1963, pp239-243.

22 In a lecture on 'The English home in the 19th century' given at the Geffrye Museum, Shoreditch on October 19 1948. *Architects' journal*, vol 108, p470.

23 See also A K Cairncross: *Home and foreign investment 1870-1913*, Cambridge University Press, 1953, p84.

24 Cairncross explains that before 1840 the 19th-century industrialists' working capital came directly from the banks and indirectly from agricultural landowners. As time went on, however, the importance of land-rent as a source of capital steadily diminished, 'at first because of the rise of industry and commerce, and later because of the long depression in agriculture after 1874'. These circumstances led the landowners to be 'replaced by a "stock and bond-holding aristocracy" as the chief owners of wealth and the chief accumulaters of capital'.

25 *Select Committee on Town Holdings*, 28 June 1887, p494, para9647.

26 'Monopolies benefit but the few, and are a calamity to the many. In the succeeding chapters . . . which describe my visits to the Portman, Grosvenor and Bedford estates will be revealed the cruelties, wrongs and outrages arising out of the ground monopoly in London.' Frank Banfield, *The great landlords of London*. Spencer Blackett, 1890, p22, reprinted from the *Sunday times*.

27 Seymour J Price: *Building societies, their origin and history*, Franey & Co, 1958, pp19-20.

28 Roger Gill: *Till we have built Jerusalem*, University of Sheffield, PhD thesis, p259.

29 Building Societies Act 1874, Public General Acts, 37 & 38 Vict, 1874, chapter 42, clause 37.

30 This statement is an inference only. It is possible, but I think unlikely, that the grouped houses in North Oxford were built first and sold afterwards. The records of the St John's College Estate include information about sales of land in North Oxford to three local architects: Frederick Codd, S Lipscombe Seckham and W Wilkinson (who was also the estate's surveyor). The houses which these men built included the georgian crescents of Park Town, built by Seckham in the mid-fifties, and a number of semi-detached pairs as well as individual houses on their own plots. These last are varied in shape and complex in their design. A simple repetitive form is fundamental to the economics of speculative building, and Codd, Seckham and Wilkinson would hardly have built as they did if their business had consisted only of building houses for sale. (I have to thank Mr C J Hewitt for allowing me to study his notes on the development of this area.) For a description of North Oxford see David A Hinton: 'An early garden suburb, North Oxford in the 19th century', *Country life*, vol 156, 1974, p845.

31 John B Papworth: 'Remarks on English villas', in J Britton and A Pugin: *Illustrations of the public buildings of London*, 1825, p83.

32 J M Richards: *The castles on the ground, the anatomy of suburbia*. John Murray, 2nd edition 1973, p13.

33 Walter Besant: *London in the nineteenth century*, p62, quoted by Olsen in *The growth of victorian London*, p210.

34 Olsen: *Town planning in London*, p75.

35 Olsen: *The growth of victorian London*, p23.

36 F M L Thompson, op cit, p241.

37 Olsen: *The growth of victorian London*, p239. A school was, however, built despite the objections.

38 'Generally speaking it may be accepted as an axiom that the class of house to which this work is devoted must have the Main Entrance and at least one of the Reception Rooms in the front, and the Kitchen and its Offices towards the back.' Charles Snell: *Modern suburban homes*, 1903, p5.

39 Olsen: *Town planning in London*, pp145-147.

40 I have to thank my friend Mr Peter Lucas for this information.

41 *Select Committee on Town Holdings*, p33, para765.

42 Peter Collison: 'The Cutteslowe Saga', *New society*, April 25 1963, p19. The walls were built in December 1934 and demolished 25 years later.

43 Builders felt it 'best to conform to the existing type of house-planning as less costly and more likely of being remunerative . . . leaseholders are content with building as their forefathers have done'. *Building news*, vol 32, 1877, p357.

44 Eg, Lonsdale Square, Islington, by Richard Cromwell Carpenter, an admirable if somewhat earnest design; or de Beauvoir Square, Hackney, a more light-hearted example whose architect I have been unable to trace.

45 *Building news*, vol 3, 1857, p383.

46 Summerson: *Georgian London*, p290. Barry and Decimus Burton seem to have been exceptions to this rule, but their work in the speculative field lay outside London, and Sir John's book deals with the metropolis.

47 'We might almost imagine we were within the precincts of some convict establishment or military barrack—that railing wall and barricade formed the limit of our existence in their interminable prospect. We suffer a sense of oppression as we cast our eyes down the miles of stereotyped perspective of Cromwell Road or Queen's Gate in which balustrade and hackneyed fenestration in stock brick and stucco are supreme, the flat stretch of wall being broken only by ionic porches, which look like sentry-boxes in the lengthened vista.' *Building news*, vol 31, 1876, p357.

48 'I have had an indirect influence on nearly every cheap villa-builder between this and Bromley; and there is scarcely a public house near the Crystal Place but sells its gin and bitters under pseudo-venetian capitals copied from the church of the Madonna of Health or of Miracles. And one of my principal notions for moving my present house is that it is surrounded everywhere by the accursed Frankenstein monsters of, indirectly my own making.' Letter from Ruskin to the *Pall Mall gazette*, March 16 1872.

49 Very little is known of the history of town gardens. A note in the Garden Exhibition held at the Victoria and Albert Museum in the summer of 1979 declared that 'historic town gardens are almost an extinct species and today the history of gardening is chartered largely through the gardens of country houses'. The best that the exhibition organizers could do to illustrate the eighteenth-century town garden was to show a large-scale map of Guildford, dated 1739. The map indicated that all but four of the gardens of Guildford at that time were small, allotment-like plots, apparently given over to vegetables and herbs.

50 Summerson: *Georgian London*, p175

51 Summerson points out that the houses in Park Village are almost all in pairs, and goes on to mention a pair in Hampstead, dated 1702, as well as a layout (dated 1719-20) for semi-detached pairs at Westminster. *Architecture in Britain 1530-1830*, p320.

52 Edward Hyams, op cit, p77; see also Thomas Sharp: *The anatomy of the village*, Penguin Books, 1946, pp22, 23; and Gillian Darley: *Villages of vision*, Architectural Press, 1975, pp11, 12. Gillian Darley suggests that Sir William Chambers may have been responsible for the outline plan, if not for its execution.

53 'There is no escape from it. Mariners' humble cottages in the East End have this plan; and so have the great houses in Carlton House Terrace.' Summerson: *Georgian London*, p66. 'The usual plan of the small, three-bedroomed house is more or less the

same throughout the whole country and for that reason is known to architects as the 'universal' plan. *When we build again*, Bournville Village Trust, George Allen & Unwin, 1941, p38.

54 The date was given in a letter to the *Chelsea news* of May 6 1966 by a Mr Hurford James.

55 See the *Times of Chelsea*, January 1974, p7, and a biographical note on Dr John Samuel Phené in Chelsea Public Library. Phené's name is perpetuated in Phené Street, at the end of Margaretta Terrace and in the Phené Arms, a pub on the corner.

56 F M L Thompson, op cit, p239.

57 It is worth noting the fact that Brown (at Milton Abbas) and Nash (at Park Village) took care to provide their semi-detached pairs with some unifying feature on the exterior in order to make them look like single dwellings. See Summerson: *Architecture in Britain 1530-1830*, p320.

58 See Gillian Darley, op cit, p12.

2 SLUMS, PHILANTHROPY, TRANSPORT AND REFORM

1   *Working-class speculative housing:* In the previous chapter we sought to describe some of the characteristics of early and mid-victorian middle-class speculative housing and to discuss the factors which influenced its form. We should realize, however, that the victorian speculators did not build only for the middle classes. Indeed, most of their activities were concerned with providing for the lower classes of society—the artisans and the poor.

The manner in which such accommodation had been provided during the georgian era varied from place to place. Thus while the poor of London lived in single rooms designed originally for middle and upper-class accommodation, those in the contemporary industrial cities occupied housing intended from the first for the working-classes.[1]

During the first part of Victoria's reign this pattern was maintained. In St Giles the poor continued to live in rookeries of run-down middle-class housing, while in the midlands, the north and the capital's southern and eastern suburbs the speculative builders were providing living-space (we can hardly call them homes) for the bursting working-class populations of the Industrial Revolution.

The form of such development varied in accordance with local conditions. In the case of Nottingham, the land which surrounded the city was under the control of burgesses and freemen who, despite many efforts to dislodge them, consistently refused to commute their common lands for building. As a result of this early green-belt policy, the city's boundaries remained unchanged between 1720 and 1841, despite the fact that its population grew over five times during that period. Its inhabitants were crowded into courts,

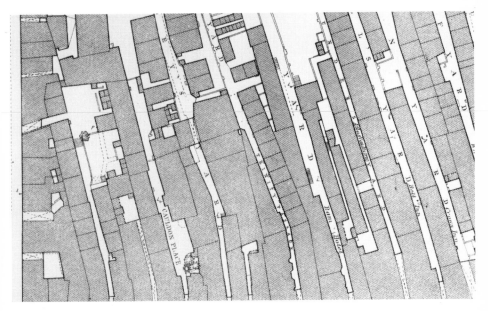

30: *Part of central Nottingham mapped in the late nineteenth century.*

47

alleys, dark grim streets and even caves carved out of the soft local sandstone. However, not all the working people of Nottingham stayed within the city; some spilt over the green belt and formed new satellite communities beyond it. The traditional industries of Nottingham were lace-making and hosiery-manufacture, and the new overspill-housing was designed to meet the needs of the framework-knitters. Thus the houses of Hyson Green included workshops for the lace-making machinery (on the second floor) as well as living-accommodation (on the ground and first floors), attics which might be used either as a store or as sleeping-space for children or journeymen,[2] and, most exceptionally for their time, long front gardens.

Not all the new housing of Nottingham's satellite villages reached the standard of Hyson Green. Some, though proportionately not very much, was back-to-back. In this Nottingham provides a contrast with Leeds, where a firm tradition of back-to-back housing was established at the end of the eighteenth century; a tradition which survived until 1937, and which seems to have resulted partly from the system of land-uses of the inner city, and partly from the pattern of farming and land-ownership on the fringe of the built-up area. The inner city of Leeds was a place of closely packed houses, shops and inns backed by long narrow yards. These yards were gradually filled with lean-to dwellings built against the yard walls, leaving between them only a narrow passage to provide access. The housing type which resulted was used later for new developments on the fringe of the town. Here the system of land-ownership was one of individual smallholdings: single narrow fields which were sold, one at a time, for building. The areas so provided

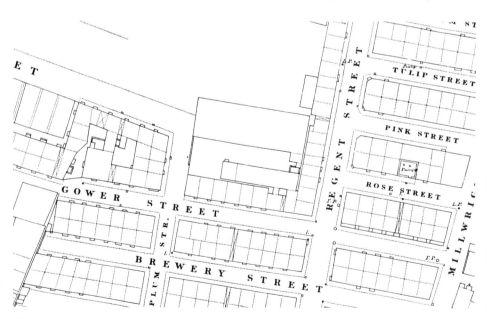

31: Back-to-back housing in Leeds, mapped about 1860.

48

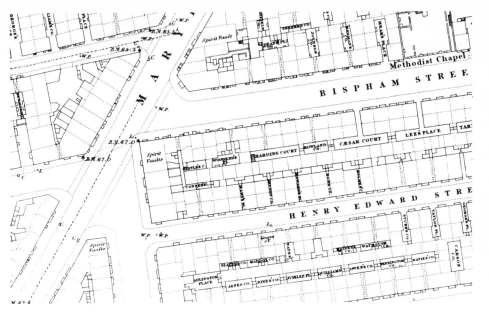

32: Court houses and front houses in Liverpool, about 1860.

were too small for effective development, and the result was an incoherent patch-work of disconnected alleyways lined with back-to-backs and 'half-backs', lines of cottages one room deep, so pressed against the edge of the field that there was no room even for a back alleyway.[3]

Liverpool was more affected than Leeds or Nottingham by the demographic pressures of nineteenth-century industrialism. It had to accommodate not only its own population-growth but periodical floods of Irish immigrants, many of them refugees from the famine of 1846. To provide for the city's surging poverty-stricken population, Liverpool's speculative builders went in for back-to-back housing arranged, like that of Leeds, in small courts. The houses were three stories high, and consisted of two rooms, ten or eleven feet square, and a garret. The courts were between six and fifteen feet wide. In addition there might be a cellar, which was always sub-let. Access to the courts was by a narrow passage or archway, while the far end was closed by the back or side of an adjoining building so the court formed a cul-de-sac with a narrow opening. Together with these 'court-houses', Liverpool's speculative working-class housing included streets of so-called 'front houses'. These were less claustrophobic than the court-houses; they were built about twenty-four feet apart, but their dull, almost anonymous character must have made them even grimmer in appearance. Like the court-houses, they were equipped with cellars, and 'it was in this kind of accommodation that the post-1835 Borough's cellar population was concentrated'.[4]

London was different again. Here land was too scarce and valuable to be squandered on separate dwellings for the artisan-class, much less for the really

49

poor. Building new dwellings for multiple occupancy was not an economic proposition, and the succession of London Building Acts defined standards of dimensions and construction which made it impossible for back-to-backs to be built, and indeed for anyone but the middle classes to afford a new house. Furthermore, the leasehold system inhibited development for high-density working-class housing. The lower-density middle-class estate would maintain its reversionary value throughout the term of the lease, while the higher-density working-class housing would be poorly constructed, badly maintained, subject to decay, and so an unsuitable candidate for an improved ground-rent. James Noble, writing in 1836, warned landowners that 'the inferior or fourth-rate dwellings merely secure a ground-rental for the time being: and probably from the introduction of indifferent materials and slight character of construction become prematurely dilapidated if not ruinous before the expiry of the building term, *and consequently an improved rent to the freeholder would be visionary*'.[5]

In consequence of these influences, London's working-class speculative housing occurred in areas such as Stepney, Poplar, or Bethnal Green, where land-values were less than in the centre and the Building Acts inoperative or loosely enforced—in places like Portland Town adjacent to St John's Wood, a district in which, owing to some oversight on the part of the landlord's agent, the building-leases were not framed in such a way as to prevent such development; or in districts like Somers Town, which lay on the northern fringes of Bloomsbury, and whose inhabitants provided the services needed by the middle-class residents to the south.

The restraints of the Building Acts created a type of house described in 1834 by the *Architectural magazine* (vol 1, pp38-9) as consisting of two rooms, one up and one down. 'They have generally from 12 to 14 feet frontage and are from 12 to 14 feet deep, having an access on the ground floor in front of the lower room and steps outside at the back leading to the upper room. Three, four or more have a yard and other conveniences in common. Dwellings of this description are rarely properly drained or ventilated, and therefore form nurseries for the cholera and all other diseases. They are usually let at from 3s to 4s per week each room.'

2 *Cholera and the victorian slum:* Much of Somers Town must have been like this. It was described in 1844 as a vast assemblage of 'put-up houses already falling into decay'.[6] By the late sixties it had been demolished to make way for the railway construction north of St Pancras.[7] It was clearances such as these, whether for railways, for commercial development, for the construction of wide new thoroughfares like New Oxford Street, or for the demolition of insanitary accommodation under the Torrens and Cross Acts,[8] which caused the worst of London's overcrowding. Those evicted did not, as had been hoped, spread thinly throughout the capital. They settled nearby, making the adjacent slums worse than ever.

The slums, whether they took the form of Leeds' back-to-backs, Liverpool's courts and cellars, or London's rookeries, were crowded, damp, filthy and insanitary. Furthermore, they were, as had been noted by the *Architectural magazine*, breeding-places for cholera, a disease which had reached Britain from India in the late 1820s and which by 1832 had gained a serious hold in many parts of the country. Its spread was due in large part to the squalid housing conditions in which the great bulk of the population lived. The following contemporary description of a part of Leeds in 1842 gives some idea of the problem which faced the sanitary reformers of the time.

'The courts and culs-de-sac exist everywhere, the building of houses back-to-back occasions this in a great measure. It is in fact part of the economy of buildings that are to pay a good percentage. In one cul-de-sac in the town of Leeds there are 34 houses, and in ordinary times there dwell in these houses 340 persons or 10 to every house: but as these houses are many of them receiving-houses for itinerant labourers, during the periods of hay-time and harvest and the fairs at least twice that number are then here congregated. The name of this place is the Boot and Shoe Yard in Kirkgate: a location from which the commissioners removed in the days of the cholera 75 cart loads of manure which had been untouched for years and where there now exists a surface of human excrement of very considerable extent, to which these impure and unventilated dwellings are additionally exposed. This property is said to pay the best annual interest of any cottage property in the Borough.'[9]

Various attempts were made to deal with this horrifying situation. Sanitarians like Chadwick sought to improve conditions by such measures as

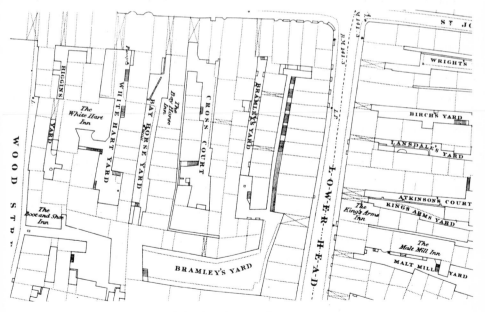

33: Part of Kirkgate Ward, Leeds in the nineteenth century.

providing proper sewerage and water-supplies, fixing minimum standards for street-widths and construction of dwellings, and appointing medical officers of health; philanthropists, such as the Prince Consort, erected experimental working-class dwellings; 'terminating benefit' and 'land' societies provided homes which were cheap enough for the artisan to buy. Optimists like James Silk Buckingham devised utopian cities in which mankind, free from the squalor of industrialism, would live a healthy and moral life; private individuals like Octavia Hill demonstrated that by proper upkeep and supervision poor properties could be improved to the advantage of both landlord and tenant; paternalistic employers built model villages for their work-people; and members of all these groups joined in the formation of the National Association for the Promotion of Social Science—a body which hoped to further 'the scientific study of the laws which govern men's habits as members of a community, and of the principles of human nature upon which the structure of society and its movements depend'.[10]

3 *The long straight street:* The courts and culs-de-sac of which the Poor Law Commissioners had written provided one of the sanitary reformers' most obvious targets. The warrens of alleyways which made up the slum areas of nineteenth century industrial cities were dark, crime-ridden, filthy and inconvenient to the stranger, who could easily lose his way among them. Furthermore, the fact that the alleyways were concealed from the passer-by made it easy for Authority to ignore their disgraceful condition. One of the more

picturesque members of the movement against these 'courts and alleys' was a certain T J Maslen, an ex-army officer of philanthropic outlook, whose book, *Suggestions for the improvement of our towns and houses*,[11] appeared in 1843, a year after the Poor Law Commissioners' Report was published.

Maslen wrote as follows (pp212-3): 'If you hear a quarrel between two women, it is sure to be up some court or alley; if you see a fight between two men, it is sure to be up some court or alley. If there is a brothel in the vicinity of any street, it is sure to be up some court or alley in the street. If there is a gambling hell, it is sure to be in some court or alley. If you hear a fiddle squealing at noon-day, be sure it is a dance of naked women in some den of infamy up a court or alley. If you hear of a gang of coiners or forgers, they are generally found up some court or alley. If you hear of a poor man's lamb (his daughter) being the victim of a seducer, you will hear it happened in some house up a court or alley. If you hear of a barbarous

34: *A slum alleyway, from Gustave Doré's* London.

murder committed upon some unsuspecting youth, it will turn out that he was decoyed to a public house up some court or alley to see some cheap silk handkerchiefs . . . In fact, courts or alleys being retired from public observation are almost always nests of poisonous filth, hiding places for thieves, and the secluded scenes of vice, depravity and desperate misery . . . I strongly recommend, for the good of all classes, that courts and alleys be abolished, and let men live in wide streets, and act openly and honestly in the sight of all.

To achieve this laudable objective he proposed (preface, pV) that 'it would be wise to trace the plans of new streets from the first as wide, as long and as straight as possible, adopting the reasonable measurements laid down in the following pages.'

Maslen was not one to skimp such matters. His 'reasonable measurements' were thirty or forty feet from the centre-line to the edge of the kerb (p109), an arrangement which would give a carriageway between three and four times as wide as today's usual practice.

Maslen was soon forgotten, and his propaganda seems to have had little direct effect. To his contemporaries he was probably a harmless eccentric who spent his retirement in the preparation of hare-brained schemes of civic improvement. His ideas about street-patterns were, however, a natural reaction to the circumstances of his age, and he probably put down in words what many of his contemporaries were thinking. The more progressive developers could, and did, adopt these ideas, modifying his proposals only in regard to the width of the carriageway. Time, however, was required before such concepts gained general currency, and their full impact was not felt until the expansion of 'by-law housing' in the eighties, forty years after the publication of his book.

Maslen, like the jubjub, was ages ahead of the fashion. His essay is a remarkable mixture of comedy in matters of detail, and prophetic vision in matters of principle. He recognised (p145) the need for a plan to include the dimension of time as well as those of space, an idea which was not incorporated in planning legislation until after the second world war—though it must be admitted that his proposed time-scale for the implementation of a plan (three hundred years) would not be accepted by today's practitioners of the town-planners' art; writing fifty years before the invention of the motor car, and a century before its impact on our cities, he advocated the segregation of vehicles and pedestrians, proposing (p13) that London should be replanned in such a way as to 'leave the one principal thoroughfare for carriages and to construct a continuous series of arcades for foot passengers only, to draw off a portion of those yet unborn millions who will otherwise swarm and block up the foot-pavements of Cheapside and the Strand'; he proposed, a century before the passing of the New Towns Act, that government should 'begin the building of ten new cities in England, each intended to contain three-hundred-thousand souls and to be colonized from the old cities; the legislature to grant two million sterling a year for twenty years for the building department'

53

(p245); and forty-five years before the passing of the first major Allotment Act he suggested (p111) that the people should be given 'a taste for and the knowledge of how to *cultivate and enjoy gardens of their own* where they might grow potatoes for their winter supper (for a roast potatoe (sic) is a capital supper) . . . which they would not eat with less appetite for having walked out of a noisy factory or mill into a sweet little quiet garden at the edge of the town. All the fields round the town in every side and immediately contiguous to the houses should be divided into about twenty-thousand squares, of a rood each, not divided by walls but by paths, and every citizen should be compelled to hire a rood of ground for a garden or pay a tax for exemption.'

4 *Model villages—Ironville:* The model village was an eighteenth-century concept. A great landowner would build such a place to house his farm-workers, or an industrialist would provide one for his employees. These early industrial villages were sited in accordance with the geographical needs of the industry concerned. Mistley in Essex was established in connection with the maltings and quays which the local landowner, Richard Rigby, built on the banks of the Stour near Manningtree. Capability Brown's Milton Abbas, and John Nash's Blaise Hamlet, were picturesque examples of the type, rural preludes to the building of Park Village in London.

Industrial villages such as Mistley were small affairs by subsequent standards, but they set precedents for later settlements which philanthropic employers established in connection with their factories. Of these, New Lanark, extended and transformed by that utopian socialist, Robert Owen, between 1799 and 1816, and Saltaire near Bradford, built by Sir Titus Salt in 1852, are the best-known. These, however, were not the only examples of such settlements. There were others, less often cited by historians of nineteenth-century planning, but not less interesting, and from our point of view more important. One of them is Ironville, a place which was founded by the Butterley Ironworks Company in the 1830s among the pits and slag heaps of the Derbyshire coalfield.

The part of Ironville which was built first is a dreary place. If its name were not sufficiently descriptive, its terraces of mean little houses are called Furnace Row and Foundry Row, as if to emphasize to their inhabitants that they live there only by courtesy of their employers. But Ironville has lovely country close by. It lies on the fringe of the woods of Codnor Park, and to the west of the settlement there is a dale known as 'Golden Valley' whose stream was dammed in the early nineteenth century to form a storage reservoir for the canal which runs through the village. The space between the dam and the village formed a convenient dump for the cinders from the Butterley Company's furnaces. By about 1850 the heap of cinders had reached the level of the dam. The heap was then flattened and a housing-estate built upon it. This estate (known as Queen Street and the Market Place, though no markets are held there) is, for our purposes, the most

54

35: Blaise Hamlet.

36: Ironville—the Market Place and Queen Street.

significant part of Ironville, for it shows the beginnings of the movement for low-density industrial housing which culminated in the garden cities of Letchworth and Welwyn, and in the post-war new towns. The houses in the Market Place are laid out on two sides of a large rectangular green, beyond which lies the reservoir and the woods of Codnor Park. The green is a waste of rank, weedy grass encumbered with clothes-drying posts, and the houses, though they are not slums, are bleak and unattractive. Nevertheless the planning of the estate foreshadows much of the best of present-day practice. The spoil-dump is put to good use, the service roads are set at the rear of the terrace-

55

blocks, and the green is arranged so that the open space of the park extends into the area of housing.

5 *The 'land societies'*: Ironville is interesting not only on account of its lay-out, but also because it was the scene of a meeting held on March 18 1850 at which it was resolved to form a society pledged 'to form one common fund by the contributions of the members for the purpose of purchasing from time to time large tracts of eligible building land, retailing the same to members at the wholesale or cost price in lots available for building purposes, or to be used as garden ground as the members may think fit'.[12] This body (The Ironville Benefit Building Society) was part of a curious quasi-political movement known as the 'land societies'.

The land societies were centered in Birmingham and flourished during the fifties and sixties.[13] A land society was a poor man's housing-association, a sort of cross between a building society and a speculative developer. They originated about the 1730s, and all had in common the acquisition of large estates and their division into building-plots. Some, which were self-help organisations, sold the plots to their members at cost-price, others 'sold or leased plots or erected rows of more or less identical houses for sale to any person willing to buy for cash down or on a weekly basis'.[14]

After the Reform Act of 1832, more land societies were formed, but this time with a political purpose—to increase the franchise to the benefit of the party concerned with establishing them. Under an Act of Henry VI, as extended by the Reform Act, the owner of a freehold estate of an annual value of not less than 40 shillings was entitled to a parliamentary vote. Both parties saw in this an opportunity to increase the register of electors to their own advantage. They formed land societies to build houses which were then sold freehold on weekly payments to their own political supporters.

The movement was started by Cobden, who ensured the capture of the West Riding constituency for radicalism and free trade by thus creating five thousand liberal votes in the area. The Anti-Corn Law League followed his example in other parts of the country, and in 1848 a certain James Taylor founded the Birmingham Freehold Land Society 'with the double object of creating votes and encouraging the working classes to invest in land and property'.[15] Taylor used to stump the country making speeches calling upon every good radical to assist the party's cause by helping to establish a land society in the district. It was at one of these meetings that the Ironville Society was formed.

The Ironville Society did not last very long, though it did build a few cottages in the nearby village of Waingroves. These buildings are scattered in a sporadic manner along the road. The passer-by would hardly notice them. They are dingy cottages in a dingy part of Britain. They are, however, of special interest to this study, for they show how the rural immigrants' habit of gardening began to influence the form and layout of industrial housing. We have seen how the middle-class desire for a pleasance originated in the early nineteenth century as a consequence of the romantic movement. At first this desire was confined to the wealthy and was practised by them, by the occupants of an occasional model village such as the Quaker settlements of Nant Head or Middleton in Teesdale,[16] or by the residents of houses such as those at Hyson Green, Nottingham. By the time, however, that the land societies became active, the cultivation of flowers had begun to affect the workers also. It provided an escape from the squalor of the industrial revolution. It was practised by all classes. The factory-owners grew orchids and the workers grew auriculas.[17]

The relationship between gardening and the land-society movement is exemplified both by the Waingroves cottages, which have front gardens, albeit small ones, and by the terms of sale of an estate at Handsworth, Birmingham, which was developed in 1869 by the Birmingham Freehold Land Society. These required that each house should be 'set back twenty yards from the footpath on the north side and ten yards on the south side',[18] arrangements which resulted in very deep front gardens.

We have already noted that gardening, and with gardening the need to arrange rear-access, provided the raison d'être of the semi-detached plan. However, not all housing is semi-detached; where a terrace-house has a back garden, some expedient has to be devised to provide an approach to the garden, the coal-shed and the back door. Present-day architects adopt various ingenious devices to solve this problem, but until recently the commonest solutions were those which originated in the mid-nineteenth century: a drive

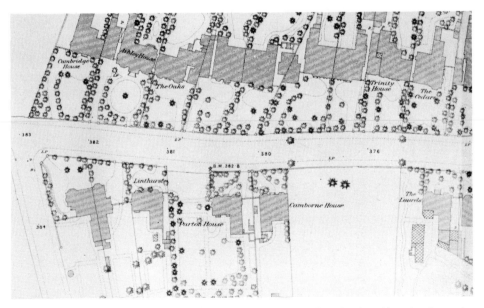

37: Trinity Road, Handsworth, Birmingham—a middle-class land-society development, 1869.

38: The same street in Walkley, Sheffield, from front and rear.

or path behind the houses (the arrangement employed at Ironville), or a terrace of mirrored pairs with a tunnel between each pair (the system which can be seen in some of the houses at Waingroves).[19]

By the period of the second Reform Act (1867), the Birmingham Land Society had become a 'sedate middle-class movement'.[20] That does not seem to have happened in Sheffield; William White's map of the city in 1869 is marked with the names of the societies which developed the Walkley district. Walkley is a hilly area, built up in an irregular manner with terraces of different lengths, together with an occasional single house or pair of cottages. The smaller societies were somewhat hand-to-mouth organizations, and it seems that they built sporadically as the money came in. Much of Walkley is drab and mean, but the houses have gardens, and here and there a tree and a curving wall make an attractive picture. The mood of the builders is reflected in the names of some of the streets. Walkley has an Industry Street, a Grammar Street, and a Freedom Road.

6   *Philanthropic housing:* The land societies were self-help organizations. They were radical in origin and were established by members of the working classes in order to obtain the franchise, while at the same time providing themselves with decent homes. In this they were the political opposite of the Artizan's Labourers and General Dwellings Company (Limited). This was a property company of philanthropic intent, which was inspired not by the radical philosophy of Cobden, but by the benevolent Toryism of Lord Shaftesbury. It was formed in 1867 'in consequence of the destruction of houses by railroads, and other improvements'. It did not sell its houses freehold. Early in its history it sold the lease, and later became a property company of the orthodox kind, building houses to rent.

The company's first venture was the Shaftesbury Park Estate at Battersea, which was founded by Lord Shaftesbury in 1872 and opened two years later in the presence of Shaftesbury, Disraeli and others. *The builder* noted (vol 30, p623-4) that 'on every estate purchased by the company a suitable space will be reserved as a recreation ground, a cooperative store will be built for the especial benefit of the tenants, and public houses will be absolutely forbidden'. In his speech when laying the foundation stone of the estate, Lord Shaftesbury declared, 'we have founded this day a workmen's city'. *The builder*'s comment was both wise and cautious: 'We are not quite certain that we desire to see workmen's cities established, we have no desire to segregate classes, but we shall doubtless have an opportunity before long to know more of the plan proposed'.

The importance of the Shaftesbury Park Estate lies not only in the fact that it was an early experiment in working-class housing, but also in the design of the houses themselves. Richard Austin, the architect, enlarged and improved the small compact plan of the mid-nineteenth-century cottage, (though his terrace-blocks were still composed of mirrored pairs like those at Waingroves). He dressed up the elevations in a 'domestic gothic or tudor'

39: Shaftesbury Park Estate, Battersea.

style, he provided a bay-window here and party-coloured brickwork there, he laid out the estate with straight roads, cast-iron railings, tiny front gardens and privet hedges, and in so doing produced the prototype of that bye-law housing which was to overwhelm our cities during the last two decades of the nineteenth century.[21]

The Artizan's Labourers and General Dwellings Company was only one of Lord Shaftesbury's interests in the field of philanthropic housing. He was also a leading member of the Society for Improving the Condition of the Labouring Classes. Besides holding meetings and carrying out propaganda, this association built experimental blocks of flats (such as the still-existing tenements in Streatham Street near the British Museum). It was also interested in the maintenance and improvement of slum property and in rural housing. In 1850 its architect, Henry Roberts, published a manual on the dwellings of the labouring classes, which included a number of semi-detached cottages designed for agricultural districts. These cottages had twin gables on the facade. The same arrangement appeared in two designs for 'suburban

60

residences' which were illustrated in an anonymous and undated pattern book of about 1855, *The builder's practical director*; it crops up again in a later pattern book, John Vincent's *Country cottages*, published in 1860, in which the gables make a shallow 'V' in the centre, spreading down further on either side, in John Birch's project for a pair of urban cottages which won the Society of Arts prize in 1864, and in the cottages built in the early 70s by Earl Cowper for the workers on his estate at Panshanger near Hertford. It was, indeed, a common feature of the dwellings which victorian landowners built on their rural estates. Such cottages provided the prototype for the houses at Bedford Park, Chiswick,[22] an estate which, like Park Village and the Eyre Estate, is of seminal importance in the history of suburbia.

7 *Bedford Park:* This estate on the western periphery of London was begun in 1875 as a speculative enterprise by a certain Jonathan Carr. Carr was perhaps inspired by the work of the Artizan's Labourers and General Dwellings Company, for *Building news* of December 22 1876 declared (p621) that he 'proposed to supply for the middle classes that which the Shaftesbury Park Estate has partially done for the labouring classes'.

His intentions are fully described in a letter (signed 'The Freeholder', but clearly written by Carr himself) which appeared in the same journal six weeks later. Carr's letter is worth quoting at some length. It not only describes what he had in mind, it indicates that the architect's 'holier-than-thou' attitude to the speculative builder was well ingrained into the profession's mind at that time, and it defines the problem which the architect who enters the speculative field has to solve—that of devising an original and attractive design which can be built as cheaply as those which the speculator is used to building by the hundred.

Carr wrote as follows (vol 32, p134): 'For the last two years the profession seems to have been united only in one point, and that is that an ordinary mortal has no right to possess anything needing construction, from a simple chair to an elaborate house, without calling in the aid of one of their own body. I must say I have become a by-no-means unwilling believer: and as from every one of the profession with whom I came in contact I heard nothing but condemnation of the present style of architecture in which suburban villas are built, I anticipated being readily able to secure for those in which I was individually interested plans that would obviate the faults grumbled at . . . I wanted plans of houses that a gentleman would be glad to live in, which should be as perfect architecturally as the most splendid house, but that the extreme cost of a detached house should be £700, and for a pair of villas £1100. Now, while I found, as I said above, every member of the profession with a sneer for 'Camden Town gothic', as the efforts of a speculative builder to be picturesque are generally called, there were few who could suggest a remedy so long as people were so inconsiderate as to want houses as such a price.'

To us Bedford Park does not appear particularly remarkable. It is an estate

40: *A pair of cottages by John Vincent.*

41: *Semi-detached cottages at Tewin, Hertford.*

42: *A pair of houses in Bedford Park, by E W Godwin.*

62

43: A street in Bedford Park.

of red-brick houses with bay-windows and gables to the road. We have seen many such buildings; but we look at it with the eye of the twentieth century, and if we find Bedford Park uninteresting, it is because thousands of imitation Bedford Parks have been built everywhere during the last ninety years. For Bedford Park was the prototype of our twentieth-century semi-detached suburbia. To us it seems a little ordinary, but to its contemporaries it was sensational. Architectural students used to visit it as those of today visit the latest experiments of Richard Rogers. It was original in a number of differents ways.

In the first place its style was new. The seventies were the years in which 'Queen Anne' was beginning to take the place of gothic or italianate as the fashionable pattern of design for domestic purposes, and Bedford Park was the first occasion upon which the style was used for a whole estate.

Secondly, there were no basements, and so no area steps to a back door on the street frontage.[23] In building his houses without basements Carr was faced with the same problem as that which caused the Ironville Land Society to provide tunnel-access to the gardens of their houses at Waingroves. The tunnel was, however, at best an unsatisfactory expedient; the semi-detached plan provided a more acceptable solution to the problem of access to the back door, the coal-cellar, the dustbin and the garden. Terraces and basements went together, and Carr's omission of the basement consolidated the semi-detached house as the standard unit of middle-class speculative development.

Thirdly, the motive of large twin gables which Carr's first architect, Godwin,

63

developed partly from earlier pattern books and partly from the rural cottages of the time, was a sharp breakaway from the clumsy gothic dormers which were a feature of such developments as the terrace at Steele's Road, Hampstead (illustration no 21), a scheme which was built at about the same time as Bedford Park. This motive, modified by floor-board tudor and diamond-paned windows became, during the nineteen-twenties, the most typical feature of suburbia. It can be seen in every town in the kingdom.

Fourthly, Carr took care to save as many as possible of the fine trees with which his site was encumbered. This point was emphasized by a contemporary article in the *Lady's pictorial* (vol 3, 1882, p314) which declared: 'The first thought of the proprietor of these hundred acres was how to spare the greatest number of trees and build artistic houses among them that might look as though they were surrounded by the growth of centuries. Here there is a medlar by the roadside, there the street curves so that it may not disturb a noble elm, and in fact, the position of the trees may have decided those of the houses.'

The effect of Carr's efforts at landscaping was illustrated by a certain Barry F Barry, who published in 1882 a chromolithograph of a view in the estate, 'Bath Road looking east'. This shows a number of tall elms in the front gardens of the houses, together with a row of young trees planted in avenue-formation along the roadside. Today the view has changed; the houses in the foreground have been replaced by the bulky edifice of a technical college. The elms have gone and the trees by the road have, like so many other avenue-trees on housing-estates, been kept small, and mutilated in the interests of light in adjoining windows and free movement for pantechnicons

44: *'The disastrous consequences of Carr's good intentions.'*

on the highway. Bedford Park illustrates the need not only to save existing trees when a suburban estate is laid out, but also to provide space for new ones to grow to their full stature.

Carr was an idealist. He employed the best architects of his time—the most notable of whom was Norman Shaw—and, as our suburbs go, Bedford Park is an attractive estate; but some of Bedford Park's least happy features were to be copied by less idealistic men who built without either leasehold control or benefit of architect. Every town in England is afflicted by the disastrous consequences of Carr's good intentions.

8 *Urban tenements:* At the same time that the land societies were building houses for their members, George Peabody (an American banker) was building working-class tenements in London. He was a rich man who devoted a portion of his wealth to rehousing the poor. The trust which he established built homes for over four thousand people during the sixties and early seventies. It was a 'generous scheme, truly humanitarian in its intentions, yet depressing in its results'.[24] The Peabody Trust's flats were bleak, cliff-like buildings, five stories high, coarse in detail and inhuman in atmosphere. Mean though they were, they were still too costly for the poor of London. In 1864 *The builder*'s correspondent remarked (vol 22, p67) that 'these apartments will not be found to meet the wants of the poor dwellers in

45: Langbourne Buildings, Mark Street, Finsbury.

Bethnal Green, and in other parts of the metropolis, who can only afford to pay a rent of from 2/- to 3/- a week and more than any other class require help and care'.

Peabody's interest in working-class housing was philanthropic. That of his contemporary Sydney Waterlow was financial. In 1863 Waterlow built in Mark Street, Finsbury, 'a pile of "chambers" of middling quality and not agreeable forms, from which he expects to receive 9% for his money.'[25] The block was called Langbourne Buildings (and was demolished in 1979). Its importance lies partly in the fact that its roof structure was an example of the use of reinforced concrete, and partly in the sheer dreariness and inconvenience of its design. The use of concrete for lintels, staircases, etc and for the roof cheapened the building considerably,[26] and thus made it an economic proposition. Reinforced concrete was not used for the floors, but the meeting at which the building was shown to the Press demonstrated that the materials was also capable of carrying floor loads.[27].

Waterlow's plan derived from some flats for the working classes which had been designed by Henry Roberts for the Great Exhibition of 1851. Following the exhibition, a number of flats were built in different parts of the country in accordance with Roberts' design. They were two-storied buildings. The twin flats on the upper floor opened off a balcony which was reached by a staircase from ground level. The small size of Roberts' blocks made them acceptable. Their staircases were mean, but they only went up one floor. Their balconies were narrow, but, since there was only one to a block, they were tolerable. Langbourne Buildings, on the other hand, was five stories high. Its rooms were gloomy and misshapen, while its multiplicity of narrow balconies and mean staircases made it a most disagreeable place in which to live.

46: Model houses for families, from the Great Exhibition of 1851, designed by Henry Roberts.

Waterlow's design was copied by other speculators during the latter part of the century. The joyless atmosphere both of these tenements and the flats built by the Peabody Trust tended to set men's minds against flat-living, and thus helped, by a kind of homeopathic reaction, to consolidate the Englishman's traditional preference for a house.

9 *The Public Health Act of 1875:* While Peabody and Waterlow were building their tenements, Chadwick and his associates were labouring in the field of sanitary-reform. This work had been in progress for many years. There were during the second half of the nineteenth century numerous Acts of Parliament dealing with sewerage, water-supplies, refuse-disposal, slum-clearance, and the establishment of minimum building-standards. To consider them all would require a monograph on the history of sanitary science; for our purpose it is enough to mention one of them only, regarding it as an example of the manner in which sanitary reform affected urban-design. This Act (The Public Health Act of 1875) was one of the finest pieces of social legislation of the nineteenth century. It brought into a single Act a number of earlier laws dealing with sanitary matters. It reformed the structure of local government, setting up local sanitary boards, which later became the rural and urban district councils of the twentieth century. It established the Local Government Board as the controlling body for questions of sanitation. It gave the local sanitary boards powers and duties covering a wide field of activities, including such matters as sewerage, the control of slaughter-houses and the collection of refuse. It had, in addition, three direct influences on building; it gave power to urban authorities to make building by-laws, it established for the first time in a public general Act the principle of building-lines, and it required every authority to appoint a surveyor.[28]

10 *Building-lines and bye-laws:* Building-lines were not a new idea. Legislation to control the alignment of new structures had been in existence ever since London's rebuilding after the Great Fire. Such legislation had, however, been confined to local Acts. The Act of 1875 was the first occasion upon which this kind of legislation was made general, but its effect was limited to infilling and to the extension of already-existing development, and it therefore had little immediate influence on the suburban scene. Suburbia, however, had no need for such regulations. Its developers had long been used to setting their houses back behind privet hedges and front gardens of a certain minimum depth. The Public Health Act did, however, establish the concept of building-line legislation firmly in the public mind, and when, in 1925, the system was extended to include all buildings along carriageway-roads, it was a natural development of existing laws.

Building-lines and bye-laws limited freedom of design. Houses could not project forward from their neighbours, because the building-line prevented such an arrangement; there could be no more narrow, romantic, insanitary alleyways, because the bye-laws defined a certain minimum width of street.

Some form of building-controls was certainly required; the jerry-builder had to be checked, but as early as 1878 certain people had begun to doubt the wisdom of restrictive legislation of this kind. In that year H Heathcote Statham uttered the following cry of dismay in a lecture to the National Association for the Promotion of Social Science:

'At present there is no doubt whatever that street architecture in London and other large towns suffers, as far as regards effect, from being too much governed. If we take a view of a picturesque street or building of old time, such as the modern architect or artist delights to sketch, and apply it to the provisions of (say) the Metropolitan Building Act, we shall find in most cases that nearly all which made the picturesque of it has disappeared. The effect of the average modern Building Act on street architecture is pretty much the same as would be the effect on the human countenance if it were to be decreed that all projections were to be cut off and the face kept flat . . . The consideration of architectural effect, in fact, does not enter the legal or official mind. In the voluminous blue-book of evidence taken by a Parliamentary Committee three or four years ago when there was an attempt to get a new Building Act for London, I have not been able to find a single question, out of the thousands asked, framed to elicit any opinion on the effect of the proposed legislation on buildings architecturally. To ensure a character of town-building at once safe and picturesque what is wanted is not a stringent prohibitive legislation, repressing the life and character of street architecture; but rather a legislation which would provide that the task should be undertaken by properly competent and conscientious persons; which would put a check on the iniquities of the "jerry-builder" (who is the cause of the existence of nine-tenths of every Building Act), and at the same time leave the competent and conscientious constructor room to carry out his ideas without vexatious interference, and to indulge his fancy in regard to picturesque effect in the confidence that such fancies would be carried out on the basis of a sound and scientific construction.'[29]

Heathcote Statham was too naive. It is easy to demand that building should be carried out by properly competent and conscientious persons, but less easy to define competence and conscientiousness, and without restrictive legislation it is very difficult to ensure that the occasional incompetent or rogue does not get away with something which ought to be prevented. Much of the dullness of suburbia is due to the existence of bye-laws and codes of practice which are needed to ensure minimum standards of health, traffic-safety or public welfare.

Some of these regulations will be discussed in later chapters. In the meantime, it is enough to note their effect, to recognise that they constitute a necessary part of social legislation, and to understand that they derive from the admirable work of our nineteenth-century sanitarians.

Admirable as their work was, it had an indirect consequence which survived for almost a century and which was implicit in Statham's pertinent remark that 'The consideration of architectural effect does not enter the legal or official mind'. The local authorities which were set up by the Act of 1875 had, as their original raison-d'être, the administration of sanitary regulations, (including building bye-laws) and the construction of roads and bridges. In these circumstances it was natural that the Act should require the appointment of a surveyor as their principal technical officer, but as the activities of local government became more complex, these men's responsibilities increased. They undertook an extraordinary variety of jobs, including the administration of street-lighting, drainage, refuse-disposal, private street-works, parks and open spaces, town-planning and housing, as well as building by-laws. No one individual, however able, could possibly cope with such a wide field of responsibility. The wiser surveyors, and more far-sighted authorities, recognised the difficulty, and either passed some of these duties to outside consultants, or formed separate departments for the purpose under the control of their own chief officers. Often, however, this was not done, and the municipal surveyor became a sort of Pooh-Bah, to whom housing and town-planning were two of a large number of duties.

Inevitably these jobs were badly executed; the surveyor lacked both the time and the qualifications to give them the attention they required, and his

47: Bye-law housing in Kensal Rise, London

69

architectural staff was usually of the poorest. (The best architectural assistants do not as a rule seek appointments in municipal surveyors' offices.) Much of our council-housing suffers from the fact that housing, perhaps the most difficult of all architectural problems, was placed in the hands of men who were unqualified by training or experience to carry it out. The sanitary reformers cleaned up our cities, but in so doing they set up as the principal local-government official responsible for building matters a man without specifically architectural training. (These comments refer to the system as it became established outside the county of London, an area which had its own code of building law and its own rather different system of enforcement.)

11 *Bye-law housing:* The bye-laws which were promulgated under the Public Health Act have given their name, the 'bye-law street', to a certain kind of nineteenth-century housing, consisting of a characterless rectangular grid of streets lined with semi-detached houses or terraces, such as were described on page 23.

This nomenclature is somewhat unfair. The bye-laws did not require that streets should be straight, merely that they should be of a certain width.[30] They did not insist that houses should be identical, merely that they should be solidly built, adequately ventilated, and reasonably fire-resistant. The dreary appearance of late nineteenth-century bye-law housing is due less to the bye-laws than to the nature of the problem and the prototypes which the speculators of the day used as their models. Small, cheap, decent, solidly-built houses were needed in quantity, and it is not easy to devise interesting or attractive layouts for large numbers of small, cheap, decent, solidly-built

48: *Bye-law housing in Kensal Rise, London.*

70

49: Noel Park, Wood Green.

houses. The georgian speculators had built most elegantly (so long as they built for the upper classes), but their houses were three or four stories high; their layouts included squares, and Repton and his followers had completed the picture with tall forest trees.

The late victorian developer could not afford such extravagances. He was not building for the gentry. His was a different customer—the small trades-man, the shopkeeper and the better-class artizan; furthermore, he was often a freeholder, he lacked the controls implicit in leasehold-ownership. Finally, he had as his exemplar the work of that most progressive of property com-

50: A cross-street in Noel Park.　　　　　51: Part of a skyline in Noel Park.

panies, the Artizan's, Labourer's and General Dwellings Company, whose estate at Noel Park, Wood Green was started in 1883 with a grid layout, to the designs of their architect, Rowland Plumbe, described in *The builder* for June 30, 1883 (vol 44, pp890, 893, 895).

This place has a horrifyingly bleak adequacy. Its wide, straight roads show the consequences of applying the precepts which Maslen had enunciated forty years earlier. It possesses the empty, haunted air of a street-scene by Chirico. Plumbe followed the example set by Nash in the Regents Park terraces, and tried to relieve the monotony by what *The builder* called (p880) 'specially designed features to break up and improve the skyline of the buildings', but such alterations of detail are futile in the context of a long straight street on a featureless level site with small houses set in rows seventy-feet apart. The houses are not ill-designed but the layout is abysmal. Unfortunately, the late victorian speculators copied not only the houses but the layout as well. The bye-law housing which they erected owes its form to the examples of Richard Austin at Battersea and Rowland Plumbe at Noel Park, rather than to the legal restrictions under which they worked.

Their houses were not bad (they were certainly better built than many which have been erected since). The typical bye-law house is a compact little dwelling, and its heavy lintels, cement ornaments and terracotta trumpery possess a coarse vigour which when seen in twos and threes can be attractive. Too often, however, one cannot consider it on its own. Bye-law houses come in interminable rows; they are all built to the same plan, with the same height of rooms, the same width of street, the same bay-windows, the same red bricks, the same slate roofs. There are thousands of them; their monotony is appalling.

12　*The 'Illustrated carpenter and builder':* The late victorian speculators could hardly have built so many similar buildings so quickly had there not been some means of communication which served them all. From the fifties

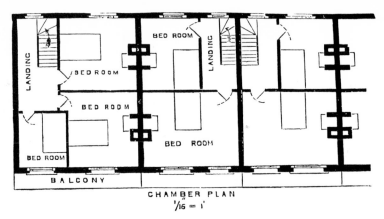

CHAMBER PLAN
$\frac{1}{16}'' = 1'$

TERRACE OF COTTAGES — BY G. M. JAY.

52: Chamber-plan of cottages for 'Alpha'.

onwards the publishers of architectural pattern-books had issued volumes of designs for suburban houses, often supported by working drawings, specifications and bills of quantities.[31]

In 1877 these pattern books were supplemented by a weekly journal. This was the *Illustrated carpenter and builder*, a publication which cost a penny and which circulated among the small builders and 'superior artizans' of the time. Its cover was embellished with perspectives of buildings. Plans of these buildings, together with specifications and details of cost, were supplied to enquirers. In addition, it contained a 'notes and queries' column. A prospective developer who required plans would write to the journal, stating his needs, and asking for suggestions. A few weeks later, a reply would be published, illustrated by a small-scale elevation and plan.

Thus page 103 of the volume of 1881 contains the following enquiry:
'I have a plot of land, 210 ft by 50 ft on which I want to build a terrace of four or five-roomed cottages, suitable for artizans. I would wish to build as many as possible consistent with appearance and convenience. I should wish all bedrooms to be entered from landing, to have no attics, to have a bay-window with balconies, a roomy entrance-hall and neat staircase to each cottage and the design of the frontage to be decidedly attractive, and is it probable that they may be built for £160 to £170 per cottage? A design or reply from any of your practical and artistic contributors would much oblige—Alpha.'

Alpha's request was soon answered. Page 137 of the same volume shows a block-plan of seven cottages, together with the following letter: 'I enclose ground plans of cottages for one half of "Alpha's" land; in the whole plot I get fourteen roomy cottages with back entrances. Of course, more could be got in but they would be pinched. I would have shown the whole fourteen

73

but they would take up so much space here . . . If the enclosed plans suit, he (Alpha) can have any information respecting them by communicating with me, or I would supply him all the necessary drawings for the fourteen houses for a very small acknowledgement. The enclosed would not cost over £170 each—G M Jay.'

Jay followed this up a few weeks later with a further letter (p249), including plans and elevations: 'I enclose chamber-plan and elevation of three of the cottages at the request of "Alpha" . . . The front elevation is designed to be executed in red and black stock bricks, the black bricks joining the strings, corners, etc. The joints of red bricks to be dressed off and pointed with black and the joints of black bricks pointed white. I hope it will suit. If not, I will give another design—G M Jay.'

Jay's drawing shows a terrace of mirrored pairs in very elaborately-patterned brickwork. There were a number of 'practical and artistic contributors' who made a business of providing drawings in this manner; among them was a certain Edward Drew who showed, in the issue of October 22 1886, a picture of a type of dwelling which was almost as ugly as the narrow house and was to become very nearly as popular. This is the bungalow with a square plan, a pyramidal roof, bay-windows, tall chimneys and an arched front door. The type probably derives from some regency gate-house, but its origin is less important than its present universality. (An earlier version, but without bay-windows or arched front door, appears in the volume of 1881. There may well be earlier examples than this, but I have not found one.) As the narrow house is the cheapest, commonest and ugliest of detached two-storey

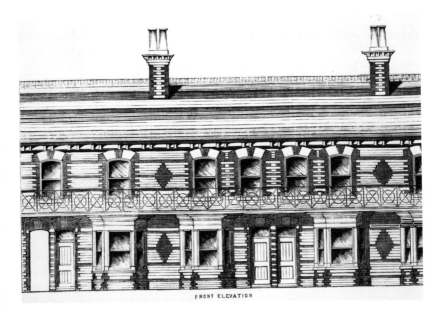

FRONT ELEVATION

53: Cottages for 'Alpha'.

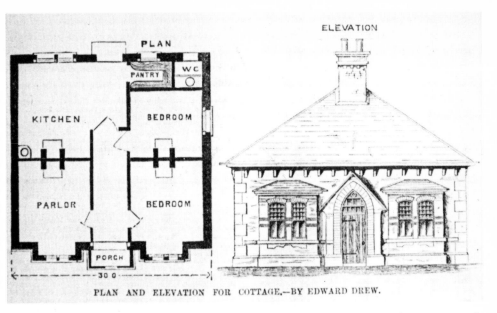

PLAN

ELEVATION

PANTRY

W C

KITCHEN

BEDROOM

PARLOR

BEDROOM

PORCH

30 0

PLAN AND ELEVATION FOR COTTAGE.—BY EDWARD DREW.

54: A square bungalow-cottage for 'Young Archie', from the Illustrated carpenter and builder, *October 22 1886.*

houses, so the square-plan bungalow is the cheapest, commonest and ugliest of single-storey dwellings.

13 *Victorian commuter transport—horse-traction and steam-trains:* The *Illustrated carpenter and builder* was the means by which the bye-law house became the universal industrial dwelling of the eighties and nineties. In this it helped to consolidate the English tradition of house rather than of flat-life, but it might not have achieved this universality had it not been for the development, during the last three decades of the century, of the horse-tram and the cheap workmen's train.

We have already noted that the spread of housing in this country has been limited only by the transport available and by the readiness of landowners to sell for building. So long as man had to walk, ride or go by coach, all but the wealthy had to live close to their places of work. A man had to be prosperous to afford his own coach and horses, and without them a house in Park Village was too far fom the centre to be a practical possibility for anybody with a regular job.

Park Village, as we have seen, was built in 1824. Five years later the first omnibus appeared, and soon a service of horse-drawn buses was providing 'genteel transportation' along the Finchley Road. These vehicles enabled the developers of St John's Wood to build their houses with scarcely any of the stables and mews which formed an essential part of the georgian estate. St John's Wood was, however, a place for the prosperous, and during the 1830s commuting was too costly for anyone else. It was a dozen years before the lower middle-class could afford to participate in the pains and benefits of daily travel. By 1849 this had been achieved. In that year 'Londoniensis', writing in *The builder* (vol 7, p572) declared that 'owing primarily to the establishment of omnibuses, many thousand families of limited income have left the city to reside in the suburbs . . . in small four, six or eight-roomed tenements with but small gardens attached to them.'

The London omnibus was, according to Olsen in *The growth of victorian London* (p322), 'an overwhelmingly middle-class conveyance. It did not start operating before eight in the morning, by which time the working classes were at work; it had a cushioned interior and an obsequious conductor; its fares approximated to those of second-class travel by rail and were too high for the working man or his family.' The tram on the other hand was (at least in London, and during the nineteenth century) a working-class vehicle.

Successful operation of horse-tramways started around 1870,[32] and soon they had become numerous enough for an Act to be passed regulating their provision. One of the clauses gave both frontagers and local authorities power to veto tramway-construction in their streets. This was done by the City Corporation, while in the West End property interests prevented the incursion of trams. In consequence it was only in the twentieth century, and then underground in the Kingsway tunnel, that the tram touched central London. 'The tramway network of London, while extensive, remained overwhelmingly suburban, and working-class suburban to the end' (Olsen, p321).

Other authorities, particularly in the midlands and the north, were less restrictive, and tramways developed apace following the Act of 1870. Leeds, for example, possessed, in 1879, a ten-minute service from the centre of the town to Kirkstall and Hunslet, together with bus connections to Adel and Scarcroft, a total distance of five miles.[33]

There can be little doubt that such transport improvements did much to assist the development of working-class housing in the suburbs, though it is, as Wohl declares, 'extremely difficult to correlate exactly the development of any particular area and, workmen's transport facilities to that area'.[34] Four points are, however, evident:

First, an hour of travel in each direction is the tolerable limit for the commuter, and the average speed of a horse-bus or tram was six miles an hour. So long, therefore, as the horse provided the only motive power, dormitory-estates were limited to a distance of six miles from the city-centre. Long-distance commuting was dependent on mechanical traction and that, until the electrification of tramways in the nineties, meant the steam-train.

Secondly, the usage, and hence the effect of commuter transport, varied from city to city. Thus, on the one hand, Wohl mentions that the Chairman of the London Tramway Company calculated, in 1884, that not only had accommodation for 20,000 people been provided along the company's South London routes, but that it had 'relieved London of an immense number of poor people by carrying them out to the suburbs'. On the other hand, Simmons, after describing the horse-drawn trams and buses of Leeds, goes on to say that such services as these had less effect on urban-development than might perhaps be supposed. 'They were of importance chiefly to the middle and lower-middle class in enabling them to live further from their work. The fares charged were usually high, too high for the men of the working class to incur as part of the expenses of life.'[35]

Thirdly, suburban growth was influenced by other factors than emigration from the crowded inner areas; shopping-facilities, local employment, whether in manufacturing or (often more importantly) in services, and immigration from other parts of Britain all had their effect.

And finally, suburbia grew as a consequence not only of radial, but also of linking transport connections. Horse-drawn vehicles provided both. The linking connections helped, in outer London, to consolidate and expand the middle-class estates which had become established around the suburban stations.

These stations had long provided the growth-points for middle-class suburbia. From the forties onwards, commuting by rail had been possible. It was, however, largely confined to London. Other cities were too small for it to be economic. Furthermore, it was a costly activity, limited to the middle-classes and consequently restricted in extent. According to Cherry, there were 27,000 rail commuters entering London in the mid-fifties, compared with a total of 244,000 daily foot and omnibus passengers entering the city,[36] while as late as 1873 a contributor to the *Workman's magazine* declared that many of the working classes never travelled by rail.[37] Such of the working classes as did commute by rail were able to do so in consequence of the introduction of cheap workmen's fares. Articles and leaflets advocating such arrangements appeared as early as 1845, but it was long before workmen's trains became established, and even then their effectiveness was limited.

We have noted the disruption of housing caused by the building of the railways, and the fact that the Artizans' Labourers' and General Dwellings Company was founded in consequence of the destruction of houses by railways and other improvements. Workmen's fares were first introduced as a means by which the results of such demolition might be mitigated. Thus in 1864, as an alternative to re-housing those displaced by the construction of a new city terminus and approach tracks, the Great Eastern Company accepted an obligation to run daily return trains between Liverpool Street and Walthamstow and Edmonton at a fare of only 2d return.[38] Other companies followed suit, clauses requiring such provision were included in Acts of Parliament authorizing railway developments and by the turn of the century this had become a general practice.[39]

A few railway companies provided workmen's fares voluntarily, and in 1883 a Cheap Trains Act was passed. This placed a general obligation on all companies to provide workmen's trains in return for a remission of passenger duty. It was, however, an ineffective measure. Action could be taken to enforce its requirements only when complaints had been received, and the courts ruled that a company could not be forced to run cheap trains against its financial interest. The Great Eastern was in fact the only company in the London area to provide a comprehensive service of workmen's trains. In consequence of this policy, bye-law housing is much commoner in London's north-east than in its southern and western suburbs.[40] Jackson refers particularly to Tottenham, Walthamstow, Leyton and the southern parts of Wood Green as railway suburbs which developed rapidly after 1870. He adds that in these districts artisans and clerks lived almost alongside the middle strata of the urban working class, in 'long terraces standardised and depressingly dull to the eye . . . built to conform to the basic standards of the 1875 Public Health Act.'[41]

14   *The National Association for the Promotion of Social Science:* Among the advocates of cheap workmen's fares was a body entitled the National Association for the Promotion of Social Science—an institution which was founded in 1857 to provide a forum for the study of 'moral and political science', in the same manner as the British Association provided an opportunity for men to investigate the mathematical and physical sciences. It met annually until 1885 in the provincial cities of Great Britain, and also held sessional meetings in London. It was a body of some influence. Among those who participated in the meetings were Gladstone, Bright, Joseph Chamberlain, Chadwick, Octavia Hill, Ruskin, Kingsley, Sir Titus Salt and John Stuart Mill.

Planning was not, of course, a direct subject of study. The yearly meetings were divided into five sections: punishment and reform, education, public health, social economy, and law-amendment. Later, a section was added on the arts. As a result of their studies, the members of the association became convinced of the need to limit housing-density as a means of improving health. G L Saunders read a paper to the association in 1865 in which he declared, 'It is already clearly demonstrated that the more you pack the people together, the greater is the amount of disease and death'.[42] The problem of how to devise an agreeable as well as a healthy environment was not mentioned; the question was one of public health and social betterment. At the final meeting of the association, the Reverend Henry Solly declared, 'There is no reason why these great populations should all be working in huge sinks of misery and vice and crime. There is hardly an existing social evil in the large towns which would not be diminished, if not abolished, by removing the people to the country (where) land could be got, and houses and factories put upon it for less than the land itself would cost in London and the suburbs.'[43]

This attention to public health and social betterment was very proper. Beauty is less important than health, and ugliness a less serious evil than vice and crime. Nevertheless, the conclusion that the evils of city life would be

78

overcome if only densities were low enough was to have a potent influence on the urban scene. It reinforced the Englishman's traditional dislike of flat-life, and helped to create the image of the small, low-density town as the ideal human environment. The National Association for the Promotion of Social Science was the philosophical precursor of the garden-city movement, just as the industrial villages of Port Sunlight and Bournville were the movement's immediate ancestors.

15 *Port Sunlight and Bournville:*[44] Of these two settlements, Port Sunlight is architecturally the more attractive, Bournville historically the more important. Both were set up in association with industries: Port Sunlight with Lever Brothers, Bournville with Cadbury's. They were thus in the direct line of descent from the earlier industrial villages such as Mistley, and Saltaire.

Port Sunlight (its name is indicative of its founder's idea) is an example of industrial paternalism *à l'outrance*. It is a place of wide boulevards, trim lawns and costly monuments. It was founded in 1887. T Raffles Davison, writing in 1916,[45] mentions that at that time its communal buildings included a church, a 'Lyceum', a cottage-hospital, a gymnasium, an open-air swimming pool, a post-office, a village inn and stores, a fire-station, an auditorium to seat 3000, the 'Collegium', the 'Gladstone Hall', the 'Hulme Hall', a club with billiard-rooms and bowling-green, and an art-gallery. It was probably the most elaborate piece of suburbia ever built. The design of its buildings is often excellent, its open spaces are wide, its public gardens are admirably maintained, it is replete with wealthy victorian paternalism.

55: Port Sunlight, Cheshire.

To us its interest lies partly in this quality (it shows what can be done with suburbia when the money is there), partly in its place in the history of the tudor revival (see above, p16), and partly in the details of its garden-layouts. A typical back garden consisted of a small yard, beyond which lay a service road and a wide area of allotments. Front gardens were arranged with a minimum of intervening fences. (Raffles Davison's illustrations show that many of the gardens originally had iron railings or low guards of hooped wire. These have now been removed. Probably they were taken away during the war.) Raffles Davison commented upon this system as follows (pp10-11): 'The general amenity of the village gains by the Port Sunlight method, whilst the special charm of individual gardens which enthusiastic efforts produce is naturally lacking . . . Of one thing however there can be no doubt; the absence of many dividing lines of fences between each cottage-frontage produces a breadth of effect along the lines of roadways which is in itself pleasing. From the point of view of the town-planner who looks for the collective result this is, of course, very satisfactory.'

Port Sunlight shows us industrial housing at its richest. Bournville by comparison seems to be rather small beer. It was a Quaker foundation. In this it followed established precedent, for Blanchland had been built by the Quaker Lead Company, and Coalbrookdale in Shropshire by that dynasty of Quaker Ironmasters, the Darby Family. Bournville, however, differed in one important respect from these earlier settlements. Though it was established by Richard and George Cadbury, and situated next to their factory, its houses were not built exclusively for their own employees. It was an experiment in housing reform, as well as an example of industrial paternalism. In 1900 George Cadbury handed over the estate to an independent body, The Bourn-

56: A view in Bournville.

80

57: Back gardens in Bournville.

ville Village Trust. He was a firm believer in the desirability of low density housing, and in the trust deed he indicated his wish that 'dwellings should not occupy more than about a quarter of their sites', and that 'at least one tenth of the land in addition to roads and gardens should be reserved for parks and recreation grounds'.[46]

Just as the design of Bedford Park was a reaction against the 'Camden Town gothic' of the seventies, so the layouts of Bournville and Port Sunlight were a reaction against the bye-law housing of the eighties and nineties. Cadbury and Lever (to reverse the phrase used by *Building news*) built for the labouring classes that which the Bedford Park estate had partially done for the middle classes. Cadbury's first houses were built only three years after Bedford Park. They were decked with brick cornices and gothic windows and were much more typical of their age (1879) than was Jonathan Carr's estate with its twin gables and tile-hanging. Soon, however, the architects of Bournville began to imitate Shaw and Godwin. The houses of the late nineties and early nineteen-hundreds are in a diluted Queen Anne Style, varied here and there with applied half-timbering. Laburnham Road, which was built at this time, has the well-kept gardens and flowering trees of a speculative builder's estate of the 1920s.

Bournville, Port Sunlight and Bedford Park were all essays in the picturesque housing-estate. None of them was entirely successful from this point

58: *A view in Bournville.*

of view. The open treatment of its front gardens, and Lever's readiness to spend lavishly on behalf of his employees, made Port Sunlight the most attractive of the three, but Port Sunlight suffered from a *folie de grandeur* on the part of its founder. Its layout is too formal, and its spaces too large for the small scale and picturesque design of its houses.

In Bedford Park, on the other hand, Carr's need to obtain the maximum return from his investment produced a street-layout without open spaces[47] and caused his buildings, admirable though they often were, to lose much of their effect. Bedford Park was a speculative enterprise, Port Sunlight a piece of wealthy paternalism, Bournville a trust under the control of the Charity Commissioners.

The trustees of Bournville could not afford Lever's extravagance, but they did not regard their estate as a speculative venture; for this reason they could space their houses more widely than Carr, and, like the Butterley Company at Ironville, incorporate greens in their layouts. The attractiveness of Bournville lies in the treatment of these open spaces. The arrangement of the houses is uninteresting, their design is generally dull, but Bournville is redeemed by its trees, its grass and its daffodils. These redeeming features are the direct result of the leasehold system under which much of the estate was developed.[48] The trust followed the tradition of the georgian landowners; they owned the freehold, inserted covenants in leases in order to achieve the founder's aims, and spent part of the income from ground-rents on landscaping and the maintenance of open spaces.

16   *Ebenezer Howard—the garden-city movement:* Cadbury built his first houses in 1879, started the Bournville estate in 1894, and handed it over to

the Trust in 1900. His work was thus exactly contemporary with that of Ebenezer Howard, the founder of the garden-city movement, whose book *Tomorrow: a peaceful path to real reform* was published in 1898 and re-issued four years later under the title *Garden cities of tomorrow*.

As Bournville was in a direct line of descent from Blanchlands and Coalbrookdale, so Howard's book followed after the writings of earlier utopians such as James Silk Buckingham. Howard suggested that a city should grow, not by adding layer upon layer of suburb around its periphery, but by establishing a ring of satellite 'garden cities', each with a population of about thirty thousand, and each with its own industries, shops and communal buildings. The book opens with a description of one such city. For our purposes its significance lies less in what this description includes than in what it omits. Howard was not an architect, nor a town-planner; he was a shorthand-writer who recorded parliamentary debates. He was concerned far less with the form of the new city than with the administrative and financial processes by which such places could be established. He believed in low-density housing, but such a belief was general among progressive housing theorists of his time, and it was in any case, marginal to his main thesis. The only mention of housing-density in the book is a statement (p54), 'that there are in the town 5,500 building plots of an *average* size of 20 feet x 130 feet, the minimum space allotted for the purpose being 20 x 100'.[49] (For comparison, the average plot at Bournville was 500 square yards, or about twice that which Howard recommended.)

Howard's theories have had a profound effect on planning throughout the world. According to the late Sir Frederic Osborn, associations for the advocacy of his ideas have been established in France, Germany, Holland, Italy, Belgium, Poland, Czechoslovakia, Spain, Russia, and the United States.[50] In Britain, Letchworth, Welwyn Garden City and the post-war new towns are all essays in the application of Howard's principles. Unfortunately, these ideas were often misunderstood by people who had not studied what he had to say, while the technological premises upon which they were based had begun to change even before his book was written.

Tomorrow was first published in 1898, in the era of steam-railways, and trams, at a time when travel from station to home or factory was slow, uncomfortable and often dirty, while travel from station to station was quick but noisy. In circumstances such as these, long-distance commuting was possible only for those who could afford it and who lived near one railway-station and worked near another. Everyone else had to walk, take a noisy tram or a jolting horse-bus, or, if they were wealthy enough, ride in a cab. In the context of such technology, a ring of satellites was the most logical system of growth for a great metropolis, but before the turn of the century the change in the systems of transport had begun.

Ten years earlier, in 1890, the first of London's electric underground lines (The City and South London) was opened, in 1888 Dunlop patented the pneumatic tyre, and in 1887 Gottlieb Daimler ran his first car. These three devices (together with the electric-traction which, expanded greatly during the next ten years), invalidated Howard's technological premises. Electric-traction and the motor-vehicle made it possible for all but the poorest workers to have a house with a garden some miles from office or factory. Suburbia ceased to be the prerogative of the few who could afford to buy a house in Bedford Park, or who happened to be employed by a philanthropic industrialist, and the garden suburb, not the garden city, became the typical housing pattern of the twentieth century.

In retrospect it seems that this phrase 'garden city' was Howard's greatest contribution to the pattern of twentieth-century housing. It summarised in two words the definition of suburbia which took me half a page! Unfortunately, such an interpretation misreads Howard's ideas. He used 'garden city' to mean a city in a garden (ie surrounded by beautiful country) not a city of gardens (ie suburbia). The movement which he founded became wedded to the ideal of low-density housing, and in 1913 E G Culpin, the secretary of the Garden Cities and Town Planning Association published a book called *The garden-city movement up to date*, in which he described fifty-five low-density housing schemes, of which only one, Letchworth, was a true garden city in the sense that Howard intended.[51]

Letchworth was founded in 1903, five years after the publication of Howard's book. It was set up by a philanthropic company, First Garden City Limited, who defined their object as the development of 'an estate of about 3800 acres between Hitchin and Baldock on the lines suggested by Mr Ebenezer Howard, with any necessary modifications'. The directors were, as one might expect, an idealistic group; several of them were Fabian socialists, and they chose as their architects two men with ideals similar to their own. These were Raymond Unwin and his partner Barry Parker, who had recently prepared a scheme for the model village of New Earswick near York, a settlement which had been founded, perhaps in imitation of Bournville, by Cadbury's fellow Quaker, Joseph Rowntree.

17 *Raymond Unwin:* The more forceful of the pair, Unwin had published, in 1901 and 1902, a couple of pamphlets (*The art of building a home* and *Cottage plans and common-sense*) in which he advocated housing-density of twenty-two dwellings to the acre. In 1901 he took part in a conference at which he met Cadbury; and later, apparently under Cadbury's influence, he changed his tune. He became a firm believer in the need for low-density housing, and at Letchworth he and Parker put the concept into practice. They made it not only the first garden city, but the first English town to consist, so far as its housing was concerned, entirely of suburbia. They consolidated Cadbury's experiments at Bournville, but built more cheaply, used land more economically, introduced the occasional cul-de-sac to save road-costs, and in doing so defined the pattern which was to be followed by housing authorities for the next forty years.

It was in this that the housing-layout of Letchworth differs most markedly

59: Cromwell Green, Letchworth.

from that of Bournville. Just as Rowland Plumbe had tried to relieve the monotony of Noel Park by 'specially-designed features to break up and improve the sky-line of the buildings', so Unwin sought to relieve the monotony of the street by designing his houses in symmetical groups. One group might have hipped roofs and dormer windows, another might have gables at each end and be set closer to the road. The intention was to create interest and a variety of street-pictures. In this Unwin was more successful than Plumbe; Letchworth is a much pleasanter place than Noel Park, but Unwin's groups of houses, though attractive in themselves, do not add up to a fine street. The whole is no more than the sum of its parts.

Letchworth was an industrial town. Its housing had to be cheap, for the industrial worker cannot afford a high rent. In this it differed from Hampstead Garden Suburb, most of which was designed from the first as a middle-class dormitory.[52] At Hampstead Garden Suburb Unwin and Parker worked in collaboration with Edwin Lutyens, the greatest architect of the time. The fact that they were building for a wealthier class than the workers of Letchworth gave them a chance to enlarge the scale of the housing, enrich its details and lay it out in a more generous fashion than was possible in the garden city. The site, a hill patched with woods on the fringe of Hampstead Heath, provided opportunities for a varied and attractive layout. The result has been highly praised. Lewis Mumford describes it as a 'superb achievement'[53] but the coherence of the plan, and the masterly handling of much of the detail hardly compensates for its weakness as a piece of spatial design.

Unwin's ideas in housing arrangements owed much to Camillo Sitte, an Austrian whose book *Der Städtebau*[54] had been published in 1889. Sitte sought to establish principles of civic-design by the study of details from ancient cities. He showed that monuments do not need to be set in the centre

85

60, 61: Cromwell Green, Letchworth, and adjoining houses.

of open spaces, that churches may be buried among other buildings, that squares do not have to be square. Sitte was an apostle of the picturesque. His ideas were a reaction against the baroque school of civic-design, with its radiating avenues, and axial symmetry. Baroque, however, was fashionable in the edwardian era (it was the time of Cardiff civic centre, the Victoria Memorial and the Piccadilly Hotel), and though Unwin's buildings were not designed in the baroque manner, his street-layouts were influenced by the current taste. The plan of Letchworth, with its radiating roads and tree-lined avenues, is more akin to Versailles than to Bloomsbury.

Unwin in fact tried to make the best of all worlds, to fuse the axial symmetry of the baroque with the picturesque ideas of Camillo Sitte, the romantic medievalism of Voysey and the open layout of Bournville. Inevitably he failed. His streets are too long, his spaces too wide for the height of his buildings. He seldom attempted to fuse landscape and buildings into a coherent whole, and the 'mièvre' style of his architecture was unsuited to the symmetrical pattern which he often imposed on small groups of houses. (Not all Unwin's work was in the mièvre mode. He also designed neo-georgian buildings, but these were usually in the central areas of his towns. For domestic work the mièvre was preferred.)

Unwin was not only a practitioner of suburbia, he was also its theoretician. In 1909 he published a book, *Town-planning in practice*, which was largely conceived as a manual for the town-expansion schemes which were expected to follow the Housing and Town Planning Act of that year. *Town-planning in practice* went through many editions during the next two decades, and for all its suggestions for the formal arrangement of informal buildings, it remains a most useful study in the art of building-layout. This was followed in 1912 by a pamphlet, 'Nothing gained by over-crowding', in which he showed that bye-law housing was economically wasteful, as well as being visually deplorable. A lower density meant less expenditure on roads and thus better value for money. Suburbia was not only healthier and better looking than bye-law housing, it was better business as well.

62: A view in Hampstead Garden Suburb.

18 H G Wells: Between the publication of Howard's essay, and the realization of his ideas at Letchworth, the novelist H G Wells published a book, *Anticipations*, in which he foretold with extraordinary accuracy many of the consequences of the technological changes which were taking place at the time. Wells recognized that urban-density and the distribution of human settlements are both directly related to the technology of communications. He foresaw that the telephone, the railway and the motorcar would combine to cause a simultaneous growth and diffusion of urban areas, until the antithesis between town and country disappeared (a circumstance which is the commonplace of much present-day social geography). He used the phrase 'urban region' to describe this new phenomenon, and he went on to declare

63: Letchworth

that 'by a process of confluence the whole of Great Britain south of the Highlands seems destined to become such an urban region, laced all together not only by railway and telegraph, but by novel roads . . . and by a dense network of telephones, parcels delivery tubes and the like nervous and arterial connections'.[55]

Wells was optimistic about the probable appearance of these urban regions. He did not think that their scattering of houses would 'follow the fashion of the vulgar, ready-built villas of the existing suburb'. He foresaw instead an individualistic suburbia of 'personal homes built for themselves even as tudor manor-houses were and even, in some cases as aesthetically right'. He considered that each district would develop its own differences of type and style. 'As one travels through the urban region one will traverse open, breezy, "horsey" suburbs, smart white gates and palings everywhere, good turf, a Grandstand shining pleasantly, gardening districts all set with gables and roses, holly hedges and emerald lawns; pleasant homes among heathery moorlands and golf links and river districts with gaily painted boat houses peeping from the osiers' (pp61-62).

It is a delightful picture, a great novelist's image of the best of the suburban ideal. The scene which Wells described was not too far different from today's wealthy commuter-areas of Farnham or Ewhurst, though he hardly paid sufficient attention to the economic implications of his concepts, and we may doubt whether the ultimate result would be, as he suggested (p61), 'far less monotonous than our present English world'. Wells was, however, like Maslen and Howard, a utopian idealist proposing imaginative suggestions for the future, and utopian idealists may be allowed a certain license in matters of this kind.

19 *Patrick Geddes:* Such idealism has long been an important part of town-planning theory. Human ecology, the other great constituent of this matrix of ideas, is of more recent origin. It derives from the work of Patrick Geddes, a Scottish biologist who constructed an all-embracing theory of civic-planning at the same time that Wells was foreseeing the probable diffusion of great cities, and Unwin was putting such diffusion into practice with his work at Letchworth. To provide an adequate summary of Geddes' teaching is hardly possible. It covered an extraordinarily wide field; Roger Gill mentions (op cit, chapter 10) that it included biology, economics, sociology, education, history, philosophy, geography, art, social reform, town-planning, social credit and the celtic revival.

Sir Patrick Abercrombie declared that his influence would never be known to the world at large: the works by his disciples—his teaching is of the sort that it does not get watered down in transmission. It is a sort of vital idea—a divine inoculation that goes on spreading its infusion without exhausting its original elan.'[56]

Geddes was a biologist whose weak eyesight made it impossible for him to use a microscope for any length of time. He therefore turned to other interests, in particular to sociology, to the inter-relationship of the social sciences, the physical sciences and the arts; and to the way in which these relationships have been reflected in the structure of cities and their surrounding regions.

To him there was no ideal city-plan. Each place had grown differently as a consequence of its geographical, social and historic background. Evolution had produced this individuality, and it was the duty of the town-planner to preserve it. To plan in this way involved an intimate understanding of both the place to be planned and the evolutionary process which had created it. To achieve such an understanding, a comprehensive survey was needed; such a survey should include an inquiry into the geography of the place and its surrounding region, as well as an investigation of its social and economic history, and a study of its present form and its existing social pattern.

This approach to planning could be applied more directly to a project for the redevelopment of some existing city, or to the planning of a large geographical region, than to the layout of a housing-estate. Geddes, for all the originality of his thought and the wisdom of his teaching, had no fresh ideas about the form of suburbia. In this field he followed the example of Unwin, but he was not an architect, and he possessed no skill in design. His book, *Cities in evolution*, contains a reproduction of his own plan for a suburban extension to the town of Leven in Fifeshire. It was, as Gill declares (p245), 'as characterless and formless as any garden suburb drawn up by a borough surveyor'.

Geddes' influence was, as we have seen, indirect. He wrote little, and it was only in India that he was able to put his ideas into practice. One of his most important works, an exhibition illustrating his ideas of civic survey was lost in 1914 when the ship which carried it was sunk by a German raider in the Indian Ocean. Nevertheless, the effect of his teaching was remarkable. He changed men's ideas. Until his time town-planning had been a matter of military strategy, of courtly display, of financial speculation, of social reform or of architecture writ large. He showed that a city-plan cannot properly be confined to the city alone, because the city cannot be considered apart from its surroundings, and its surroundings form part of an even greater whole, the geographical region. He pointed out that planning is above all a social activity. He demonstrated that cities behave like living organisms and that the planner's task is more akin to that of a gardener than that of a surveyor, a social reformer or an architect. Just as a gardener tends his plot for a few years of its history, so a planner controls his city for a brief moment during the many centuries of its existence. Just as a gardener improves his trees by studying their shape, their habit of growth and the soil which suits them, and by pruning a branch here or feeding the roots there, so a planner should improve his city by studying its present forms, its evolution and its geographical background, and by clearing slums in one place and encouraging growth elsewhere.

Geddes taught that man could only create a humane environment by

90

developing the intrinsic characteristics of a place and by studying the habits and needs of the people who were to live there. Like all great ideas it was a concept at once simple and profound.[57]

20 *Politics and housing in edwardian Britain:* Profound though it was, Geddes' teaching produced few immediate results. A group of idealists could build a garden city by floating a company for the purpose, but it was less easy to control the growth and redevelopment of existing towns. For this task new laws had to be passed, the rights of property had to be sharply curtailed, and housing had to be subsidised. Edwardian Britain was not ready for such innovations; the provision of working-class housing was still regarded as a task for the speculative builder.

There had been a few preliminary attempts at housing reform, but little had been achieved.[58] Parliament had passed a series of Acts giving power to local authorities to clear slums and to build houses, and a Housing and Town-Planning Act was passed in 1909. This Act, however, only sought to control new development in the growing fringes of towns, and the Housing of the Working Classes Act of 1890, which empowered municipalities to build houses, did not provide for any system of central-government subsidy.

Nevertheless, by the turn of the century, certain authorities had begun to use the powers of the 1890 Act to erect cottage-estates on the fringes of their cities. Thus in the London area, some fourteen authorities developed such estates during the quarter-century between the passing of the Act and the outbreak of the first world war. Of them the LCC was by far the most active. Of its earlier developments, that at Totterdown in Upper Tooting is a valiant, if not altogether successful attempt to make the best of a grid street-layout. On the other hand, the last of these projects, the Old Oak Estate near Wormwood Scrubs, was a ringer. Its formal romanticism is reminiscent of Lutyens,

64: The Old Oak Estate, Wormwood Scrubs.

and it offers what has been described as 'perhaps the finest architectural experience of all the LCC cottage-estates'.[59]

As the twentieth century got under way, people began to realise that neither the bye-law housing of the speculators nor the unsubsidized developments of the municipalities was cheap enough for the unskilled, or casually-employed labourer. If the poor were to be decently housed, central-government finance was required. Thus, in 1906, the Select Committee appointed to consider the Housing of the Working Classes Amendment Bill (a piece of legislation designed to facilitate working-class housing in rural areas) made a somewhat guarded recommendation that the National Exchequer might make a grant to assist authorities for housing purposes, adding, however, that it would prefer loans at a low rate of interest and longer periods of redemption 'on sound economic grounds'.[60]

A few years later, a Private Member's Bill designed to provide state aid for housing (The Housing of the Working Classes Bill 1912, known at the time as the Boscawen Bill, after its sponsor) achieved a second reading in the House of Commons, and in the following year the Conservative Party issued a pamphlet, 'History of housing reform', which declared that the 'traditional view that the proper housing of the working classes is a matter of state and national concern is deeply embedded in the past traditions of the Unionist and Tory parties', and that 'on the central principle of the state grant the party appears to be absolutely unanimous'.[61]

21 *The Well Hall Estate, Eltham:* The Liberals, led by Asquith and with John Burns as President of the local Government Board, were firmly against state aid for housing, but greater matters were driving them to a change of heart. War was on the way. In August 1914 an Act was passed which em-

65: Part of the Well Hall Estate layout plan.

92

66: A view in the Well Hall Estate, Eltham.

powered the local Government Board to provide houses for government employees. Ten such estates were built in England, eight in Scotland.[62]

One of them, the Well Hall Estate at Eltham is an admirable piece of design. Its style is a roughcast mièvre similar to that employed by Parker at Letchworth, but Frank Baines,[63] its architect, did not make the mistake of combining the romanticism of Voysey with a formal layout. The Well Hall Estate is the first fully-blown English example of a large working-class housing-estate in the picturesque manner. It remains one of the best. Its designers recognized more clearly than Unwin that streets are seen in acute perspective, that a street should be a unity, and that unity is not achieved by placing a series of well-designed, axially-symmetrical compositions next to each other along the road. Instead they produced an irregular romantic layout of great interest and vigour. Sir Frederick Gibberd has pointed out that its acute-angled junctions and even carriageway-widths are poor practice by modern standards,[64] but in 1915 there was no need to design for motor-traffic. More serious criticisms of the scheme are its cost (it was an expensive project) and its 'lack of any sort of provision or preparation for social intercourse, social enjoyment or social advancement of any kind', and, from the standpoint of appearance, the weakness of its landscaping. (The layout seems to have been designed in such a way as to save the existing trees, but no new trees were planted. The original trees have died over the years, and have only recently been replaced. The estate looks somewhat naked in consequence.)

In one way Baines' task was made easy. Because it was a government project, the Well Hall Estate was outside bye-law jurisdiction. Commenting on this, the *Town planning review* declared that 'His work proved what a collection of absurdities we who are less favoured have to contend with', and added, 'Thus it is a most valuable object lesson to the Local Authority and the Local Government Board' (vol 6, 1915-16, p14).

22 *A national housing policy:* The Local Government Board did not take the hint immediately. In 1915 there were other matters which engaged men's attention, but as the war drew to a close, the government began to consider future as well as present problems. A Ministry of Reconstruction was formed, and one of its first tasks was to study the nation's housing requirements.

In 1918 it issued a pamphlet which stated that at that time there was in England and Wales a shortage of between 300,000 and 400,000 houses, apart from any need for slum-clearance. Philanthropy and private initiative were inadequate to solve such a problem. The task required government money. In July 1917, the War Cabinet decided that substantial financial assistance would be given 'to those local authorities who are prepared to carry out without delay, at the conclusion of the war, a programme of housing for the working classes which is approved by the Local Government Board'.[65]

The principle of exchequer-subsidies for council-housing had been established. With such assistance municipalities could build far more easily than before, but if the central government was to provide financial aid, it had to be sure that money was properly spent. A national housing policy was required. The first decision to be made concerned density. On March 18 1918, the Local Government Board issued a circular to local authorities recommending a density of twelve or, in rural areas, eight houses to the acre.

A definition of suitable densities was a necessary first step, but it did not go very far. Details had to be filled in. For this purpose a Select Committee was appointed under the chairmanship of Sir John Tudor Walters MP. Unwin was a member of the committee and had considerable influence on its findings.[66]

The Tudor Walters Report was in many respects an admirable document. Among other things, it established standards of accommodation which are little different from those which are used today. It recommended that carriageway-widths should be varied according to the importance of the street; it suggested that building components, such as baths, windows and doors should be standardized; it proposed improved methods of building-construction, of the organization of contracts, and of the administration of the Local Government Board's housing department; it suggested that housing schemes should be prepared by a competent architect and that roads should be arranged in such a way as to canalize through-traffic on certain principal routes.

One of its most significant features was its comment on tenements or, as we should call them, multi-storey flats. It said[67] that it had received a considerable amount of evidence, particularly in reference to Scotland, as to the advantages or disadvantages of flats or cottages, and went on, 'For large blocks of tenements four or five stories high, such as have been erected in our great towns and have been commonly adopted in certain Scottish cities, no advocate appeared, though it was admitted that modified types of such buildings might be a necessity in the centre of areas already partly developed with this class of dwelling or to meet special conditions. Such blocks of tenements are not dealt with in this report.'

Flats were out. Baines' achievement at Well Hall was ignored, and Unwin's influence on the committee caused them to adopt his mixture of formal street-planning and Sitte's romanticism as their policy in regard to housing-layout. The pattern of development which the committee envisaged was a 'cottage-estate' of two-storey dwellings in blocks of two or four, spaced far apart with a road-layout like those of Letchworth and Hampstead Garden Suburb. There were to be no high buildings to provide a contrast to the rows of houses.

The committee's recommendations were substantially accepted by the government, and a year later the Local Government Board issued a manual (the *Housing manual* of 1919), which embodied their suggestions on housing layout. Unwin's ideas had become the nation's policy.

The housing problem had been studied, policy had been determined, and the war was over; an election had been won on the slogan 'Homes fit for heroes to live in', and a new government had been formed. Accordingly, the Minister of Health, Dr Christopher Addison, inaugurated the first scheme for state-aided housing. The job was to be carried out by local authorities in accordance with the precepts laid down in the *Housing manual*. The government found, however, that the manual did not alone provide sufficient guidance. Housing was a new task for most local authorities, and they needed help in the choice of types and assistance in the provision of working drawings. Thus in 1920 the Ministry of Health issued a pattern-book of plans and elevations for which it had prepared full working drawings and quantities. The preface to this volume was somewhat defensive in tone. It remarked that where these type-plans had been adopted, 'comparatively satisfactory prices have been obtained, both in open competition and for agreed-price contracts'. The implication is clear. Housing was found to be a more expensive activity than had been expected. A year later, the cost of the 'Addison Scheme' (as it was called) caused such an uproar that Addison was forced to resign. A new Minister was appointed, policy changed and state-aided housing stopped.

The halt was temporary. A fresh system of government help was established by the Housing Act of 1923, and throughout the inter-war period (except for a short interval between 1928 and 1929) municipalities built housing-estates both with and without the assistance of the central government. These estates were laid out in accordance with the principles which the Tudor Walters Committee had recommended. Financially the Addison scheme was a failure, but it caused housing-committees in all parts of the country to learn Unwin's gospel.

Their housing had its faults (we shall discuss some of them in the next chapter), but it gained the objective which had been sought by three generations of social reformers: it provided decent homes which the working classes could afford. This achievement has been summed up by an American authority in the following words: 'The techniques and the standards for thus housing great masses of the population in England which developed early in this century have spread out to modern civilization all over the world . . . Here surely is an accomplishment that history will class as one of civilization's greatest strides.'[68]

REFERENCES

1 See Chalkin, op cit, pp196-217; and Olsen: *The growth of victorian London*, p267.

2 See W G Hoskins: *The making of the English landscape*, Penguin Books, 1970, pp281-286; also K C Edwards: 'The Park Estate, Nottingham', in *Middle-class housing in Britain*, M A Simpson and T H Lloyd, editors, David and Charles, 1977, p154; also S D Chapman: 'Working-class housing in Nottingham during the Industrial Revolution', in *The history of working-class housing*, Stanley D Chapman, editor, David and Charles, 1971, pp146, 148 and 149.

3 See M W Beresford: 'The back-to-back house in Leeds 1787-1937', in *The history of working-class housing*, pp99, 108 and 109.

4 J H Treble: 'Liverpool working-class housing 1801-51', in *The history of working-class housing*, p176-8.

5 James Noble: *The professional practice of architects*, 1836, p92.

6 *The builder*, vol 2, 1844, p386.

7 See A S Wohl: 'The housing of the working classes in London 1815-1914', in *The history of working-class housing*, p18: 'So many houses were torn down during the railway boom which lasted down to 1867 and picked up again after 1875 that contemporaries likened the coming of the railways to the invasion of the Huns.'

8 The Torrens Act of 1868 gave local authorities power to demolish individual insanitary houses. The Cross Act extended the power to larger areas.

9 Robert Baker: 'On the state and condition of the Town of Leeds (in the West Riding of the County) of York', in *British Parliamentary Papers: The Chadwick report on the sanitary condition of the labouring population with the local reports for England and Wales and other related papers 1837-42*, Irish Universities Press, 1971, p997.

10 Transactions of the National Association for the Promotion of Social Science: Presidential address by G Shaw Lefevre, quoting Lord Brougham. Birmingham Meeting, 1884, p1.

11 T J Maslen: *Suggestions for the improvement of our towns and houses*, Smith Elder & Co, 1843.

12 R H Mottram and Colin Coote: *Through five generations, the history of the Butterley Company*, Faber & Faber, 1950, p61. Mottram and Coote state that a considerable part of Ironville was developed by the society, but this seems hardly possible. The Butterley Company's deed register shows that all the land upon which the village is built was owned by the company before the society was formed, and the only records of sales to the society refer to land outside Ironville itself.

13 For an account of the land societies in Birmingham see S D Chapman and J N Bartlett: 'The contribution of Building Clubs and Freehold Land Societies to working-class housing in Birmingham', in *The history of working-class housing*, pp239-244.

14 Seymour J Price, op cit, pp49-50.

15 Roger Gill, op cit, p121.

16 For an account of these two villages see Gill, op cit, pp137-139.

17 See J Street: 'How to succeed in gardening', *New society*, vol 2, no 47, August 22 1963, p9.

18 Chapman and Bartlett, op cit, p243.

19 Two terraces of mirrored pairs with tunnel-access to a yard at the back appear in a pattern book of 1859—Samuel Hemming's *Designs for villas, parsonages and other houses*.

20 Chapman and Bartlett, op cit, p243.

21 For detailed account of the company's activities, see John Nelson Tarn: *Five percent philanthropy*, Cambridge University Press, 1973, pp56-58.

22 Bedford Park is well documented. See, among others, Walter L Creese: *The search for environment*, Yale University Press, 1966, pp87-107; Girouard, op cit, pp160-176; 'The first garden suburb': *Country life*, December 7 and 14 1967; and *Bedford Park: the first garden suburb*, Anne Bingley, 1975. The last two are by my friend T Affleck Greeves, the architect and artist who drew the title-page and chapter head pages for this book.

23 This point is noted by John Burnett: *A social history of housing 1815-1970*, David and Charles, 1978, p202; and by Marc Girouard: *Sweetness and light*, p151. Girouard suggests that basements were omitted 'less out of consideration for servants than for reasons of health'. He refers to a lecture to the Social Science Association in which the lecturer, Dr B W Richardson, had proposed a 'City of Health' in which basements were forbidden, and adds that, according to an article of 1883 in the *Bedford Park gazette*, basements were left out following Dr Richardson's recommendations. Burnett mentions that the innovation was 'unusual so near London'—an interesting comment which implies that ground-floor kitchens were common in the provinces, but not in the capital. He ascribes the idea of bringing the kitchen out of the basement to Norman Shaw, Philip Webb and George Devey. This could be so, but Webb and Devey did not build in Bedford Park, and Shaw was not the first of Carr's architects.

24 Nikolaus Pevsner: 'Model houses for the labouring classes, *Architectural review*, vol 93, 1943, p127.

25 *The builder*, vol 21, 1863, p198.

26 'The use of ordinary materials, the builder states, would have increased the cost of the building *by at least 25 percent*(?) and so rendered a good return on it impossible'. Ibid.

27 *The builder*, commenting on the fact that no architect was employed on the design, declared, 'We can believe that an architect with a reputation to lose might have hesitated before constructing a roof as this is described if aware that it would be used as a meeting place for sixty or seventy gentlemen around a table'. Ibid. For an acount of Langbourne Buildings see John Nelson Tarn: *Five percent philanthropy*, Cambridge University Press, 1973, pp50-52.

28 Public Health Act, 1875, Public General Acts, 38 and 39 Vict, 1875, vol 42, chapter 55, clauses 155 and 189.

29 Heathcote Statham: *Transactions* of the National Association for the Promotion of Social Science, Cheltenham Meeting, 1878, pp658-659.

30 A minimum width of thirty-six feet was specified for a new street intended for carriage-traffic—see *Knight's annotated model bye-laws of the Local Government Board*, Knight & Co, London 1883, p47.

31 See H J Dyos: *The speculative builders and developers of victorian London*, Victorian Studies vol II, Indiana University Press, 1968, p661. In a footnote he lists five such pattern-books.

32 I have to thank Mr Alan A Jackson for this information.

33 Jack Simmons: *Transport: a visual history of modern Britain*, Vista Books, 1962, p57.

34　A S Wohl: 'The housing of the working classes in London, 1815-1914', in *The history of working-class housing*, p30.

35　Simmons, op cit, p57.

36　Cherry, op cit, p44.

37　J Parsloe: *Workmen's magazine (1873)*, p288, quoted by H J Dyos: 'Railways and housing in victorian London', *Journal of transport history*, November 1955, p93.

38　Alan A Jackson: *Semi-detached London*, George Allen and Unwin, 1973, p24.

39　For an account of these arrangements see Dyos: 'Railways and housing in victorian London', p91; and Jackson, op cit, p24.

40　'The Great Eastern Railway Company . . . is the only company which offers reasonable facilities for the travel of the working class; and the result is that ever-increasing numbers of the working-class population are practically forced along the lines of the Great Eastern Railway; so that while there is an enormous working-class population in that one direction, there are, in the north, west and south of London, within a much less distance from the Bank of England, large tracts of land not developed for the erection of houses—sometimes within the county boundaries.'—the Valuer of the LCC speaking in 1898 for that body's housing committee, quoted by Wohl, op cit, p31.

41　Jackson, op cit, p22.

42　G L Saunders: *Transactions* of the National Association for the Promotion of Social Science, Sheffield Meeting, 1865, p454.

43　Quoted by Roger Gill, op cit, pp103-104.

44　For accounts of these two settlements, see Gillian Darley, op cit, pp70-76, and J N Tarn, op cit, pp156-161.

45　T Raffles Davison: *Port Sunlight, a record of its artistic and pictorial aspect*, London, 1916, pp21-22.

46　*The Bournville Village Trust*, Publications Department, Bournville, undated (probably about 1939), p8.

47　Bedford Park adjoins Acton Green, but this was a public open space before the estate was built. Carr himself provided no public greens.

48　'Houses were sold, and land was let for building on 99 year leases—an arrangement which is still in force although about half the houses on the estate are let.' *The Bournville Village Trust*, p10.

49　Ebenezer Howard: *Garden cities of tomorrow*. Faber, 1946.

50　Page 22 of his preface to the 1946 edition of Howard's book. For an account of the effects of Howard's influence on planning in Germany, France and Russia, see *Architectural review*, vol 163, 1978, pp333-363; articles by Nicholas Bullock, James Read and Catherine Cook.

51　Howard himself became concerned at the confusion between the terms 'garden suburb' and 'garden city'. In a letter to the *Times*, published on March 26 1919, he complained that 'The careless use of two terms meaning quite different things has seriously retarded the growth of the garden-city movement, a movement started with the express object of increasing the productive powers of the nation and of solving the twin evils of the over-growth of great cities and the decay of rural districts'.

52　Of the original estate of 240 acres, 72 were set aside for the working classes. George Herbert Gray: *Housing and citizenship, a study of low-cost housing*, Reinhold, 1946, p59. See also Burnett, op cit, p204.

53　Mumford, op cit, p497.

54　The full title of the book is *Der Städtebau nach seinem Kunstlerischen Grundsätzen*, a phrase which Mr Charles I Stewart, its translator, renders as 'City-building according to its artistic foundations'. His own title for the book is briefer. He calls it 'The art of building cities'.

55　H G Wells: *Anticipations of the reaction of mechanical and scientific progress upon human life and thought*, Chapman & Hall, 1902, p61. (In the previous chapter Wells had discussed the effect of motor-transport, and had concluded that a new road-system was shortly to be established.)

56 Quoted by Philip Boardman: *Patrick Geddes, maker of the future*, Carolina University Press, 1944, p252.

57 This summary of Geddes' teaching is not to be found in any library. It is rather the subjective interpretation of one who has received, albeit at third hand, a particle of that divine inoculation to which Abercrombie referred.

58 'Briefly put, it may be stated that the constructive powers possessed by local authorities in regard to housing were for the greater part ineffective just where they should have been most effective, viz, in securing a great increase in the building of houses.' Henry R Aldridge, *The national housing manual*, The National Housing and Town-Planning Council, London 1923, p130.

59 Tarn, op cit, p142.

60 *Reports of committees*, vol IX, 1906, pp36-37.

61 *History of housing reform*, National Unionist Association of Conservative and Liberal Unionist Organizations, 1913, p70. See also the *Times*, December 4 1913.

62 Richard Reiss: *The home I want*, Hodder and Stoughton, 1918, p166. According to Simon Pepper and Mark Swenarton: 'Garden suburbs for munition workers', *Architectural review*, vol 163, 1978, p368, 10,284 permanent houses were built on 38 different sites throughout the country.

63 Baines was one of the principal architects employed by the Ministry of Works. He was responsible *inter alia* for the Ministry's working-class housing. His assistants were A J Pilcher, G E Phillips, J A Bowden and G Parker.

64 Frederick Gibberd: 'The design of residential areas', in *Design in town and village*, Ministry of Housing and Local Government, HMSO 1953, p46.

65 'Reconstruction problems 2. Housing in England and Wales', p2. This seems likely to have been an underestimate. Dr Marian Bowley states that at the time of the armistice there was probably a deficit of about 600,000 houses without allowance for slum clearance. It should be noted however, that her figure includes Scotland, while that of the Ministry of Reconstruction refers to England and Wales only. Marian Bowley: *Housing and the state (1919-1944)*, Allen & Unwin, 1945, pp12, 17.

66 'His most widely influential contribution to planning may be considered to be in the report drawn up by the committee on housing of which Sir John Tudor Walters was chairman (1918) and in the Ministry of Health's *Housing manual* (1918).' Barry Parker's note on Unwin in the *Dictionary of national biography*, 1931-1940, p877. (In this Parker made a small slip. The *Housing manual* was published in 1919 by the Local Government Board, not in 1918 by the Ministry of Health). Baines was also a member of the committee, but he resigned a month before the report was submitted. See also Mervyn Miller: 'Garden-city influence on the evolution of housing policy', *Local government studies*, November/December 1979, pp5-21.

67 *Report of the Committee on Building Construction and Dwellings for the Working Class* (The Tudor Walter's Report), Local Government Board, Reports from Commissioners, (Command 9191), 1918, vol VII, p24, para 84.

68 Gray, op cit, p60.

3 THE COUNCIL,
   THE SPECULATOR AND
   THE MOTOR CAR

1 *The characteristics of inter-war municipal suburbia:* The character of inter-war municipal suburbia was defined by the Tudor Walters Report and the *Housing manual* of 1919. The theme was Unwin's. It derived, by way of Gretna Green, Letchworth and New Earswick, from Cadbury's experiments at Bournville, the writings of Camillo Sitte, the baroque layouts of Versailles and Karlsrühe, the picturesque architecture of Voysey, Shaw, Godwin and Nash, the experimental speculation of Jonathan Carr, the utopias of Ebenezer Howard and James Silk Buckingham, the paternalistic housing of certain industrialists, the philanthropy of Lord Shaftesbury, the studies of the National Association for the Promotion of Social Science, the labours of sanitary reformers, the journalism of the *Illustrated carpenter and builder*, and the politically-inspired self-help of the land societies.

The theme had faults of landscaping, (such as the emphasis on avenue-planting of small trees), a predilection for an intractable architectural problem (the semi-detached house), an encumbered floorscape (caused by the fragmentation of the area between the houses by front gardens, hedges, pavements, verges, kerbs and carriageways), aesthetic inconsistencies (such as the imposition of symmetry on groups of houses which could only be seen in acute perspective), weakness of scale (due to the multiplicity of two-storied houses), poor spatial design (caused by the rigid application of building-lines, the frequent use of the semi-detached house and the insistence on a minimum distance between the fronts of houses), lack of contrast, (due to the absence of tall buildings or forest trees), dubious social implications (caused by its failure to consider the influence of housing patterns on social relationships) and a characterless architectural style.

These were its faults, but to damn Unwin's ideas in this manner is hardly just. For a balanced judgment it is necessary to study the problem more fully, to determine not only what happened, but why it happened, to discover why the floorscape was encumbered, why all houses were two stories high, why they were widely spaced, why large trees were not planted, and why the semi-detached house was preferred.

2 *The recommended designs:* As we have seen, the semi-detached plan provided a ready solution to the problem of access to garden, back-door, coal-shed and dustbin. These were the reasons for its origin, they remain the reasons for its continued popularity, and they were no doubt the reasons why over two-thirds of the plans illustrated in the *Housing manual* and the Ministry of Health's pattern-book were for semi-detached houses. Most of these schemes were negative, mealy-mouthed pieces of architecture. Conceived in an unhappy blend of neo-georgian and mièvre, they lacked both the thoughtful detail of the one and the sentimental romanticism of the other. Their planning was adequate, their form economical, their proportions poor. Their style was copied by public authorities throughout Britain, and now every town and village has its estate of two-storied council-houses with hipped roofs, multi-paned casement windows and tiny hoods over the front doors.

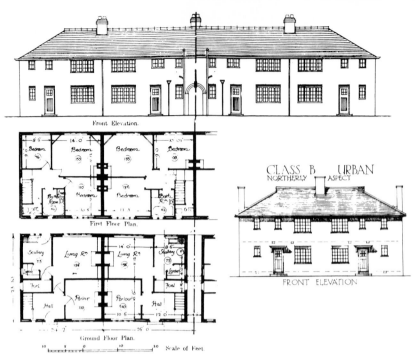

Front Elevation.

First Floor Plan.

Ground Floor Plan.

CLASS B URBAN
NORTHERLY ASPECT

FRONT ELEVATION

Scale of Feet

67: Designs from the Housing manual *1919.*

The preference for the semi-detached house was, from the standpoint of appearance, the theme's most regrettable feature, but it was also the characteristic which possessed the firmest basis, both in functional need and in popular demand (see illustration no 43). The semi-detached house not only solved the problem of rear-access, it was the symbol of the new freer pattern of suburbia. Terraces were associated in men's minds with squalid industrial slums, or the arid monotony of bye-law housing. Furthermore, terraces usually meant mirrored pairs with tunnel-access to the garden, and though such an arrangement was often employed, it was at best a cheap but awkward expedient. The tunnels were draughty, gloomy and dank. They had to be shared by adjoining tenants, and such shared responsibilities sometimes led to disputes and ill-feeling between neighbours. Finally the terrace of mirrored pairs was a difficult problem in design. The mirroring of the plan produced a similar mirroring of the elevations, and so made it impossible for the architect of such a building to achieve the even rhythm of the georgian street. Such terraces were usually designed in blocks of four or six houses (ie, two or three pairs). The block of four was a more difficult problem than the block of six. It formed a symmetrical composition whose central, and hence most obvious feature was the entrance to the tunnel. The tunnel thus obtained a disproportionate prominence, and the pattern of the facade contradicted the requirements of the plan.

104

The tunnel was not, of course, the only available solution to the problem of rear-access in terrace-housing; a service-road at the back provided an alternative means by which the coalman could deliver his goods and the refuse-collector reach the dustbin. Such arrangements were, however, somewhat unsatisfactory, they were expensive (since they involved duplication of the road-system, and also, if the job were done properly, of the street-lighting), and they were insecure for the tenants (since the access-road provided a ready hiding-place for thieves and hooligans). The *Housing manual* specifically advised against such arrangements, declaring that,'Save in exceptional circumstances, back roads should not be provided, but access from the front should be arranged to the back garden of each house'.[1]

The manual presumably recommended the two-storied house because bungalows were costly in land, foundations and roof-structure, while houses of three stories or more were unpopular. The three-storied house was acceptable in a society in which there were servants to carry coals and polish floors, but in a working-class family the extra storey meant an extra staircase to sweep, extra steps for the elderly to climb, and extra trouble for the mother carrying a tray of food to a sick child upstairs.

3 *The space between the houses:* The combination of two-storied housing, hipped roofs and the semi-detached plan not only produced indeterminate spaces and a monotonous, jagged roof-line, it also led to a certain weakness of scale. To design handsome estates made up of such small unattractive buildings was not an easy job. The task would have been simpler if it had been possible to relate the scale of the space between the houses to the scale of the houses themselves.

This however was not to be. The Tudor Walters Report had recommended that no house should be less than seventy feet from the one opposite. This regulation made it impossible to create the dramatic contrasts of the medieval town. The rule derived, like so many of the factors which have created suburbia, from the well-intentioned efforts of sanitary reformers. It was held that sunshine is necessary to health, that every room must therefore have its quota of sunlight, that if this is to be obtained a minimum distance between houses must be defined, and that this distance should be calculated in accordance with the length of shadow cast by the sun at noon in mid-winter.

The report pointed out (p15, para 59) that on south-facing slopes a shorter distance and on northern slopes a longer distance would be required to give equal results, and went on,

'Where two-storey houses are concerned . . . a general width of 70 feet between the houses should be regarded as the desirable minimum, otherwise in winter very little sunshine will reach the lower rooms. The closing in of this width to 50 or 60 feet by projections may, however, be justified at times for various reasons, and, so long as it is for short lengths, will have only a slight effect on the available sunlight. The following diagram refers to the latitude of London and to a south aspect. Further north, or with an east and west

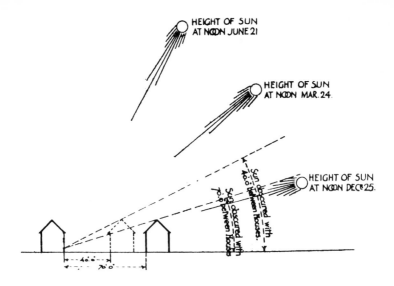

HEIGHT OF SUN
AT NOON JUNE 21

HEIGHT OF SUN
AT NOON MAR. 24

HEIGHT OF SUN
AT NOON DEC. 25.

Sun obscured with
40.0 between houses.

Sun obscured with
70.0 between houses.

68: Diagram in the Tudor Walters Report illustrating the basis of the seventy-foot rule.

aspect, the results will be less favourable.'

The logic of the argument was perhaps somewhat shaky. It implied that there would be sunshine at noon in mid-winter (and this at a time when pea-soup fogs occurred frequently), that there would be no trees between the houses to obscure sunlight, that housing-authorities would be ready to vary the spacing of their buildings in accordance with latitude, aspect and direction of slope, and that economy in the use of land and 'considerations of architectural effect' were of less importance than the winter insolation of certain rooms. But whatever its logic, the influence of this part of the report was profound. The principles which it expressed received official approval in the *Housing manual*, and accordance with the manual was the criterion upon which state assistance for housing-schemes was provided. In consequence the seventy-foot rule was applied everywhere, though its origin, the reasons which lay behind it, and the committee's qualifying phrases were quickly forgotten. It became an unwritten, unexplained, but universally accepted code of practice, and it extended throughout Britain the unhappy proportion of building-height to intervening space which was the besetting fault of Unwin's housing-layouts.

From the standpoint of landscape this intervening space should ideally have been a crisply-defined area like a university quadrangle, with a floor-scape of paving or grass equipped with paths to give access to the houses, shrubs to provide masses of foliage or flowers, and a few tall trees to afford a contrast to the even monotony of the roof lines. Instead the space stretched loosely along the roads and leaked out between the terrace-blocks or the pairs of semi-detached houses, while the floorscape was dissected by hedges, broken up with lawns and flowerbeds, split into roads, verges, pavements and gardens, and dotted with rows of lamp-standards and avenues of small flowering trees. These encumbrances derived from the requirements of public authorities, building-line legislation, the need for road-safety and the traditions of avenue-planting and of the front garden. There were good legal, social or technical reasons for each of these influences, but together they set the designer of suburbia a most intractable problem.

The suburban front garden originated, as we have seen, in the regency period, as a feature of the middle-class speculative estate. It began to be introduced into industrial housing during the 1850s, and by the 1920s had become an inevitable feature of housing-layout. It consisted of a tiny patch of grass, paths to front and back doors, one or two beds of roses or snapdragons, and a privet hedge to divide it from its neighbours and protect it from wandering dogs and unruly children. Each curtilage was regarded as an island entire unto itself. The tenants sprayed their roses, mowed their lawns, weeded their paths, and ignored the fact that their own garden was part of a larger whole which included the road outside, the pavements, the verges, the other houses in the street, and the avenue of flowering cherries planted by the municipality when the estate was laid out.

Such an attitude is readily understandable; the garden was their own, while the appearance of the street was the council's job, not theirs. The council however had no brief on such matters. The Tudor Walters Report did not discuss landscaping, and the single paragraph on the subject in the *Housing manual* (para 29) did not suggest that the appearance of the individual front garden should be subordinate to that of the whole street. The manual's advice was limited to generalities about ecology, pious hopes about the preservation of existing trees, and the suggestion that trees and shrubs should be 'placed in positions suitable to the size of their ultimate growth and where they will contribute to some definite effect'.

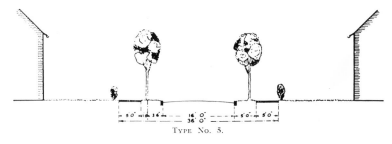

TYPE No. 5.

69: Road-section diagram, from the Housing manual *1919.*

The diagrams of road sections indicate what the authors had in mind: trees sixteen feet high with a spread of six feet are shown planted in the verges. Unwin and his colleagues were properly anxious to avoid the butchering of forest-trees which so often occurs when they are planted along carriageways. To achieve this they did not follow the example of Repton and suggest that large trees should be grouped in open spaces, for to do so would have

107

involved development at a much lower density than the recommended figure of eight or twelve houses to the acre. A fully-grown London plane, planted among others, has a spread of at least fifty feet, and groves of such trees, spaced out in the manner of the georgian squares, must necessarily take up a large part of any estate. It would not have been possible to adopt such an arrangement of planting, provide gardens of the size suggested in the manual and at the same time achieve the recommended densities.

The authors of the manual solved this problem by retaining the avenue, but proposing small trees instead of big ones. Since Repton's time the victorian plant-explorers had been at work collecting specimens from all parts of the world. This increased the varieties of tree available to the estate-developer, and suburbia became a place of Japanese cherries and purple-leaved plums—a pretty, exotic vegetation which was in flower for but two weeks of the year, whose branches did not interfere with traffic, and whose scale was inadequate to provide a contrast to the houses or to relate happily to the spaces between them.

Avenue-planting had begotten the verge; the trees of the avenue had to be set in soft soil, and it was natural to connect these unpaved squares so that they formed narrow strips of grass between road and foot-way, thus providing bands of green in the desert of road-metal and artificial stone. Soon, however, the verge developed a functional as well as an aesthetic purpose. It afforded a buffer between the pavement with its pedestrians and the road-way with its (possibly erratic) horse-drawn traffic, and it provided a convenient position in which to set underground services. At first, space was only needed for gas and water-mains; later, other services such as electricity-cables and telephone-lines had to be provided also. To run such services through gardens involved administrative difficulties; wayleaves had to be arranged with each tenant, and maintenance or alterations meant entering property, digging up lawns and disturbing rose-beds. It was easier to set the services in the public land which lay between the edge of the carriageway and the garden fence. A width of some ten feet was needed to give space for them all. The most convenient way of providing for this equipment was to pave only that part which was needed for a footway, leaving between pavement and kerb a verge of soft ground in which workmen might dig for suspected faults.

The laying of these services beside the road reinforced the arguments for planting small trees. Not only did the branches of large trees obscure light and interfere with traffic; their roots lifted pavements, disturbed underground services and made maintenance more difficult. The avenue begat the verge, but once established the verge helped to define the form taken by the avenue.

The other underground service, sewerage, affected housing-layout in a different way. Sewers require less maintenance than mains and cables, and for this reason they were usually set under the roadway rather than below the verge. Sewers, however, unlike mains and cables, have to be laid to a fall.

The layout of a sewerage-system must therefore be arranged to run downhill. This requirement meant that the sewers were either disposed without reference to the road-pattern, or, more commonly in new estates, that the road-pattern was laid out with easy downhill gradients in such a way that the sewers could conveniently be set beneath the streets.

The gradients required by sewers were not very different from those suitable for roads, and in general the influence of sewers on road-patterns has probably been favourable, for the need to place them under roads has often led the designer of a housing-estate to adjust his roads to the configuration of the land. On the other hand, the verge, for all its functional advantages, was not an attractive part of the suburban scene. It helped to fragment the floorscape between the houses, it was not wide enough to form an effective greensward, it was difficult to maintain, and it could easily degenerate into a ragged strip of weeds and mud.

Building-line legislation had, as we have seen, a long history, but until 1925 its effect was limited to the control of infilling and the extension of existing development. In the early twenties, however, circumstances changed. The sudden expansion of motor transport after the war took place on roads which were of a size and width designed originally for horse-drawn traffic. These highways had to be widened in order to cope with the extra load. Such widening involved expense to the authority concerned, both in connection with the road-construction itself, and also in regard to compensation when adjoining buildings had to be acquired and demolished. To avoid the latter expenditure the County Councils' Association arranged for legislation to be enacted to give them 'power to prescribe a building-line even when there is no idea of widening particular roads in order to safeguard themselves when a road is to be widened twenty or thirty years hence'.[2] When it was passed, however, the Road Improvement Act of 1925 gave power to prescribe building-lines, not only to county but also to other highway authorities. It was interpreted as authorizing the council concerned to define building-lines on all roads, no matter where they might run, or how likely they were to carry a large volume of motor-traffic. When applied to an area of housing, this interpretation of the Act made it impossible for a developer to lay out his estate in the manner of Bloomsbury or Bath, and suburbia became the inevitable consequence of highway-legislation applied to the layout of two-storied housing.

The problem of providing for vehicles in suburbia was not, however, only a matter of allowing for possible road-widening. Safety requirements at road-junctions led to the 'sight-splay' a diagonal chamfering of the plot-boundary in order to provide an unobstructed view at the street-corner. This was certainly an essential device, but it created a most difficult visual problem. The space at junctions became blurred. Instead of being defined and clear-cut, it was a shapeless negative volume which had no edges and which leaked in an indeterminate manner down the adjoining roads.

The requirements of underground services, the tradition of avenue-planting,

70: Inter-war municipal suburbia—an estate at West Drayton, Middlesex.

the front garden, the limitations of building-lines, of sight-splays and of the seventy-foot rule, and the convenience and economy of the two-storied semi-detached house, all helped to define the appearance of inter-war municipal suburbia, but its sameness and extent derived from social and economic rather than legal or functional influences.

The municipal housing-authorities encountered the same problem as that which faced the builder of the bye-law streets. They had to provide large numbers of small, cheap, decent, solidly-built houses, and, like their predecessors, they found it impossible to provide such houses without producing wide areas of repetitive monotonous building.

They can hardly be blamed for this. The character of their housing was controlled in the manner and for the reasons which have been described. Their job was, within this system of control, to provide mass-housing suitable for a single social class. This meant large estates, and the multiple repetition of a limited number of house-types. Such repetition, with such control, could hardly avoid tedium. The architects of these estates often tried hard to make them look attractive, and the best projects, such as Barry Parker's Wythenshawe Estate at Manchester, or the London County Council's Doverhouse Road Estate at Roehampton, are skilful variations on Unwin's theme.

4 *Social and aesthetic characteristics:* Tedium of appearance was municipal suburbia's most obvious fault, but it was not its only failing. The council-estate not only looked dull, it was also a dull place in which to live.

110

Unwin and his followers did not ignore the social aspect of housing, but they failed to appreciate the complexity of this part of their problem. They believed that an estate was well planned if it consisted of decent, inexpensive homes, arranged with an eye to architectural effect, laid out at a density of twelve to the acre and provided with sufficient schools, churches and shops. To them low density was the social basis of good housing. Men should live not in congested unhealthy slums, but in the airy freedom of suburbia. They forgot that though the slums were crowded and insanitary, they were also intimate, friendly places. Relatives kept in close touch and neighbours were at hand to help in cases of illness, or to 'sit in' while parents were away for an hour or two.

Suburbia lacked this neighbourliness. Its inhabitants tended to keep themselves to themselves. It was an isolated, unnatural society, established on the edge of the town, made up of people chosen by accident of need and administrative convenience, and formed, not only of a single social class, but often of a single age-group. The young family was catered for, but there was seldom sufficient variety of dwelling-size to accommodate all types of household. The elderly and the children were often forgotten. Grandparents became separated from their children, maiden-aunts lost touch with their nephews, and the nuclear, rather than the extended family became the centre of society.

Such artificiality was certainly undesirable, but it could hardly have been avoided in the circumstances in which municipal suburbia was built. Council-housing was a social service, it provided homes at minimum cost for those in the greatest need. The demands of the young family were more urgent than

71: Inter-war municipal suburbia, Dagenham, Essex.

72: *Inter-war municipal suburbia, Dagenham, Essex.*

those of the elderly and the childless, so the young were naturally served first. Houses were built for them, they left the congested centres where they were brought up, and many subtle webs of family and friendship were destroyed.

This destruction of established social relationships would have been less serious in its results if the pattern of housing recommended by the *Housing manual* had been such as to encourage social cohesion, but the manual's recommendations ignored this aspect of housing-layout. The authors can hardly be blamed for this omission; in 1919 the sociology of suburbia was an unexplored branch of an undeveloped science. Unwin and his followers were pioneers in a new field of human activity and it was natural that they should make mistakes. Their errors were serious, but only one of the faults listed at

73: *Back-garden use in municipal suburbia, Dagenham, Essex.*

112

the beginning of this chapter was without mitigating circumstances.

Their building was repetitive, but repetition was an inescapable part of their problem. Their architecture was dull, but they were working to a minimum budget at a time when England's vernacular architecture had reached its nadir. Their efforts at landscaping were negligible, but the front garden was almost a statutory requirement, and between the wars the avenue still dominated the landscape of the street. Their spatial design was poor, but their thinking was conditioned by the hideous congestion of the slums, the convenience of the semi-detached house and the requirements of the delivery-vehicle. Their housing was small in scale, but the two-storied house was the most convenient and economical of dwellings. The silhouettes of their streets were often harsh and jagged, but the semi-detached plan provided the most satisfactory solution to the problems of access to garden, dustbin and back door. Their estates lacked contrast, but contrast implied flats (which were unpopular) or tall trees (which were impractical in the context of the recommended densities).

Their errors can be explained and understood, and they were probably inevitable in the circumstances in which Unwin and his followers worked, but their theme had another failing which can be less easily excused. This was its aesthetic inconsistency—a characteristic which was typified by the manner in which symmetry was imposed on groups of houses which could only be seen in acute perspective. Suburbia represented a romantic ideal; the symmetry of the baroque city was contrary to its spirit, as well as being inappropriate to streets where the perspective view was more important than the facade. Furthermore, the picturesque approach to townscape possessed both a basis of theory (in *Der Städtebau*) and a practical exemplar (in the Well Hall Estate). If the layouts in the *Housing manual* had followed the example of Baines rather than that of Unwin, the appearance of England's inter-war council-housing would be better than it is.

Formality of design is hardly ever suitable to suburbia, but the patches of symmetry which abound in Letchworth and Hampstead Garden Suburb possess a saving grace; they can be recognised by anyone wandering through these estates. The pattern may be inappropriate, but it is sufficiently small in scale to be appreciated by the passer-by. Not every estate was designed in this way. Sometimes the system of layout which the *Housing manual* suggested was misinterpreted by the authorities when they tried to put it into practice. They understood that the rectangular grid of bye-law housing was uneconomic, that culs-de-sac saved road costs, that symmetry was fashionable, and that streets might be curved. They interpreted these requirements to mean that housing estates should be laid out in geometrical patterns like a piece of cheap linoleum or a seventeenth-century parterre. Such models are, however, hardly suitable for an arrangement of houses. Linoleum is designed to be seen from above, and the formal garden at Villandry can be viewed from a raised terrace, but it is only from an aircraft that the geometrical precision of the Wollaton Park Estate, Nottingham can be appreciated.

74: *Wollaton Park Estate, Nottingham.*

In their pursuit of such aerial geometry the planners of these estates ignored both the conformation of the land and the *Housing manual's* injunction about the preservation of trees and hedges. Every other canon of authority was faithfully observed. Densities of twelve to the acre were maintained, houses two-stories high were built in blocks of two, four or six at a time. No house was less than seventy feet away from the one opposite. The house-blocks toed the building-line like guardsmen, or were set forward and back in patterns of strict symmetry, culs-de-sac proliferated, flowering trees were planted along the carriageways, and houses were designed in the hybrid, emasculated style of the manual's prototypes.

5 *The back gardens:* The symmetry which was typical of inter-war municipal suburbia derived from the symmetrical terraces of the georgian and regency periods; but while the backyards of the georgian terrace were separated by high brick walls, the back gardens of municipal suburbia were divided by fences of wooden posts and galvanized-steel wire. These gardens did not consist simply of lawns, herbaceous borders and cabbage patches. They were areas where washing was hung out to dry, and where the tenant could pursue hobbies which were out of place indoors. They might contain greenhouses, sheds for use as workshops or the storage of garden tools, cotes for pigeons, aviaries for canaries, as well as clothes-drying posts with their lines of underwear, sheets and babies' napkins. Individually such gardens could be kept tidy: collectively they were a mess. The fences which separated them defined their boundaries, but they did not give privacy to the tenants, nor did they form a screen to hide the muddle next door.

A succession of such muddles can often be glimpsed at a street-corner where a side-street adjoins the garden of the end-house. If, as frequently

114

75: *Back gardens in an estate near Syon Park, Isleworth. Stylistically the houses appear to be post-war, but the cars are an interesting example of garden-lumber!*

happens, this garden is not screened from the road, the public can see not one garden only, but a series of them one behind the other, an ugly chaos of backs which complements the dreary tidiness of municipal suburbia's street-frontage.

6 *Municipal flats:* The absence of flats from municipal suburbia has already been considered. It was due to the Englishman's traditional preference for a house, a preference which was powerfully reinforced by the evidence submitted to the Tudor Walters Committee. Municipalities built flats between the wars, but they were laid out as the committee recommended, in the central areas of big cities 'already partly developed with this class of dwelling'.

On sites such as these the cost of lifts set a limit of five stories to the height of the building. Staircases were expensive also, so their number was kept as low as possible. The flats were usually reached by means of shared-access balconies (enlargements of the tiny balconies of Henry Roberts and Alderman Sydney Waterlow). Their blocks were planned in a formal manner, often around three sides of a court, which was laid out in the current fashion of axial symmetry. The architectural character of the blocks was unattractive. The fact they were often built on small, awkwardly-shaped sites made it difficult to design pleasant spaces around them, while their facades consisted either of bands of access-balconies or cliffs of brickwork perforated with neo-georgian sash-windows. At first, the flat-blocks were neat enough, but as time went on their trim quadrangles became cluttered with clothes-drying posts, washing-lines and nondescript wooden shacks, and their grass lawns were replaced with asphalt to make hard-wearing play-spaces for children.

76: *The Ossulston Estate, Somers Town.*

The London County Council's Ossulston Estate near St Pancras Station is a typical example of such housing. The Ossulston Estate does not possess the vapid monotony of Wollaton Park; its higher density gives it a more active, bustling atmosphere than exists at the Nottingham estate. Nevertheless, both estates have the same unsuitable formality of layout, while the echoing courtyards of the one are even less humane than the semi-circular roads and radiating avenues of the other.

7 *The transport revolution and its consequences:* The Ossulston Estate was a re-development project. It took the place of an area of rookeries which had lain on the site. The existence of these slums was due not only to the inadequacy of water supplies, the lack of drains and the operation of laissez-faire economics. They were also the consequence of poor transport facilities.

At the start of the industrial revolution, when there were no trains, buses or cars, the worker had to live within walking-distance of his job. We have already seen how the technological assumptions which underlay Ebenezer Howard's garden-city theory were made obsolete by the changes in transport technology which occurred about the turn of the century. These changes were accelerated by the first world war. The needs of the army caused the motor-vehicle to develop rapidly, while at the same time many men became familiar with its mechanism and used to coping with the administrative problems of large transport-fleets. On demobilization these people naturally sought to make use of their skills in civilian life. They established bus and coach services which soon superseded the horse-bus (and later the electric-tramcar) as the typical systems of public transport by road.[3]

This expansion of bus services combined with the housing shortage and a

116

period of agricultural depression to cause a sudden explosion of suburbia. Just as victorian suburbia had been based on the horse-bus, the horse-tram and, more rarely, on the railway-stations, so inter-war suburbia outside London and larger provincial cities was largely based on bus-routes. The pattern of building which resulted from the motor-bus was, however, different from that which depended upon the steam-train or the tramway. Trams and trains are inflexible devices. Their rails are expensive to lay, and once set down can hardly be moved. Furthermore, trains are slow to accelerate and take time to come to a halt. Stations have therefore to be placed wide apart if the trains are to travel at maximum speed for any distance.

Buses, on the other hand, can change their routes at short notice, can stop where they will, and can wander wherever there may be a reasonable road. Rail-transport resulted in clumps of housing based upon the stations; bus-transport resulted in ribbons of housing which stretched from town to town and from clump-suburb to clump-suburb. The ultimate consequences of the two forms of development were similar. The clumps of housing based on the railway-stations tended to spread until the clumps coalesced into a single, large built-up area. The ribbons of housing based on the bus-routes have often grown in depth until the spaces between them have become filled with suburbia. It was in the interim period, before the clumps coalesced or the ribbons spread, that the difference in development-pattern showed most clearly. The clump-pattern possessed a certain coherence as a consequence

77: Inter-war ribbon-development at Wistaston, Cheshire.

of its tie to the railway-station. It also enabled the open country between the settlements to remain untouched. Ribbon-development on the other hand ravaged the countryside without giving its dwellers the benefits of a rural, an urban, or even a suburban environment. Sir Colin Buchanan has called ribbon-development 'perhaps the greatest disaster the long-suffering face of our country has had to endure', and has gone on to describe its effect in the following words:

'The housing and social conditions in which it resulted proved bad in every way. Houses, bungalows, shacks, shops and petrol filling-stations sprang up in motley disarray; verges, hedges and trees disappeared; views and outlooks were utterly destroyed. The free flow of traffic became impeded by standing vehicles and crossing pedestrians, and these ribbon-developed roads became death-traps in the full sense of the term. Though there was superficial convenience in having the bus at the front door, there came a time when bus stops had to be regulated in the interests of traffic; they became widely spaced, and to many people it meant a long walk to the nearest stop. Access to town, to work and to school were not the easy matters they promised to be at first. Low rateable values tended to be balanced by increased travelling costs. Peace and quiet at the back of the houses were rudely balanced by traffic noise and confusion at the front, for only in the rarest cases was anything better than the normal shallow urban building-line observed. Though water, gas and electricity were usually provided by their purveyors, the provision of sewerage was frequently a matter of great difficulty for the local authority, and so there developed a large-scale reliance on cesspools, with all the unpleasantness that these involve.'[4]

Ribbon-development was, however, the natural consequence of motor-transport, of a depressed agriculture, and of weak planning-control. To the farmer, bungalows were often a more profitable crop than corn. For the developer, it was easier to build along an existing highway than to lay out roads of a new estate. To the householder, ribbon-development seemed to provide the ideal combination, easy access at the front and a view over open countryside at the back. To the local authority, ribbon-development was a bolting horse which it could neither control nor halt. Town-planning legislation was ineffective, and it was not until 1935 that Parliament sought to strengthen the authorities' hands by passing the Restriction of Ribbon-Development Act.

This Act helped to limit the spread of ribbon-building, but it was concerned with transport rather than with planning and land-use. It sought to cure the disease by treating the symptoms, and its effectiveness was thereby limited. Furthermore, it came too late.

By the time the Act was passed the damage had been done. The tragedy of ribbon-development was not so much that it happened (some form of linear growth was perhaps inevitable), but that it occurred so suddenly. The countryside was spoilt, the roads impeded, and deplorable houses erected before men realised what was happening and what might be done to prevent

118

such development or to make it decent and humane. For, as Buchanan points out (p60), 'The strange thing about ribbon-development is that something of a case may be made in its favour. Had the architecture been good, the houses set well back on service-roads separated from the main road by pleasant glades of trees, then perhaps we should have had experts from abroad coming to study our linear suburbs, so cleverly arranged with good transport to town at the front door, clean open country at the back, and withal merely skimming the road-frontages off the farms without chewing savagely into them.'

At the same time that suburbia was ribboning along main roads and country lanes, it was also spreading around towns in the irregular manner of English urban growth. The character of inter-war suburbia had been determined by a group of victorian and edwardian architects and social reformers; but its shape, that vast, sprawling, formless extension of the town was, (except around London) the consequence of motor-transport. Speculators and municipalities did not need to build near a railway-station or a tram-line. They could buy one or two fields anywhere on the fringe of a town and lay out an estate upon them in the certainty that the local bus-company would extend its route to provide a service for new housing. Says Buchanan (pp64-65), 'It only requires a visit to a large provincial town at the rush-hour to see the astonishing intensity of the bus services, and to realize that these vast suburban accretions are completely dependent upon motor-transport for journeys to work, to school, to shop and to market, to cinema and football match.'

But not around London—for the capital was a special case. Here there were electric-trains as well as trams, buses and cars. An electric-train is quicker to accelerate and can stop more swiftly than one powered by steam. It can also run underground for long distances without asphyxiating its passengers. These characteristics not only make electricity a more satisfactory system of traction than steam for the frequently-stopping suburban train, they also enable such trains to travel below ground and thus serve the centre of a city without disturbing the roads, buildings, sewers and water-mains which either lie on the surface or reside just below it.

The heavy clay of the London basin provided an ideal material for such burrowing. The deep tubes of the London Underground had been laid during the first decade of this century, and the shallow tunnels and cuttings of the Metropolitan District and Inner Circle lines had been electrified at about the same time. Soon these railway companies began to extend their lines by coming to the surface and spreading into the countryside beyond the town. The station at Golders Green was opened in 1907. The success of this project led (in 1923 and 1924) to the extension of the line through open country to Edgware, where a station was built in virgin meadowland. Developers erected shops and houses nearby, bus-services were started, and soon the rural pleasances of North Middlesex were lost in a deplorable scrabble of speculative tudor.

119

UNDERGROUND

SANCTUARY.

"'Tis pleasant, through the loopholes of retreat,
To peep at such a world; to see the stir
Of the great Babel, and not feel the crowd;
To hear the roar she sends through all her gates
At a safe distance, where the dying sound
Falls a soft murmur on th' uninjured ear."

William Cowper.

THE SOONEST REACHED AT ANY TIME

GOLDERS GREEN

(HENDON AND FINCHLEY)

A PLACE OF DELIGHTFUL PROSPECTS

At the same time that London's Underground was extending into Middlesex, Hertfordshire and Essex, the Southern Railway's lines in Kent, Surrey and Sussex were being electrified. This led to a similar spread of suburbia to the south of London. A small part of this spread was due to the activities of the London County Council, whose St Helier, Bellingham, Downham and Mottingham estates were erected in the area served by the Southern Electric. Very much more of it was due to the activities of speculative builders, 'who invariably advertised that their particular estate was contiguous to an electrified line'.[5]

The effect of this electrification was startling. H P White[6] points out that at the dawn of the railway age, London south of the Thames was no more than an extended bridgehead, and goes on (pp4-5), 'Even in 1857 Dickens, in describing a railway journey to Dover, could speak of the train passing into the country about New Cross. Since then building has spread ever southward.

NORTH HARROW ESTATES

SEMI-DETACHED Brick-Built Villas within 3 minutes of North Harrow, 5 minutes West Harrow Stations. Train journey about 16 minutes Baker Street or Marylebone.

3 Bedroom Houses from **£750** Leasehold.
£920 Freehold.

3 Bedroom Houses, Large Type **£850** Leasehold.
£1,040 Freehold.

4 Bedroom Houses **£950** to **£1,450.**

Repayments as Rent arranged.

ADVANCES are being granted on this property by The Middlesex County Council under The Housing Acts, 1890—1924.

Electric Light.   Large Gardens.
Rates 8/- in the £ per year.
Pinner Parish.   Facilities for Garage.

A. CUTLER, *Builder,*

Estate Office, Pinner Road, North Harrow.
Phone—Harrow 139.
Hundreds have been satisfied.

SAY YOU SAW IT IN "METRO-LAND."

79: An advertisement from Metroland, *1925.*

Extensive as was the London of 1914, a real growth since had been spectacu-
lar, very largely stimulated by the constant extension of electric services.
The continuously built-up area now extends right up to the North Downs
beyond Orpington and Croydon. Rural villages of 1914, among them Bexley,
West Wickham, Sutton, Malden and Ashford (Middlesex) have become large
towns with thousands of small or medium-sized houses. Beyond the North
Downs and as far up as the Thames erstwhile market towns, Sevenoaks,
Dorking, Guildford and Woking, have swollen to several times their popu-
lation of a century ago. Scattered semi-rural suburban areas such as Crow-
borough and Haslemere have come into being, and even coastal towns,
Brighton, Bognor and others harbour their quota of London commuters.'

White probably overstates his case a little. There is no doubt that electrification was one of the principal agents of London's expansion to the south,
but buses and cars played their part also, and some of the growth was
certainly due to natural extension of the market-towns, and to the drift of
population to the south east, rather than to migration from London. He
does not however ignore the motor-vehicle entirely. Elsewhere (p10) he
notes that 'outer suburban rail-services and the ubiquitous private car, this
time in the role of feeder rather than rival, have led to the spread of building
throughout the rural areas of the region. It has been termed the "rurbani-
zation" of southern England.'

This use of the private car for commuting, either in association with railways (in the larger cities) or directly to office or factory (in the smaller
towns), has increased greatly since the second war. It started between the
wars when the wealthier classes sought to escape both the congestion of city
life and the formless monotony of the suburbs by building homes far out in
the country. Wives would ferry their husbands to station or office, while
children were sent to boarding-schools or carried back and forth in the
family car. The gardens of such houses were large (sometimes over an acre in
extent). The houses themselves were generally hideous, though they might
sometimes be masked by tall trees and thickets of undergrowth.

Sometimes a speculator would lay out an estate of this kind. He would
buy an area of land, build the roads, and sell plots upon which the purchasers
would erect their own houses. Sometimes the houses would be built in
ribbon-formation along country lanes. In either case a rural suburbia was
created. The inhabitants of such places were neither townsmen nor villagers.
They possessed the wealth of the squire, but lacked both his status and his
place in the local community. In an extreme case, as in the Hertfordshire
village of Tewin, the immigrants became so numerous that two distinct
societies were created, each with its own part of the village and its own social
activities.[7] Such social schizophrenia is certainly undesirable, but the wealthy
immigrants to these villages came nearer than anyone else to achieving the
suburban ideal. They had comfortable country homes, but thanks to the
motor-car they were able to enjoy the amenities of the town.

Sometimes whole districts were made up of such affluent houses. Towns

122

such as Reigate and Woking were transformed by the combined influence of the electric-train and the motor-car into aggregations of upper-middle class suburbia, while in the provinces any village which lay within fifteen miles of a town was likely to become a refuge to which the wealthy would escape from the squalor of industrialism.

The wealthy were not the only people who used the motor-vehicle to provide a means of escape from the city. Elderly and retired people often moved out into the country in an effort to live cheaply and thus eke out meagre pensions or savings. Others sought a 'place' in rural surroundings where they could spend weekends and summer holidays, while a few who were weary of town life built homes in the country so that they might enjoy the independence offered by a rural small-holding. Speculators and the manufacturers of prefabricated houses were ready to provide for such demands, and soon large areas were peppered indiscriminately with the cheapest and poorest of dwellings. Southern Essex was one of the places most affected by this kind of development. The settlements of Laindon, Pitsea and Billericay consisted 'to a greater or less degree of a central area . . surrounded by an expanse of bungalow or shack-development scattered over an exceedingly wide area of country'.[8]

Buchanan, who worked there during the early thirties, describes it as follows: 'There was a large area near Billericay where someone had pegged out an estate on a considerable scale and where the roads existed as muddy, unmade tracks. Here and there, and not by any means confined to the vicinity of the hard public road, plots had been sold and bungalows or shacks erected, without gas or electricity or main drainage or any real convenience for shops or schools, and too remote even for the tradesmen to penetrate. The link with civilization was provided by the bus-service on the nearest main road or by ramshackle car. A half-finished building-estate is a depressing place, but infinitely worse is the estate that obviously never will get finished, will never have the shopping centres, cinemas, churches and schools so optimistically marked on the plan.'[9]

Deplorable though they were, these places were not the worst examples of such shackland. The speculators of Laindon, Pitsea and Billericay ruined a wide area of south Essex, but south Essex is not among the most attractive parts of Britain. It was on the south coast, and particularly at Peacehaven on the South Downs, that inter-war suburbia reached its nadir. At Peacehaven the South Coast Land and Resort Company Ltd (a body which described itself as 'one of the most enterprising town-planning organizations of modern times')[10] caused a stretch of open down on top of the channel cliffs to be spattered with development like that at Billericay. There can be few English landscapes less suited to such exploitation than the 'blunt, bowheaded, whalebacked downs' of Kipling's Sussex. Peacehaven's flimsy shacks were set on a naked plateau. There were no trees to mask them from the public eye, and no hedges to give shelter from the channel gales. It must have been almost as uncomfortable to live in as it was disagreeable to look at. Its

80: Peacehaven, about 1935.

developers not only created one of the ugliest townships in England, they destroyed a lovely landscape in the process.

Peacehaven and the Laindon-Pitsea-Billericay area provide an interesting contrast in ways of dealing with such shack-development. The latter place now forms part of the site of Basildon New Town. At Basildon the shacks have been demolished, new roads have been laid out, a pedestrian shopping-centre built, and some very fair municipal housing erected. At Peacehaven the shopping-centre still lies astride the main coast road, the shacks remain and the spaces between them are being filled with more bungalows. These, though more solidly built, are just as ugly as the original shanties. At Basildon a ruined landscape is being converted into a town which is decent throughout, and occasionally even inspired. At Peacehaven the original shantytown has been consolidated into a horror-comic of mid-century suburbia.

Peacehaven is not only an example of how the revolution in transport technology caused suburbia to spread. It also shows how that same revolution caused a change in the materials of which suburbia was constructed. The walls of Peacehaven were not built, like the local cottages, of Sussex flints. Most of its bungalows were prefabricated shacks of timber-framing covered with asbestos cement. Building, from being a craft industry using local materials, was starting to become an assembling industry using materials brought from a distance. Bricks, tiles, stone and timber are clumsy goods and expensive to move from place to place. As a consequence of this, the vernacular housing of the past has always been constructed of local materials. The tile-hung farmhouses of the Weald, the brick squares of Bloomsbury, the plastered cottages of East Anglia, and the stone streets of Bath were all built of local stuff. This fact gives such buildings a certain ecological rightness; they are constructed of the same materials as the land around them. This use of local materials was changed, first by industrial technology and then by the railway and the motor-lorry.

The history of this change is exemplified by that of the fletton, the smooth, brindled, salmon-pink brick which is used throughout the midlands and the south of England in those parts of a building where appearance is of no consequence. The fletton brickfields form a band which runs south-westwards from Peterborough, through Bedfordshire to Bletchley. Their clay is unusual in that it contains small nodules of carbon. The clay thus possesses its own fuel, so that in firing the bricks burn themselves.

By 1936 the output of flettons was 'probably equal to between one-third and one-half of all common bricks made in England'.[11] The brindled salmon-pink of the fletton makes it a most unattractive facing material. The brick manufacturers sought to overcome this disadvantage, first by giving the fletton a textured 'rustic' surface, and later by facing it with a cosmetic layer of sand. The sand-faced fletton did not come on to the market until just before the second world war, but by 1936 its sister, the rustic fletton, had started to invade suburbia.

As with fletton bricks, so it was with other building materials. The economics of mass-production, and the ease by which materials could be transported by goods-train and motor-lorry, completed the destruction of local architectural idioms which had been started by the stylistic fashion-parade of the previous century.

81: A postcard advertising Peacehaven.

The transport revolution not only affected the materials of which houses were built and the manner in which cities spread. It also influenced the way in which they were laid out and the accommodation which the developer had to provide. Suburbia's inhabitants sometimes possessed cars, and the car required a garage. Garages, however, did not form part of the inter-war municipal estate. Council-housing was built for the working-classes, and the working-classes could not afford cars. It was in speculative and individualistic suburbia that the garage first became a feature of housing-layout. In speculative suburbia its most important effect was to consolidate the national preference for the semi-detached house. Garages cannot easily be incorporated in a terrace; in such a building the garages take up space on the ground floor and compel the developer to adopt house-designs which are certainly unfamiliar, probably inconvenient and sometimes unprofitable. With semi-detached housing this problem does not arise. In such circumstances all that needs to be done to provide garage-space is to set the pairs of houses a little further apart. Garages can then be fitted in, either by placing them between the back door and the site-boundary, or by setting them further back (usually in line with the rear wall of the house) and providing a narrow drive beside the building.

Most earlier inter-war speculative housing did not include garages, but, as time went on and car ownership became more frequent, developers saw the need to provide for it in their more affluent estates. Sometimes garages were built at the same time as the houses, and were sold with them; sometimes sufficient space was left beside the house, so that the purchaser could build his own garage when he acquired a car. In either case the effect on the street-picture was similar. Houses were more widely spread, the silhouette of semi-

82: Peacehaven today.

126

detached suburbia more jagged, and its spaces more indeterminate than before.

Just as the provision of garages aggravated the ugliness of suburbia's silhouette, so the need to provide paved approaches to them intensified that fragmentation of the floorscape which was one of the most unhappy features of the suburban scene. The verge ceased to be a narrow green strip, punctuated with lampposts and flowering trees, and became instead a series of oblong patches of grass separated by wide bands of concrete leading to the garage gates. These bands not only divided the verge, they broke the smooth line of the kerb, and spoilt the appearance of the footway by interrupting its regular pattern of paving slabs. The verges of municipal estates were often broken by paths, but the paths were narrower, and they interrupted neither the line of the kerb nor the pattern of the footway. It was in speculative estates that the difficulty arose, a difficulty which was but one aspect of a greater problem: the design of speculative suburbia.

8 *The characteristics of inter-war speculative suburbia:* The essential difference between council-housing and speculative development is its purpose. The one is built by a municipality as a public service, the other by a development company for the more mundane object of making money.

Building is expensive, and the speculator's business is one of heavy outlays and quick returns; as a consequence of this he is chary of taking risks. He builds what will sell. This has always been the case. We have seen how the speculators of the eighteen forties were unwilling to adopt the fantasies of Richard Brown's domestic architecture, and how the georgian terrace survived beneath a veneer of italianate stucco or Ruskinian gothic until the architectural revolution caused by the building of Bedford Park.

The speculators of the inter-war period were as conservative as their forbears, but unlike their forbears they were not the only builders of houses. During the previous century almost all house-building had been speculative. The victorian speculators had erected slums to be let to the working-classes, as well as villas to be purchased by the well-to-do, but after 1919 things were different. Working-class housing had become the preserve of the municipality. Building houses to let was no longer profitable, and the speculator's business was virtually limited to the building of middle-class houses for sale.[12]

The heavy outlays and quick returns of the speculator's business not only make him conservative in his thinking, they also cause him to be sensitive to the idiosyncracies of his customers. The customers of the inter-war speculators possessed one overriding idiosyncracy; being Englishmen, they were class-conscious. The inhabitant of Ruislip or Pinner, buying his semi-detached villa on mortgage, regarded it not only as his home, but also as the symbol of his position in society. To be saleable, a speculative house had to be emphatically middle-class, but if it had to be middle-class it also had to be cheap, for the speculator's customers were seldom wealthy. Jonathan Carr's desire for houses 'that a gentleman would be glad to live in, which would be as perfect architecturally as the most splended house, but that the extreme cost of a detached house should be £700 and for a pair of villas £1,100' was the same (allowing for a change in the value of sterling) as that of his successors fifty years later. They had, in fact, to devise a pattern of housing which was attuned to the romantic ideal of suburbia, which fitted in with their conservative outlook, which was cheap to build, and which was at the same time an easily recognised middle-class status-symbol.

If the speculator's housing was to fit in with his conservative outlook, it had to be built according to the universal plan; if it was to provide for car-ownership, as well as access to garden, fuel-store and dustbin, it had to be semi-detached. If it was to be cheap, it had to be two-storied and built of the most inexpensive materials; if it was to be effective as a status-symbol, it had to be built in a recognisable style, and one which was as different as possible from that of council-housing; and if it was to be attuned to the suburban ideal, the inspiration of its style had to be romantic. The pattern of building which resulted from these requirements was at once elaborate and mean.

This combination of elaboration and meanness was encouraged by the manner in which government intervened in the finance of private development. During the first part of the inter-war era, successive administrations offered subsidies to developers who built for the lower end of the market. Thus the Housing (Additional Powers) Act of 1919 granted lump-sum subsidies up to a maximum of £160 for houses up to 920 square feet in area. The opportunities so provided were taken up by the speculative builders of the time and the 'Notes and queries' columns of the *Illustrated carpenter and builder* regularly included house-designs whose penny-pinching plans met the requirements of the 'subsidy-house' and whose romantic, half-timbered gables provided the necessary middle-class cachet.

We must remember that there were at this period four architectural styles in use for domestic purposes: the tudor, the mièvre, the neo-georgian and the debilitated Queen Anne. Of these, neo-georgian was, from the speculator's standpoint, the least suitable. Its mouldings and multi-paned sash-windows were expensive; its trim formality was out of keeping with the suburban ideal, and the fact that it was sometimes employed for council-houses made it useless as a middle-class status-symbol. By the same token, the hybrid neo-georgian-mièvre of the *Housing manual* was an unsuitable idiom for the speculator. Pure mièvre was better. It was a romantic style, it lacked the associations of council-housing, it could easily be adapted to variants of the twin-gabled, semi-detached tradition which derived from Godwin's villas at Bedford Park, and it was cheap to build. Mass-produced timber casements, pebble-dash on flettons, and a roof dipping down over the front door were inexpensive elements from which to make up a house.

If mièvre was, from the speculator's standpoint, a more suitable style than neo-georgian, tudor was a more suitable style than mièvre. It was

128

hardly more expensive to build, it was even more emphatically different from council-housing, it could easily be developed from the debilitated Queen Anne of the edwardian era, and it possessed associations which mièvre lacked. By providing leaded lights to his windows and nailing creosoted floorboards to the gables above his bays, the speculator was able to set up associations of ideas in his customer's minds. He made them think that, despite Passchendaele and the Somme, despite the coal strikes, despite the millions of unemployed, despite the dreary round of cooking and housework, they, the middle-classes of Britain, were the heirs of Merrie England—a golden age of thatched cottages with roses round the door, of oxen roasted on the frozen Thames, and of Drake playing bowls on Plymouth Hoe.[13]

Many people have mocked at speculative tudor, and many more have reviled

83: A cover from Metroland, *1925.*

it. It was without doubt the most extraordinary architectural-vernacular which England's builders have ever employed, and it was certainly a principal constituent of speculative suburbia's ugliness, but it was no more a revival than the other styles which were current at the time; and its romanticism, both of design and of association, was in tune with suburbia's romantic spirit.

84: The romanticism of speculative tudor.

This romantic spirit was fostered by the rise in the status of women which was epitomised by the Representation of the People Act of 1918. The influence of female emancipation on architectural taste has never been studied, but it must have been considerable. It was directed, naturally enough, at the home, which woman 'claims . . . as her special sphere and demands the right to choose'.[14]

Ideal home, a magazine aimed at a middle-class, principally feminine readership, was founded in 1920, and soon the speculator's customers were provided with illustrated articles about half-timbered houses set in woodland glades. The illustrations in *Ideal home* were always of individual houses, never of streets; the magazine was concerned with targets, rather than attainments, with the ideal home in its perfect garden, rather than with the speculator's 'semi' in a suburban road.

It may also be that this attention to individual houses helped to make the magazine more attractive to its women readers. Thomas Sharp suggested that woman is by nature far more individualistic than man; he says, 'She has a sense of property and a desire to display it . . . that is far more highly developed than his, she is at once more conservative and more open to the appeal of small novelty: aesthetically she has few or none of the makings of a citizen'.[14] This is not the place for a skirmish in the battle of the sexes, but there is no doubt that the building-society movement helped to foster the householder's sense of property, while the designs which the speculators employed provided for a combination of conservatism and a demand for

130

85: Inter-war speculative suburbia—the Kingston by-pass and its hinterland.

minor novelty in their customers.

These paradoxical requirements had to be achieved at minimum cost. To this end the speculators built as cheaply as possible, maintained the accepted styles of mièvre or tudor, and the accepted form of the semi-detached house, and sought individuality by secondary, cosmetic changes. To save expense they often built the front wall of a pair of houses in a facing brick, leaving the sides and rear in pebble-dash or flettons, while to seek individuality they might change the texture of a roughcast wall or the pattern of half-timbering on a pair of gables. There was in fact little else that they could do so long as

86: The Kingston by-pass.

131

social snobbery, the convenience of access to garden, the requirements of the motor-car, the economics of development and the depth of their customer's pockets, the constraints of planning-schemes prepared under the Acts of 1906, 1919 and 1932, controlled their designs and impelled them to build estates of cheap semi-detached mock-tudor houses at a density of about eight to the acre.

It will be seen that the speculative developers possessed even less freedom of design than the architects of municipal suburbia. If it was not easy to make up a handsome estate from the small, unattractive buildings recommended in the 1919 *Housing manual*, it was far more difficult to make anything of the grotesque status-symbols of the speculators. The designer of a speculative estate had to solve all the problems of municipal suburbia and at the same time to provide his customers with that combination of symbolism, conservatism of design, and appeal to womanhood which was the peculiar requirement of houses built for sale. The task may not have been impossible, but it was certainly more complex than that of the georgian developers. The builders of Bloomsbury worked within the framework of a fine architectural tradition; they built for an aristocracy, they did not need to worry about motor-cars or the seventy-foot rule, or the social symbolism of mock-tudor. Furthermore, the georgian developers were sometimes speculative architects, while the character of their buildings was determined by the conditions of the leases upon which they bought their land.

9 *The disappearance of the speculative architect:* We have seen how the systems of development control by leasehold tenure and by the regulations of the terminating-benefit societies gradually disappeared during the second half of the nineteenth century, and how, after about 1850 the more reputable architects had drifted away from estate-development and house-agency. The change was slow. Wilkinson, Codd and Lipscombe Seckham were speculating in North Oxford in the early 1870s, and as late as 1920 the RIBA's Code of Professional Charges included clauses regarding fees for negotiating the purchase and sale of estates and property.

By this time, however, the change had occurred. The architect's job had become separate from that of the contractor or speculative developer. The position was formalized on May 3 1920, when the Council of the Royal Institute approved an amended code of professional practice. The preamble and the first three clauses of this document read as follows:

'In order to place on record the considerations which govern the conduct of honourable architects and the customs accepted and observed by the Architectural Profession the Council of the Royal Institute of British Architects declares the practice of Architects to be as follows:

1 PERSONAL AND INTER-PROFESSIONAL OBLIGATIONS

(1) The architect is both an artist and a technician. He designs the construction, the internal and external proportions, arrangements, decoration

132

and accessories of buildings, directs their execution and regulates the expenditure upon them.

(2) The profession of architect is liberal and uncommercial. It is incompatible with the business of a contractor, manufacturer, dealing in (or agent for) materials used in buildings or of an auctioneer or house-agent.

(3) An architect is remunerated solely by his fees and is debarred from any other source of profit in connection with the works and duties entrusted to him.'

The code was clearly not a new departure. It defined, and gave official support to a practice which already existed. It seems to have caused little stir at the time. It was first published in the *RIBA journal* of July 31 1920. *Building news* ignored it entirely. *The builder* of August 6 and *Architect's journal* of August 11 quoted it without comment, while a letter in the *RIBA journal* of August 28 describes it as a 'very excellent code'. The only serious criticism appeared in two leading articles (dated August 13 and 27) in *The architect* but these objected not to the principles behind the code, but rather to its tone and to certain matters of detail.

Nevertheless, it was a momentous document. At the beginning of the inter-war period, at the time when the architectural traditions of the georgian era had been killed by social change and stylistic experiment, when the disappearance of leasehold tenure, and of the terminating benefit societies had destroyed any effective system of development-control and the communal maintenance of open space, when the activities of nineteenth-century sanitarians had set strict limits on the designer's freedom, when the motor-bus and the electric-train were about to cause the city to overrun the countryside, when a depressed agriculture was making the farmer ready to sell his land, when the emancipation of women had created a new demand for individuality of design, when there was a shortage of about half-a-million homes irrespective of slum-clearance, when the car and the delivery-van were setting fresh problems for housing-layout, when the building of houses for sale had become a matter of providing not only a home but also a status-symbol—that is to say, at the moment when the house-building industry was most in need of leadership from the architectural profession, the profession's institute defined the practice of architects in terms which would have excluded the activities of John Wood at Bath or of the Adam brothers at the Adelphi.

By the resolution of May 1920 the architects retired from speculative development and left the field open to surveyors, estate-agents, financiers and building-contractors. These men saw little need to spend money on architect's fees. House-designs were standardized, plans could be drawn by an unqualified assistant, or obtained either from a pattern-book or through the *Illustrated carpenter and builder*. On the occasions when an architect was called in, he was a minor figure. The leaders of the profession had long ceased to be interested in work of this kind. As a consequence, the developers employed second-rate men, who possessed neither the ability to seek new solutions to the suburban problem, nor the drive to press them forward in the face of their clients' conservatism and the restrictive codes of the sanitarians and traffic-engineers.

We have seen how the Public Health Act of 1875 caused much of our council-housing to be placed in the hands of men without a specifically architectural training. The Code of Practice of May 1920 had the same effect in the speculative field. It widened the gap between architect and speculative builder which Jonathan Carr had noted fifty-four years earlier. It was perhaps the greatest blunder in the history of our architecture.

The consequences of that blunder are about us. Every town in Britain has its estate of semi-detached houses, with hipped roofs, tudor gables above the bays, pebble-dash on the walls, brick arches over the entrances, boundary-hedges of golden privet and avenues of flowering cherries. Municipal suburbia was extensive, monotonous and dull, speculative suburbia was extensive, monotonous and restless. It was the combination of extent, monotony and restlessness which made inter-war speculative suburbia so hideous in its appearance and so alarming in its spread. Every part of its was restless. The contrasting black and white of its half-timbering, the jagged regularity of its silhouette, the variety of its facing materials, the fragmentation of its front gardens, carriageways and pavements, the shapelessness of its spaces, the patchy colours of its hedges and boundary walls, the spottiness of its lamp-standards and flowering trees—all contributed to a scene which was both unsettled and invariable.

For wherever it might be, speculative suburbia was the same. One road, or one suburb, is to the eye of a stranger identical with another road, or another suburb. Ruislip is indistinguishable from Cowley, Mapperley might just as well be in Bristol as in Nottingham. Not only were the avenues of speculative suburbia as monotonous as the streets of bye-law housing, their layout was no better, their architectural detail was worse and they were even more pervasive. Nearly three million houses were built by private enterprise between the wars, the great majority by speculative building.[15] Among them all it is difficult to find a single decently-designed estate.

10 *Common house-types:* The pair of semi-detached houses with twin gables was by far the commonest housing-unit which the speculators employed, but it was not the only one. They sometimes built terraces, elaborating them with bay-windows and irregular roofs in order to differentiate them from council-housing, and they also built detached houses and bungalows.

Two types of such buildings have already been described: the narrow house, and the square bungalow. In addition to these, there were three other types in common use: the 'double-fronted' house, and two types with L-shaped plans and corner entrances, one of them two-storied, and the other single-storied. All five plan-forms resulted from the need for economy of road-costs, and this caused houses to be deep and narrow also. The double fronted

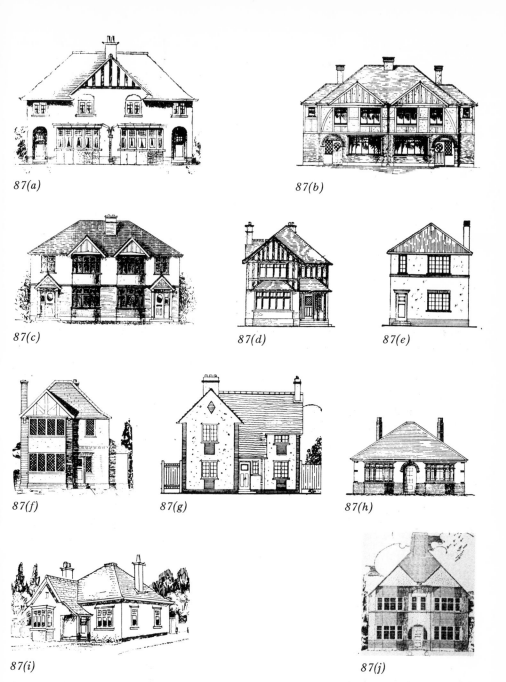

87(a)

87(b)

87(c)

87(d)

87(e)

87(f)

87(g)

87(h)

87(i)

87(j)

87: *A series of designs from the* Illustrated carpenter and builder. *(a) Semi-detached houses, c1925; (b) Semi-detached houses, c1932; (c) Semi-detached houses, c1925; (d) Narrow house, c1925; (e) Narrow house, c1925; (f) Narrow house, c1925; (g) L-plan house, c1925; (h) Square bungalow, c1928; (i) L-plan bungalow, c1925; (j) Double-fronted house, c1924.*

house derived from georgian precedents. It had a symmetrical facade, with an entrance door in the middle. There was a staircase at the rear and the principal rooms were arranged on both sides of a central hall. Many georgian vicarages and farmhouses were built in this way, but a plan suited to an eighteenth-century vicarage was not very satisfactory for an inter-war commuters' house in suburbia. The formal symmetry of the double-fronted house did not go with the fashionable styles of mièvre and tudor, and the fact that it required four downstairs rooms to give the plan a rectangular outline made it an awkward problem in design for a household which had no need for a maid's sitting-room. The L-shaped plan avoided these difficulties. Houses of this type were arranged like the narrow house, but their front rooms projected beyond the line of the entrance porch, which was thus lodged in the corner between hall and living room. The plan fitted the narrow suburban site, it provided for the normal family requirement of dining-room, living-room and kitchen, and it gave a building with an irregular roof, and so enabled the builder to equip his houses with tudor gables or eaves at first-floor level. The L-planned bungalow, like the L-planned house, derived from the need to combine a central entrance with an odd number of rooms on the ground floor. In the case of the house there were three such rooms. In the case of the bungalow there were five.

These three types, together with the narrow house and the square bungalow, have been the commonplaces of detached suburban housing since the first world war. They appeared at different times: we have seen how the double-fronted house derived from the country vicarage, the narrow house from the georgian terrace, and the square bungalow from some regency gatehouse. None of them is intrinsically attractive. The narrow house and the square bungalow are two of the ugliest dwellings ever devised by man. The two L-planned types are hardly better. Even the double-fronted house is seldom successful in suburbia. Its formal symmetry demands a solitary setting with trim lawns and spreading beeches, rather than a forty-five foot suburban plot with a thirty-five foot building-line, which was the most the speculative builder could afford.

11 *The characteristics of individualistic suburbia:* The five standard house-types were not only used by speculative builders. They were also employed by those who bought empty plots and built houses upon them suited to their own requirements.

The individualistic suburbia which resulted from this system of development varied from the small plots and shack-housing of Jaywick to the large gardens and spacious homes of Leatherhead and Woking. Most commonly it took the form of ribbon-development, or of an estate composed of plots between forty and sixty feet wide upon which were built houses of the types described above. Such estates were twentieth-century versions of the victorian pseudo-arcadias described on page 25. At densities of about six to the acre their landscapes did not possess sufficient trees to create an arcadian

88: Inter-war individualistic suburbia—Salmon Street, Wembley.

setting and their buildings were not large enough to give scale and dignity to the scene. Their houses were ugly in shape, their silhouette was even more restless, and their atmosphere no less invariable than the houses—the silhouette and the atmosphere of speculative suburbia.

The planning of such an estate was, indeed, an even more complex problem than the planning of a speculative suburb. The need to build detached houses on narrow plots resulted in unattractive building-forms and front gardens without tall trees, while the fact that each plot-owner was able to build the house of his own choice made consistency of design impossible. A speculative estate could be designed in a coherent fashion since it was built all at once by a single development company; an individualistic estate, built by many different people to their own requirements could hardly avoid muddle and confusion.

This problem was recognised at the time, and in the better-class estates landowners would sometimes seek to maintain standards of development by imposing conditions when they sold their house-plots. These might require

89: Salmon Street, Wembley.

137

that only architects be employed to design the houses, that bricks and roofing-tiles should be of a certain colour, that no building should cost less than a specified amount, and that any project should be approved by the vendor's architect before building started. Such conditions, though they might prevent the worst excesses, were inadequate to achieve an attractive environment. They did nothing to control landscaping, and they did not prevent different architects from designing in different ways. The power of the vendor's architect was more imaginary than real. A skilful and persuasive man could do much to improve the appearance of an estate, but such people were rare. The developer's concern was usually with the status and wealth of his estate rather than with its scenic quality, and his architect would normally do little except rubber-stamp a scheme which had been prepared by one of his professional colleagues and was costly enough to conform to his client's standards.

Consistency of design might have been achieved had architects been allowed to sell building-plots on condition that they were commissioned to design the houses, but the RIBA's code of practice forbade such commercial activities. Architects were no more able to emulate William Wilkinson at Oxford than to follow the example of John Wood at Bath.

Very occasionally a single architect did design a group of individualistic houses, and a landscape setting to go with them, but when this occurred it was the result of a specific commission by people who wished to live close together, rather than the consequence of an estate-developer's policy. Thus in 1936 Miss Mary Crowley and her brother-in-law Cecil Kemp built at Sewell's Orchard in the Hertfordshire village of Tewin a group of three houses arranged

90: Sewell's Orchard, Tewin.

138

91: Arcadia at Tewin Wood, Hertfordshire.

in a carefully designed setting. Of these houses, two were built for members of their own family, and the third for a close friend.[16]

Also in Tewin, about half a mile from Mary Crowley's houses, a stretch of woodland was laid out as a building-estate in plots of one-third of an acre or more. Just as the six-to-the-acre individualistic estates of the time followed upon the pseudo-arcadias of the previous century, so Tewin Wood followed upon such places as Kenwood Park, Sheffield. Like Kenwood Park it is a 'natural treescape in which the houses are but incidents, and the gardens small clearings in the forest', but its roads are straight instead of curved, its plots are separated by hedgerows or wire fences instead of by high stone walls, and its houses are smaller, cheaper and less well-built than those of Kenwood Park. Furthermore, the fact that it had no effective system of design-control caused its houses to be built in a remarkable variety of forms, style and architectural quality. Nevertheless, for all the confusion of its building Tewin Wood is an attractive place. Trees hide its houses from the surrounding countryside. Its plots are big enough to make possible the use of wide-frontage housing types, and its spacious gardens, with their birches, chestnuts and thickets of rhododendrons, make it a true twentieth-century arcadia.[17]

Tewin Wood is an example of arcadia in its purest form—an individualistic estate of wealthy houses, developed at a very low density in a woodland setting. Such purity was rare. Woodland estates were relatively uncommon,

139

92: *Tewin Wood.*

and when they occurred they were not always built at the low density of Tewin Wood. Wooded sites were not popular for building purposes. Builders found that roots interfered with the digging of foundations and the exca-vation of drainage-trenches, and house-owners soon discovered that tall forest trees are troublesome things to have near one's windows. For these reasons the speculators tended to avoid woodland, or, if they found them-selves developing in such a place, they would usually begin by clearing every tree off the site. Even when a speculator left the trees for posterity, his customers had to fell them as they died or became dangerous. Furthermore, tastes vary, and houses change hands. The original owner of a woodland house might have been happy with a garden of birches, rhododendrons and hazel thickets, but his successor often preferred herbaceous borders, veg-etables and a tennis-lawn.

Such destruction is the inevitable result of fragmented control of land-scaping. Unless his activities are subject to covenants (which are difficult to enforce), or to tree-preservation orders (which are uncommon in suburbia), the freehold-owner of a suburban house can hardly be prevented from felling his trees or surrounding his front garden by a hedge; yet some such control is necessary if the space which he occupies as a garden is to form part of a design for the whole street. For suburbia consists not only of buildings, carriageways and pavements, but also of trees, grass, hedges and flowers. The garden, and particularly the area between house and pavement, is an important part of the whole. If a suburban scene is to possess coherence, its landscaping must be designed as carefully as the houses themselves, and the maintenance of this landscape cannot safely be left to the disparate whims of many individuals.

12 *Leasehold-development—Welwyn Garden City:* We have seen how, after the first world war, the building of houses to let became the preserve of municipal enterprise, and how leasehold-tenure gradually died towards the

140

end of the nineteenth century. As a consequence of these changes, the related design of landscape and buildings could only take place in municipal suburbia and in those speculative estates where land was still sold on lease. The *Housing manual* had, however, been very restrained in its discussion of landscape, and leasehold speculation was exceptional. The related design of landscape and buildings was therefore restricted to those rare cases in which a municipality was ready to go beyond the manual's advice, or where there was a leasehold-developer who was prepared to experiment.[18]

Examples of such leasehold-development are to be found at Welwyn Garden City, a settlement which was started after the first world war in accordance with the theories of Ebenezer Howard. Its principal architect, Louis de Soissons, was a man of French extraction, and partly of French training (a fact which may account for the arid formality of Parkway, Welwyn Garden City's main avenue). In their housing-layouts Louis de Soissons and his colleagues followed closely upon the tradition established by Raymond Unwin, though their preferred architectural style was neo-georgian rather than mièvre. The working-class housing of Welwyn Garden City is an admirable essay in Unwin's manner, while its middle-class houses are, like those of Hampstead Garden Suburb, often deployed in symmetrical groups.

The houses in these groups are generally smaller than those in the garden suburb (their owners had less to spend); they are usually detached instead of being arranged in terraces (garages had often to be provided at Welwyn, while Hampstead Garden Suburb was built before the days of the motor-car), and their detailed handling was nowhere as skilful as that of the garden suburb's central square. For all their ability the architects of Welwyn did not possess the genius of Edwin Lutyens. Nevertheless, the best parts of Welwyn Garden City possess real charm, and a feeling for the unity of landscape and buildings which Unwin seldom achieved.

93: The Orchard, Welwyn Garden City.

Louis de Soissons and his colleagues sought this unity by employing a landscape-architect and by arranging their housing-layouts in such a way as to preserve as many trees as possible. In addition, they often followed the example of Lever at Port Sunlight by omitting boundary-hedges to the front gardens and providing a lawn between the pavement and a narrow flowerbed at the base of the house-wall. Sometimes this lawn was enlarged to form a rectangular green with houses on three sides, the road on the fourth. A path around the green gave access to the houses.

Layouts of this kind may be seen in many of the cottage-estates built by the London County Council between the wars. These house-groups are much pleasanter in appearance than the more orthodox housing—with road access, front gardens and hedges—in which they are set, but their effect is still not satisfactory. Spatial relationships and the continuity of floorscape are spoilt by the presence of the road along one side of the green.

These difficulties were overcome at The Orchard, Welwyn Garden City, where the green (which was here spangled with trees, mature apples and a group of ash) was set behind a short cul-de-sac. The Orchard possesses the tranquil charm of a group of almshouses. The floorscape between its houses is not interrupted by roads or cut up with fences. The tall ashes provided a contrast to the small, domestic scale of the apple-trees and of the buildings around the periphery. (The ash-trees were felled in the 1960s, but have not been replanted.) The flowerbeds give bright patches of colour, and the houses are simply and decently designed. It is an admirable scheme.

13 *The Town & Country Planning Act, 1932:* The Orchard was a venture by the Welwyn Garden City Company. It was the result of co-operation between an idealistic developer and skilful architects (Louis de Soissons and Arthur W Kenyon) in conditions of leasehold-tenure and the exclusion of the motor-vehicle. Such a combination of circumstances was highly exceptional. While it was being built, suburbia 'vague, wasteful, formless, incoherent . . . slobbered over the counties'.[19]

To this end, preservation societies sought to raise public opinion against the depredations of the speculative builders, the Garden Cities Association carried out propaganda in favour of Ebenezer Howard's theories, and Parliament passed two acts: The Town and Country Planning Act of 1932 and the Restriction of Ribbon Development Act of 1935.

The Restriction of Ribbon Development Act has already been discussed. It was, as we have seen, an example of transport rather than of planning-law. The other Act, The Town and Country Planning Act 1932, was not the first piece of town-planning legislation in Britain. As early as 1909 Parliament had passed a housing and town-planning Act, and there had been others since, but it was the first serious attempt to provide a comprehensive mechanism for the control of land-use. Its preamble defined its purpose as being *inter alia* 'to authorize the making of schemes with respect to the development and planning of land whether urban or rural.[20]

142

This is not the place for a study of planning-law, and for our purpose it is enough to note that the Act was passed, to summarize its intentions, to record that it failed to realize the hopes which had been placed upon it, and to understand the reasons for this failure.

Under the Act of 1932, planning was a function of the county boroughs and county districts (ie municipal boroughs, and the rural and urban district councils). These bodies were empowered to prepare 'planning-schemes' which were to be the plans for their areas. The map which illustrated a planning-scheme, and formed its most important part, was drawn to a large scale (25 inches to a mile). When it had been prepared, a scheme had to be published and submitted to the Minister of Health (who could hold a public enquiry into any objections). On being approved by the Minister the scheme had to be laid before Parliament. It thus became a local Act controlling development in its area. A landowner who suffered loss in consequence of the operation of a scheme could claim compensation against the local authority, and an authority which increased the value of a landowner's property by bringing a scheme into effect or carrying out works under it could claim 'betterment' against him. Betterment was not defined in the Act, but an expert committee which studied the problem a few years later declared that it meant 'any increase in the value of land (including the buildings thereon) arising from central or local government action whether positive, eg by the execution of public works or improvements, or negative, eg by the imposition of restrictions on other land'.[21]

It was recognised that the preparation and approval of a scheme would take time, and that during this period development might occur which would prejudice the scheme's ultimate form, (a factory, for example, might be built across the line of a proposed road). Intending developers were, therefore, required to seek permission for any development which was proposed during the interim period between a council's resolution to prepare a scheme and the scheme's approval by Parliament. Such applications for permission were called 'interim development-applications'. These applications were dealt with on an *ad hoc* basis. In making its decision upon an interim development-application the council considered not only its own intentions in regard to its proposed scheme, but also the views of any other bodies which might have comments to make on the proposal, (eg a river board in the case of a proposal affecting floodland, or a panel of local architects in the case of a project of doubtful architectural merit).

The Act was found to have a number of failings. In the first place it was rigid; a scheme once prepared could not easily be varied to suit changing circumstances. Secondly, it was negative; schemes prepared under the Act could (with great difficulty) prevent bad development, they could not promote good development. Thirdly, it was administratively unsatisfactory; the authorities which were responsible for putting the Act into effect were for the most part small and somewhat parochial in outlook. (They were able to group themselves together for planning purposes into joint committees

143

responsible for the planning of several adjoining county boroughs or districts; but the members of these committees tended to regard themselves as delegates of their own authorities, rather than as members of a new and larger unit of local government.) Every authority imagined itself as growing in size, wealth and prosperity, and there was a natural tendency to zone more land for development than would actually be required. Finally, a scheme's powers of control were limited by the need to pay compensation to a landowner whose property was barred from development. In theory it should have been possible to offset these compensation expenses by money received as betterment. In practice, however, betterment was found to be very difficult to obtain, whereas compensation could hardly be avoided. The only way that an authority could escape payment for compensation was to zone for housing purposes any land which the owner might some time imagine himself developing. Thus dreams of municipal aggrandisement and anxiety about compensation expenses combined to destroy any logical basis for schemes prepared under the Act.

The effect of these hopes and fears was summarized by the Scott committee[22] in words which epitomise the fantasy of planning during the period between the wars: 'By 1937 . . . the amount of land (in England and Wales) which had then been zoned for housing in schemes that had reached an advanced stage of preparation (considerably less than half the schemes which were actually being prepared) was large enough to accommodate a population of nearly 300,000,000 people additional to our present population of 41,000,000.'

REFERENCES

1 Local Government Board: *Housing manual on the preparation of state-aid housing schemes*, HMSO, 1919, p6, para 24.

2 Lord Strachie moving an amendment to the Roads Improvement Bill: House of Lords Debates, 1925, vol 62 (July 13 to Dec 22) pp274-5.

3 The last of the London General Omnibus Company's horse-buses was withdrawn in 1911. Some of Thomas Tilling's buses remained until the outbreak of the first world war. See Charles E Lee: *The horse-bus as a vehicle*, British Transport Commission, 1962, pp24-26. In the provinces tramways continued well into the 1960s.

4 C D Buchanan: *Mixed blessing, the motor in Britain*, Leonard Hill, 1958, pp60-61.

5 One of the principal developers was the Metropolitan Railway Company Estates Ltd. An advertisement in *Ideal home*, April 1925, states that the company 'have opened up high class residential estates in various districts adjacent to their stations', and goes on, 'The company's estates offer an excellent choice of locality in which to reside and possess unusual facilities, the latest enterprising achievement being the electrification of the railway from Harrow as far as Rickmansworth.' *Ideal home*, vol 11, no 4, p69. See also Jackson, *op cit*, pp225-228.

6 H P White: *A regional history of the railways of Great Britain. Vol 11, Southern England*, David & Charles, 1964.

7 For an excellent social study of Tewin in the 1950s see R E Pahl: The two-class

village', *New society*, February 27 1964, (in which the place is disguised as 'Dormersdell'). Also the same author's *Urbs in rure, the metropolitan fringe in Hertfordshire*, London School of Economics, Geographical Papers no 2, 1965.

8   Patrick Abercrombie: *The Greater London Plan*, para 319, p131.

9   Colin Buchanan, op cit, pp63-64.

10   In an advertisement in *Ideal home*, vol 6, 1922, no 1, p9, which described Peacehaven as 'The garden city of hills by the sea', and went on '£1 will secure you a trip from London to Peacehaven via Brighton, luncheon at Peacehaven and an option on a plot of freehold land'.

11   'Varieties and manufacture', by J K Winser, *Architectural review*, vol 79, 1936, p234.

12   For an explanation of the economic reasons behind this change see Marian Bowley, op cit, pp85-93 and 175-177.

13   'The English half-timbered homestead seems to epitomise the traditions of the race.' *Ideal home*, vol 6, 1922, p194.

14   See Thomas Sharp: *English panorama*, Dent, 1936, p83.

15   Marian Bowley, op cit, p271. Dr Bowley does not distinguish between houses built by speculators for sale and those built by house-owners for their own occupation. According to R L Reiss: *Municipal and private enterprise* housing, Dent, 1945, p15, the figure was 3,135,000.

16   See F R S Yorke: *The modern house in England*, Architectural Press, 1937, pp27-29. Sewell's Orchard originated a fashion for houses with mono-pitched roofs set at an angle of about fifteen degrees, a fashion which became popular among the younger architects of the 1950s. (I have to thank Miss Crowley, now Mrs D L Medd, for information about how these houses came to be built.)

17   This description refers to that area of Tewin Wood which was laid out between the wars and developed partly at that time and partly between 1945 and 1960. It does not include the area developed after 1960 as a speculative estate.

18   There were occasional exceptions to this rule. Welwyn Garden City contains a number of examples of landscape-control by developers building houses to let. These were built by housing-companies registered under the Friendly Societies Act. Such bodies were able to borrow money at cheap rates from the Public Works Loan Board. They bought land on lease from the Garden City Company, built houses to let, devised a landscape setting to go with them and carried out front-garden maintenance themselves. In recent years these houses have been sold to their tenants, who now maintain their own front gardens. So far a coherent landscape pattern has been preserved, but no one can tell how long this situation will continue.

19   Sharp, op cit, p86.

20   The Town and Country Planning Act 1932, 22 Geo 5, chapter 48.

21   Ministry of Works & Planning: *Expert Committee on Compensation & Betterment. Final report* (The Uthwatt Report), Command 6386, HMSO, 1942, para 260.

22   Ministry of Works & Planning: *Report of the Committee on Land Utilisation in Rural Areas* (The Scott Report), Command 6378, HMSO 1942, para 144.

4 THE NEW BRITAIN OF
'AFTER-THE-WAR'

1 *Post-war planning legislation*: The unemployment of the 1930s was not evenly distributed throughout the country. South Wales, Tyneside and West Cumberland were more seriously affected than Birmingham or London. The young men of these areas saw little hope for the future in towns where grass grew in the streets and the dole queue was a centre of social life. They left home and sought their fortunes in places which were less severely smitten by depression. Jarrow, Cockermouth and the Ebbw Vale were crowded with unemployed at the same time that Oxford was becoming an industrial city, Middlesex an agglomeration of semi-detached suburbia, and Lichfield a part of greater Birmingham.

This combination of heavy unemployment in some areas with the simultaneous growth of conurbations elsewhere appeared to be economically wasteful, socially deplorable, and strategically dangerous. It was a complex matter about which little was known. On March 9 1937, the Minister of Labour announced the government's intention to appoint a Royal Commission to investigate the problem, and two-and-a-half years later the commission (known as the Barlow Commission after its chairman, Sir Montague Barlow) issued its report.

The Barlow Report,[1] the Uthwatt Report (on compensation and betterment) and the Scott Report (on the use of land in rural areas) together provided the basis of Britain's post-war system of town and country planning. To consider them all, together with the Acts of Parliament which followed them, would require a treatise on planning-law. For our purposes it is enough to note the following points.

The Barlow Committee reached the conclusions that 'in view of the nature and urgency of the problems before the Commission, national action is necessary', and that 'the continued drift of the industrial population to London and the Home Counties constitutes a social, economic and strategical problem which demands immediate attention' (p201, para 428, sections 1 and 5).

The Scott Committee's recommendations included proposals that planning should become the responsibility of a non-departmental Minister of cabinet rank, that the primary local-planning unit should be the county or the county borough and its surrounding area, and that local-planning authorities should be able to prepare their plans without fear of liability for compensation.

The Uthwatt Committee proposed an ingenious solution to the compensation and betterment problem, which included the suggestion that the state should acquire the rights of development in all land lying outside built-up areas.

Between 1945 and 1980, Parliament passed a total of some sixty-nine Acts whose purpose was to make possible new and more effective systems of control over the location of industry and the use of land, to reform the law concerned with land-ownership and the protection of amenities, and to enable government to build new towns and to collect betterment. There is no need to weary the reader with a catalogue of this mountain of legislation, but we must mention some of it—notably the Town and Country Planning Act 1947, which set up new machinery for the preparation and approval of development-plans, the compulsory purchase of land, the control of land-use and the acquisition by the state of development-rights in land; the Town and Country Planning Acts 1968 and 1971, which reformed those parts of the 1947 Act which dealt with the preparation and approval of development-plans; the Finance Act 1974, which taxed development-gains or, in planning jargon, betterment; and the Leasehold Reform Act of 1967, a measure which emasculated the system of leasehold-tenure for speculative house-building.

Under the Town and Country Planning Act 1947, planning ceased to be the responsibility of the smaller authorities and became instead the task of the county boroughs and county councils. The plans which these bodies prepared were not, as previously, 'planning schemes' which became local Acts of Parliament illustrated by maps at a scale of 25 inches to a mile. Instead they were 'development-plans', whose maps were drawn to a scale of six inches to a mile in urban, or one inch to a mile in rural areas, and which were subject to revision every five years. The use of land was controlled by a system similar to the interim development-control of the Act of 1932. Public authorities were given increased powers of compulsory purchase, and in an effort to solve the problem of compensation and betterment, the Act provided that the state should acquire, for the sum of £300 million, the development-rights of all land.

From this change a number of consequences arose. In the first place, the fact that development-rights were no longer held by the landowner meant that a planning authority could refuse permission to develop without fear of compensation. Secondly, the fact that these rights now belonged to the state made it equitable for the state to require a developer to pay for the right to carry out his development, (this payment was called a 'development-charge'). Thirdly, the fact that ownership of land no longer included owner-ship of development-rights meant that land should change hands, whether by free bargaining or compulsory purchase, at a price which ignored its potential value for development. This price was called the 'existing use-value' of the land.

In practice it was found that the Act of 1947 achieved a success in its system of land-use control, that it was far less effective as an instrument for achieving decent standards of design, that its mechanism for the preparation and approval of development-plans was clumsy and inefficient, and that it failed in its attempt to solve the problem of betterment. This last has indeed proved the most intractable of the issues investigated by the Barlow, Scott and Uthwatt committees. Ever since 1947, betterment and compulsory purchase for development have provided the material for a series of statutes introduced by successive Labour and Conservative administrations. These Acts sought on the one hand to obtain for the community at least some part of any increase in the value of land which might arise, and on the other to free developers from the expense and the bureaucratic meddling which go with such governmental interference in the land-market. I have no wish to weary the reader with an account of this tedious ping-pong game, but it is perhaps necessary to make two points: first, that the establishment in 1965 of capital gains tax as an accepted part of our fiscal system caused better-ment charges to be a less controversial issue in the late 60s and 70s than was the 'development-charge' of the Act of 1947; and secondly, that the Com-munity Land Act 1975 (the contribution of the Labour Government at the time to the ping-pong game) included an ingredient of positive planning as well as those of betterment and compulsory purchase. We shall discuss the opportunities offered by this still-born statute later, but in the meantime we must return to the immediate post-war period and consider the Greater London Plan of 1944.

2 *The Greater London Plan 1944*: While the Uthwatt Committee was investigating the intricacies of compensation and betterment, a team led by Professor (later Sir) Patrick Abercrombie was preparing a plan for Greater London.[2] The Greater London Plan was one of many projects, rich in photo-graphs, optimistic in tone, and inadequate in survey, which were prepared during the last years of war and the first of peace.

Together with the County of London Plan (which had been issued a year earlier under the joint names of Patrick Abercrombie and J H Forshaw (the architect to the London County Council), it included the whole of the counties of London, Middlesex, Surrey and Hertfordshire, as well as parts of Essex, Kent, Berkshire, Buckinghamshire and Bedfordshire.[3] The area covered stretched from the market town of Royston in the north to the wealthy suburbia of Haslemere in the south, and from the old established industrial borough of High Wycombe in the Thames Valley to the new shacklands of Pitsea and Billericay in the Essex lowlands.

The plan's principles derived from the theories of Ebenezer Howard, the teaching of Patrick Geddes, and the practice of inter-war municipal housing. Its immediate background was the findings of the Scott and Barlow Com-mittees and the current theory that Britain's population was about to decline. Its assumptions included the statements that 'in consonance with national trends, the total population of the area will not increase, but on the contrary will be somewhat reduced' (p5, para 19); and 'that new powers for planning will be available including powers for the control of land-values' (p5, para 21), (an assumption which freed Abercrombie from the need to consider questions of compensation when he prepared his proposals).

Abercrombie's other assumption, about a reduction in the area's pop-ulation, was found to be incorrect; the population of the area did not fall as had been expected. This assumption did, however, define his task. It was one of devising a scheme for the redistribution of an existing population, rather than for the accommodation of additional population. He pointed out (p22, para 78) that the structure of Greater London beyond the boundary of the London County Council area took the form of concentric rings 'of which four can be distinguished from the centre outwards, each with a lessening degree of urbanisation'. He defined the four rings as 'the inner urban ring, the suburban ring, the green-belt ring and the outer country ring'. His plan consisted essentially of proposals for the decentralization of population, combined with suggestions for limiting the growth of London's continuously built-up area. To achieve the latter, he proposed a green belt which would form a wall preventing further outward expansion; to achieve the former he proposed that the population of the suburban ring should remain static—'The only increase in population is contemplated through the possible building up on the vacant frontages' (p34, para 108a)—that the population of the green-belt ring should be allowed to grow only to the extent necessary for rounding off the existing towns, and to provide for some of the 'immediate post-war requirements of the London County Council and the County Borough of Croydon' (p36, para 109), and that the outer country ring should become a reception area for people who moved outwards from the county of London and the inner urban ring. To accommodate this increased population, certain existing towns in the outer country ring were to be allowed to grow, and in addition ten new towns were proposed. Abercrombie suggested that the housing in these new and expanded towns should be built at net residential densities of between thirty and fifty persons per acre. This was a more flexible version of the twelve houses to the acre which had been recommended by the Local Government Board twenty-six years earlier.[4] It was in accordance with the recommendations of a study group of the Ministry of Town and Country Planning, a body whose report on site-planning and layout in relation to housing was published in 1944.

3 *The Dudley Report*: This report took the form of an addendum to a report on the design of dwellings which had been prepared for the Minister of Health by a committee under the chairmanship of Lord Dudley.[5] The Dudley Report covered much the same ground as had been covered by the Tudor Walters Report twenty-six years earlier. Like the Tudor Walters Report, it recommended (p10, para 18), 'in the absence of special circumstances the Minister of Health should require all local authorities to employ a trained architect in connection with their housing schemes'. Also like the Tudor Walters Report, it noted the unpopularity of flats, but it did not, like the earlier study, suggest that they should be confined to the centres of large cities. Instead it declared that, 'while flats are open to many objections for families with children, they are less objectionable for other persons. There is need therefore for a mixed development of family houses mingled with blocks of flats for smaller households' (p13, para 35). Elsewhere it declared, 'We believe that the remedy for the depressing appearance and surroundings of some of the earlier blocks of flats is to be found in the mixed form of development ... involving as it does a mixture of blocks of flats with two-

152

storey houses. This form of development makes possible more intimate and varied grouping of the buildings around churches, shopping-centres, public-houses and community buildings; more imaginative use of open space and of the contours and natural features of the site; more attractive gardens, and more diversity in the height of blocks and in the treatment of roof lines' (p20, para 74).

To us the Dudley Report is of less interest than its addendum, the *Report on site-planning and layout in relation to housing*, to which we have already referred. This document was the first official study of the problems of housing layout since the investigations of the Tudor Walters committee. It was made up of six parts: the relationship of housing and town-planning, neighbourhood-planning, space about buildings, roads and car-parks, archi-tectural form, and planting in streets and public places. The most significant feature of the report was, perhaps, its emphasis on the social aspects of housing-layout. It declared that the tendency for large towns to absorb smaller communities 'has caused a partial breakdown of that feeling of neighbourhood and community which is one of the fundamentals of social well-being' (p58, para 13). It went on: 'The position is even worse on most of the large housing-estates built both by the housing authorities and private enterprise in the period between the wars. There it often happens that all forms of community-provision, even the pubs and the shops, are inadequate to induce any growth of neighbourhood feeling, and even the physical arrangement of the place presents as many obstacles to it as the older towns do' (p58, para 14). It suggested that the 'desirable social unit' should be the 'neighbourhood'—an area with a population of between 5,000 and 10,000, possessing an 'organization of its physical form which will aid in every way the development of community life and enable a proper measure of social amenities to be provided' (p58, para 15). It pointed out that, 'The obvious way to delimit neighbourhoods is by adapting their boundaries to barriers such as railway-lines and main highways, and by the creation of features such as open spaces of the parkway type' (p59, para 16).

The report went on to discuss the detailed requirements of such neigh-bourhoods. It suggested that they should vary in density according to their position in the town. It did not adopt the Tudor Walters committee's attitude of uncompromising opposition to high-density housing, but it rejected the densities of 136 and 200 persons to the acre which Abercrombie and Forshaw had proposed for central London. For central areas it suggested a net residential density of 100 persons per acre, and continued, 'In very few cases, and then only in large concentrated urban areas, should it be necessary to re-build at 120 persons per acre' (p61, para 19). On the other hand, the densities suggested for 'open development' and 'outer-ring' housing were the same as those of the Greater London Plan: between thirty and fifty persons to the acre.

The report proposed that neighbourhoods should contain a mixture of income and population groups,[6] that they should possess 'some principal

153

focal point, some definite "centre" (p62, para 25), and that their open spaces should be 'systematized and closely related to the dwellings' (p61, para 23). It suggested that these open spaces might form a 'continuous park and playground pattern which, besides incorporating topographical features, would be within easy reach of every house, and so would offer opportunities for walks along a system of pedestrian ways' (p61, para 23); and it pointed out that these walks could also provide safe routes for children travelling between home and school.

One of the most important parts of the report was that on road-layout and parking. It declared that if the site-planning of housing-estates is to be imaginative, 'it must be based on a thorough study of the characteristics of the site to be planned and on an appreciation of the site-requirements of the buildings to be erected' (p65, para 34). It proposed that the road layout of such estates should avoid both 'curling picturesque roads' and the 'rigidly geometric patterns' of inter-war housing. Buildings and their approaches should be thought of together, the 'pattern of domestic roads should generally be of a free and varied rectangular kind' (p65, para 36), and space should be provided for car-parking on a generous scale. The report discussed, without reaching any definite conclusions, the advantages and disadvantages of culs-de-sac. It suggested that more consideration might be given to the 'branch' system of planning, (the arrangement by which houses are approached by a short footpath leading from a carriageway road). It declared that there were 'striking advantages' to be obtained from the system employed 'in the well-known example of Radburn in the USA, where the basic principle of design is the separation of vehicular and pedestrian traffic' (p66, para 40)—a separation which was achieved by combining footpath-access to the front doors with service culs-de-sac leading to the back gardens—and it mentioned a number of other systems of layout, including 'the square', the 'loopway', the 'modern informal' and that in which the houses 'have a much smaller individual garden which abuts on to a communal garden' (p67, para 44), such as that used three-quarters of a century earlier in the Kensington Park Estate.

The report also investigated the question of daylighting in regard both to flats and to houses. It pointed out that courtyard-planning of flats causes overshadowing and accentuates noise. It therefore advocated other shapes: the T, the cruciform, the Y, the (broken) H, and the group of single blocks planned in parallel, with gaps to provide longer views and improve the penetration of sunlight. It considered that an angle of light at cill level of 15 to 18 degrees provided a reasonable working rule for the spacing of buildings; it showed that this rule gave spaces between houses of 73 feet 6 inches for two-storied houses with roofs at 45 degrees, and 42 ft 6 inches for similar houses with flat roofs. It continues: 'Though these figures may be satisfactory for lighting, they are not necessarily satisfactory for the provision of adequate outdoor amenities for persons inhabiting the buildings; and they show in this respect the unsoundness of basing any argument for low densities purely on grounds of securing daylight or any other single amenity' (p64, para 32).

The authors of the report might have gone on to consider the aesthetic implications of such rules, but like the Tudor Walters Committee they forgot that housing-layout is more a matter of space and scale than of form and pattern. The architectural section of the report consisted largely of a study of the comparative advantages of terraced and semi-detached houses. The authors reached the conclusion that most of the advantages popularly associated with the semi-detached house were illusory. Internal sound transmission was a matter of building construction and planning, and there was little to choose between the two types of house in regard to privacy. The argument that the semi-detached plan provides garage-space between the houses was dismissed in a sentence: 'Garages can, of course, equally well be provided in terrace-housing, for they may be incorporated in the house-block, bedrooms being provided above them' (p70, para 57). The authors admitted rather grudgingly that the semi-detached plan possessed one real advantage– 'the ease with which an approach to the back door can be provided', but they apparently considered that such access could be satisfactorily achieved by providing ground-floor passages between the houses.[7]

The report went on to point out the advantages of the terrace from the standpoint of street-architecture and to plead for large-scale grouping of houses, together with either a harmony or a carefully designed contrast of form and materials in the associated building: 'Variety for its own sake, and between building and building can only in the end produce monotony. But variety between street and street, and between neighbourhoods is readily possible and is the true kind of variety for urban design' (p71, para 58).

In its discussion of tree-planting the report emphasized the need to preserve existing trees and to understand the local ecological system. It declared that expert advice should be obtained in the early stages of the design and that proper provision should be made for subsequent care and maintenance. It pointed out that heavy foliage is out of place where it screens buildings and robs them of sunlight, and it condemned the unintelligent lopping of deciduous trees; but, like the section on architectural form, the section on planting did not pay sufficient attention to questions of scale and space. It ignored altogether the influence of underground services on landscape-design, and it did not discuss avenue-planting in housing-estates. Its main emphasis was laid on the omission, or at least the suppression of the front-garden fence. It declared (p73, para 68): 'Probably the greatest individual obstacle to the creation of successful urban-landscape effects in domestic streets is the ubiquitous front-garden wall or fence, we in England are especially prone to assert our rights of property, and to do so aggressively if necessary; but the spiky railing and the tall privet-hedge are over-elaborate defences for the small front-garden, and certainly their presence hinders that marriage between building and landscape setting which could make our towns very much more beautiful than they are'.

It will be seen that the addendum to the Dudley Report sought to provide a theoretical basis for the layout of housing-estates. Many of its suggestions were admirable. It was the first official document to discuss the social effects of different housing arrangements, to argue the case for terraces rather than semi-detached houses, to appreciate the need for variety of design and continuity of floorscape, and to accept the principle that the design of suburbia should be based upon a marriage between landscape and building. But it paid insufficient attention to the legal, social and administrative obstacles to this marriage, it glossed over the practical advantages of the semi-detached house, it did not discuss the peculiar problems of speculative and individualistic estates. Apart from a brief reference to Radburn, it did not propose a means by which a housing-estate could avoid the ugliness of vehicular carriageways and the dangers of motor-transport, it made no suggestions as to how suburbia could escape the monotony which is implicit in the provision of many thousands of small houses, and its recommendations on planting and architectural form ignored the fact that townscape is more a matter of space and scale than of form and lineament.

4 *Sharawaggi*: The report's principal suggestion in regard to urban design was the recommendation that the planning of housing-estates should be based upon a thorough study of the site to be planned. This proposal, which derived from the teaching of Patrick Geddes, was elaborated, by the editor of the *Architectural review*, into that journal's profession of faith.[8] The *Architectural review* rejected the garden-city ideal. 'As a physical solution to the problems arising out of the industrial revolution it is about as efficient as the pikes handed out early in the war to stop Hitler's Panzers', but, the article went on, 'so far the modern scientific town-planners have failed to provide an alternative picture comparable in realism, vividness or simplicity.'

The alternative picture which the editor proposed was the application to urban areas of the principles inherent in the picturesque landscape of the eighteenth century. Such urban landscaping was dubbed 'sharawaggi', a word first employed in 1685 by Sir William Temple as a transliteration of a Chinese term for irregular gardening. The basis of sharawaggi was "to plan irregularly, to disdain formality, to contrive beauties that shall be great and strike the eye, but without any order or disposition of parts as shall be commonly or easily observed, to improve a scene *according to the manner suggested by itself, and without regard to symmetrical arrangement'*.

Although sharawaggi was derived from the tradition of English landscape-gardening, it was in fact a rediscovery of the principles first described by Camillo Sitte, together with an application to urban conditions of the landscape-architect's preoccupation with the 'genius loci', a preoccupation which was in precise accord with Geddes' teaching.[9] Sharawaggi was not a system designed for suburbia, and indeed its author had specifically condemned the ideals of Unwin and Cadbury; it was rather a general theory which could be applied as much to the redevelopment of a city centre, or to

156

the Festival-of-Britain Exhibition, as to a residential neighbourhood. But sharawaggi, despite its author's disclaimers, was in the true tradition of suburbia. Not only were its picturesque principles in accord with suburbia's romanticism, but the article which described it accepted suburbia's basic premise: that building and planting should be mingled, not separated. One of its illustrations contrasted a treeless row of Georgian houses with a picturesque street, 'whose chimneys, odd roof-angles, protruding bows, trees and shrubs, chiaroscuro and distant eye-catcher closing the vista constitute a genuine piece of urban *langscape*'.

5 *Road-layout*: Sharawaggi was a matter of appearance. Its advocates did not suggest that it would solve the technical problems of urban design. Such questions were not the province of the architectural journalist. One of them, that of road-layout, was the subject of a report issued in 1946 by a departmental committee of the Ministry of War Transport. This essay, *The design and layout of roads in built-up areas*, covered a wide field. It included such matters as traffic-surveys and road-safety, as well as studies of road-design and the effects on traffic of various types of vehicles. Its section on road-junctions contained diagrams defining appropriate dimensions for sight-splays, and included two brief but important pieces of advice. The first declared (p52, para 281), 'It is undesirable that roads shall join each other at an acute angle, and in the planning of new roads right-angled junctions should as a rule be provided'; and the second recommended (p54, para 292), 'In the planning of the road system of neighbourhood units, housing and industrial estates, it is generally desirable that the minor roads should be so located that their junctions with the more important roads of these units and estates do not form cross-roads'. Cross-roads, and the acute-angled junctions which were a feature of the Well Hall Estate, were to be avoided; while the spatial design of road intersections was to be determined by a code of practice based upon road-safety alone.

The report did not ignore the appearance of roads, but it failed to appreciate the complexity of this aspect of road-design, and it paid insufficient attention to the aesthetic implications of its advice. Thus that part which dealt with trees and shrubs did not question the propriety of avenue-planting, while those on underground services, kerb-design and road-equipment hardly considered the effect of these matters upon the appearance and the landscaping of streets. The recommendations of the committee were not all put into practice, but those which were carried out, and in particular those which have been mentioned, had the same effect in the field of road-design as the bye-laws which were issued under the Public Health Act had had in the field of housing. Both were necessary, the one to secure healthy conditions and to minimize the danger of fire, the other to ensure road-safety and to ease the tasks of those responsible for underground services; but both made it difficult to achieve an environment which was attractive in appearance as well as being healthy and safe. In one respect, however, observance of the committee's recommendations was a precondition of planning consent. The Act of 1947 provided sanctions which ensured that such conditions would be obeyed.

This Act had provided the planner with an administrative mechanism. The addendum to the Dudley Report had furnished him with a set of principles upon which to work. The editor of the *Architectural review* had supplied him with a general theory of urban-design, and the Ministry of War Transport had advised him upon certain details of road-layout. He lacked only exemplars upon which to base his projects.

6 *Spatial enclosure*: The first attempt to provide such exemplars was hardly satisfactory. It had been made in 1944, when the Ministry of Health published a *Housing manual* based on the findings of the Dudley Committee. The manual of 1944 followed the example of the manual of 1919, but whereas the earlier study had been issued after the first war was over, the manual of 1944 was published under war-time conditions. It was, in consequence an ill-produced and uninspiring document. The houses which it illustrated had for the most part been built between the wars in the insipid style of the time, while the layouts which it proposed showed little advance upon the work of Unwin at Letchworth or of de Soissons at Welwyn Garden City. It did, however, include one important piece of advice (p16, para 36): 'The device of placing buildings to close the view at bends and right-angle turns has often been used to advantage, and a similar effect may be obtained in a square if the roads entering it are not opposite to one another. Culs-de-sac and quadrangles should not be too narrow, nor on the other hand too wide to give a sense of enclosure.' In these hesitant bureaucratic phrases the manual enunciated a principle of profound importance. It declared that spatial enclosure is a desirable quality in building-layout.

This principle was studied in more detail by Dr Thomas Sharp in a book, *The anatomy of the village*, which was published in 1946. Sharp's purpose was not to offer prototypes for suburban planning. His book was rather an essay in the tradition of Camillo Sitte's *Art of building cities*, but one which was concerned with the English village, rather than the continental town. He pointed out that the post-war era would be a period of social and technological change in the countryside, and that new forms were needed to meet these new requirements. 'But,' he went on (p6), 'a study of the principles of design, whether they were conscious or unconscious, which have given our English villages their beauty, their charm and their character may well elucidate principles that will be useful in our new building.'

Sharp distinguished two salient village-types, the roadside, and the squared. The one, a ribbon on both sides of the village street, the other a group of cottages, a church and perhaps a pair of gate-houses arranged about an open space. He pointed out that the beauty of both types derived not only from their quiet simplicity, the consistent scale of their housing, and the manner in which they were adapted to their sites; but also from their mature forest-trees, the continuity of their buildings, their absence of kerbs, their narrow unfenced garden-strips between house and footpath, and the enclosed character of their street-pictures.

It was this last quality which gave the English village its special charm. Sharp analysed this quality (as it applied to the roadside village) in the following words (p9): 'The village which merely borders a straight road so that, approaching the village, one can see through it and out beyond it before one actually gets into it, starts with a handicap which not even the most beautiful buildings can overcome. Fortunately, this does not often happen in English villages. Whether the buildings were built to line an already crooked road, or whether the road was made crooked by having to avoid curiously-situated buildings, it is difficult to say; but, whichever way it was, most English roadside villages seem somehow to *contain* their road rather than to be merely a string of buildings pushed aside by it. The road may curve gently away from the straight, or it may take a sharp and sudden turn; in either case the village is thereby transformed into a *place*; a place with a way in and a way out and not merely an incident on the roadside.'

The enclosed space was not perhaps the most important of Sharp's discoveries in the field of village-planning, but it was the one which had the greatest influence on suburbia. *The anatomy of the village* sent men back to the rural origins of the suburban tradition. It demonstrated that there was a practical alternative to the arid geometry of Wollaton Park Nottingham, or Unwin's formal symmetry, and it re-established the principle that spatial-design provides the aesthetic basis of housing-layout.

7 *The Housing Manual of 1949*: This principle was embodied in a study for the layout of a new residential area which was illustrated in a second *Housing manual*, published in 1949. The manual of 1949 was a great improvement on that of 1944. Its illustrations were well chosen, its layouts imaginatively designed and it was attractively produced. One of its features was a schedule of proposed minimum widths of streets. This schedule included the recommendation that footways should be six feet wide and should 'not be used as the principal means of access to any building which is more than 150 feet from a carriageway measured along the footway' (p141). Such a canon was necessary. Footpath-access had received official approval—the addendum to the Dudley Report had spoken favourably of the 'branch' system of planning—but such access, though economical in roadworks and attractive in appearance, was inconvenient for certain services. A limit was needed beyond which the dustman should not have to carry his bin, nor the coalheaver his sack. The manual's suggestion that this limit should be set at 150 feet was reasonable; but this rule, together with the need to provide rear-access to the houses themselves had an unexpected result: England's housing-estates came to be designed around the dustbins.

On the question of rear-access to houses the Dudley Committee had been brusque and decisive. 'In some areas,' the report declared (p19, para 71), 'notably in mining districts, it is customary to provide a back lane for the delivery of fuel etc, and for the removal of refuse. This is expensive and undesirable. We recommend instead a ground-floor passage between every two houses in the terrace.' The manual of 1949 included a number of tunnel-access houses among its type-designs, but it also showed other solutions to the problem: a combined passage and store leading from the front of the house to the back, a three-storied house with a ground-floor garage providing access to the rear, and a variant on the narrow house which was linked to its neighbours by a store and covered passage with a bedroom above. The terrace of mirrored pairs remained, as before, the most typical unit of municipal suburbia, but other, more agreeable, forms were slowly beginning to take its place.

The placing of garages was another question which was considered in the manual. Ideally a garage should be set next to the house which it serves. This, however, meant semi-detached houses which were costly in frontage and ugly in appearance, or terrace-houses with ground-floor garages which were of doubtful popularity. Furthermore, in 1949 it appeared unlikely that every household would have a car. The motor-vehicle was still the prerogative of the middle-classes. In these circumstances it seemed wiser, as well as better-looking and more economical, to arrange garages in blocks, so that tenancy of a house did not necessarily involve tenancy of a garage. Nevertheless, the authors of the manual realised that assumptions of future car-ownership were hypothetical. They therefore not only recommended that garages should be arranged in blocks, but suggested also that space should be left for additional blocks of garages to allow for increased car-ownership in the future. Unfortunately, however, this advice was generally ignored by the authorities when they began to build. To leave land unused appeared to be wasteful, and in a period of recurrent economic crises it seemed absurd to provide for more than 25% of car-owners on a working-class estate. Nevertheless, within a few years the affluent society had become established, and today the municipal suburbias both of the inter-war period and of the 1950s are littered with parked cars.

The manual's suggestions about the placing of garages, its advice on street-widths, and its proposals in regard to rear-access, together with the recommendations of the other bodies which had investigated housing-layout, combined to provide the basis for its most important feature. This was the study for the layout of a new residential area which we have mentioned above. The plan which illustrated this project (figure 4, facing p26) was a serious effort to carry out the precepts of the Dudley Report, to adapt sharawaggi to the requirements of the low-density housing-estate, and to relate Thomas Sharp's spatial discoveries to the needs of suburbia. Unlike the plans in earlier manuals, this was clearly a scheme for a genuine site. The peculiar characteristics of the place had been carefully considered (a road, for example, was aligned to accord with a bank of trees), vistas were closed, and the estate was laid out as a number of linked spaces, rather than as a geometrical pattern or a succession of building-groups. These spaces took the form of greens set irregularly about a neighbourhood centre. The project included a few semi-detached houses, but the great majority of the housing consisted of two-storied terraces with occasional three-storied houses to give variety of scale. Old people's bungalows, and flats of three and eight storeys provided for the different age-groups of the population. There were no fenced front-gardens and little avenue-planting. Allotments were set behind the houses, while garages were grouped in blocks and placed, like the allotments, out of sight.

8 *The Anglo-Scandinavian style*: The type-designs in the manual of 1949 were not, like the photographs in the manual of 1944, essays in the neo-georgian mievre of the inter-war municipal estate. A taste of neo-georgian remained in places (four schemes showed pitched roofs set behind parapets), but most of the designs had the gabled roofs, the undivided casements, and the straight eaves of a new architectural idiom.

It will be remembered that, between the wars, three architectural styles were in common use for domestic purposes: tudor, neo-georgian and mievre. In addition to these, a new kind of house might very rarely be discovered. This was a white box-like building with a flat roof and metal windows in horizontal bands. The work of such men as Walter Gropius, Le Corbusier and Frank Lloyd Wright began to be imitated in this country. The younger architects deliberately turned their backs on the traditions inherited from Norman Shaw, and tried to divise a new 'functionalist' architecture based on

94: A 'functionalist' house of the 1930s.

161

first principles. Its form was to be derived from the exigencies of plan and structure; its character was to be the result of the industrial civilization of the twentieth century; its materials were to be those that industry had produced—glass, steel, reinforced concrete and bituminous felts.

After the war these architects were in the ascendant. They found, however, that in the easy optimism of their youth they had not paid sufficient attention to questions of finance. The white-rendered boxes of the 1930s were costly to maintian, steel and glass were more expensive than brick and timber, a house with an irregular plan and a flat roof cost more to build than one of a simple oblong shape with gables and a straight ridge. Furthermore, clients were servantless and not so wealthy as before. In consequence the domestic architects of the post-war era employed their ingenuity not on seeking a new architecture suitable to an industrial society, but on providing the maximum of comfort for the minimum of cost. To this end a style was evolved whose most evident characteristic was its economy. Mouldings were avoided. Texture was the thing, for textures can be obtained easily and cheaply. Weatherboarding was contrasted with brickwork. Renderings, tile-hanging, exposed concrete and pantile roofs provided varied surfaces at low cost. It was (and indeed is, for it still survives) a dull pattern of architecture, for penny-pinching is almost inevitably dull in its results. The style derives in part from some of Voysey's smaller houses, in part from housing in Scandinavia (where local traditions of design were absorbed by the industrial revolution, instead of being destroyed by it as they were here), and to a very limited extent from the work of such masters as Gropius and

95: The 'Anglo-Scandinavian' style.

162

Le Corbusier. It does not, so far as I know, possess a name, and, since a name may help to identify it, I call it in this essay the 'Anglo-Scandinavian' style.

9 *The characteristics of post-war municipal suburbia*: The layout which was illustrated in the manual of 1949 was a theoretical scheme. Its authors did not have to persuade unwilling members of a housing-committee that front-garden fences were better omitted or that the three-storied house was a desirable form of dwelling. The architects to municipal authorities had a more difficult task. They were faced with the Englishman's profound conservatism in housing matters. They soon discovered that three-storied houses were unpopular, that the large greens which had been shown in the manual's scheme were expensive to maintain, and that the eight-storey flats which it recommended were an impractical building form. They were too high for lifts to be omitted, and too low to make the best use of them.

In consequence of such matters the *Housing manual*'s suggestions were found to be less attractive in practice than they had appeared in theory. Nevertheless, the manual's influence was felt. Post-war municipal suburbia abandoned the formal geometry of the inter-war estate, gabled roofs took the place of hips, an occasional three-storied block of flats, or a group of old people's bungalows, gave some variety of roof-line, vistas were closed, mature trees were preserved, occasional greens were provided, front-garden fences were omitted more frequently than during the inter-war period, and semi-detached houses less often employed. On the other hand, the floorscape of the post-war estate was still fragmented, space was still needed for under-ground services, houses were still two storeys high, building-line legislation still prevented the architect from setting his houses close to the highway, while sight-splays and the seventy-foot rule (which had been maintained as a means of ensuring privacy[10] still stood in the way of his achieving bold spatial contrasts and that 'sense of enclosure' which the manual of 1944 had recommended. Post-war municipal suburbia was a substantial improvement on the inter-war estate, but one which still suffered from many of its faults: weakness of scale, poor spatial design, a divided floorscape, social fragmentation and a wide repetitive monotony.

10 *The new towns*: Every town and village in Britain has its estate of post-war council-houses. The best, though not perhaps the most typical examples of such municipal building can be found in the first generation of new towns.[11]

The layouts of these estates were based on a thorough study of local conditions. Their street-pictures were carefully considered. Avenue-planting was reduced to a minimum, forest trees were placed wherever space might allow, back gardens were screened from the road, front fences omitted or suppressed, houses were often set at right-angles to the road, or staggered so that the end-gables should stand out boldly across the line of vision, and the

96: Post-war municipal suburbia—part of the Broadwater neighbourhood, Stevenage.

97: Broadwater, Stevenage.

most strenuous efforts were made to achieve variety of form and texture in the buildings.

But for all the ingenuity of their architects and the skill of their landscape-designers, the new towns are wearisome in appearance. Architectural variety is a matter of contrasting spaces, changes of scale and mixtures of land-use; it is not to be achieved by varying the materials of walls, or the silhouettes of terraces. Opportunities for spatial contrast were, however, restricted for the reasons which we have described; the scale of the buildings was limited by

164

the need to provide the great majority of the accommodation in the form of two-storey dwellings; to mix land-uses was contrary to the planner's ideology, and the very size of the new towns made their architectural monotony inevitable. However extensive it may be, a town which has grown up over the centuries cannot help but possess some variety of character. It consists of streets and buildings which have been erected at many different times for many different purposes. A new town, on the other hand, is built at a stroke. It inevitably consists of a large built-up area designed in a single architectural idiom, and its housing is necessarily made up of many similar dwelling units. Such a place can never achieve the charm, interest and surprise of an old city. Try as he may, the architect of a new town can hardly prevent its housing from possessing the air of a vast municipal estate.

This might have mattered less if the scale of the housing had been large. Terraces four-storeys high possess a certain intrinsic dignity, and when suitably designed they can be given an urban character. But the atmosphere of the new towns' housing was cozy rather than dignified, while the pattern of their layouts and the architecture of their two-storied dwellings derived from rural, not urban, prototypes. The new towns are less like towns than vast overgrown villages.

Just as the small-scale housing of the new towns derived from the small scale of the inter-war cottage-estate, and their monotonous appearance followed after the tedium of the inter-war municipal housing, so the social fragmentation of inter-war council-estates was matched by a similar fragmentation in the new towns. The young couples who moved to Bracknell or Crawley were as isolated from their parents and friends as had been those of the previous generation who had left the central London slums and emigrated to Dagenham or Watling. It had been hoped that the dwellers in the new towns would soon develop an allegiance to the neighbourhood in which they lived, but the neighbourhoods did not quickly develop a community-spirit. The immigrants took time to strike roots in their new environment, the coming of television caused people to stay at home and watch the screen rather than go out to a pub and meet their fellows, a population of 5,000 to 10,000 was found to be too large to form an immediately effective social unit, and mixtures of income and population groups produced more social strain than social stability. Neighbourhood theory did not, indeed, prove to be the immediate success that its advocates had hoped for, but it was probably unreasonable to expect that this would happen. The inhabitants of the new towns were, after all, born and bred elsewhere. Furthermore, the Englishman is reserved by nature. He takes time to settle down and make friends. The experience of Dagenham[12] suggests that communities do become established in the end. This is, indeed, beginning to occur, and it should not be too long before the neighbourhoods of the new towns have developed that social consciousness for which their designers hoped.

Nevertheless, the enclosed spaces of the post-war estate provided a more intimate environment than the long straight roads and geometrical curves of inter-war council-housing. The greens and culs-de-sac of the new towns did not possess the bustle and excitement of the slums, but they were places in which it was easy to strike friendships. People made contacts among their neighbours, children played on the concrete aprons before the garage-blocks, and the close rather than the neighbourhood became the effective social group. Furthermore, we can be sure that the appearance of the new towns will improve with time. The quality of their environments depends as much upon their trees as upon their buildings, and their trees are not yet fully grown. The effect of a landscape-scheme cannot be properly assessed until the planting is mature, and this seldom occurs during the designer's lifetime. The new towns will never possess the distinction of Bath or Bloomsbury, but in comparing them with such places one should consider how Bedford Square must have looked when the plane trees were young.

11 *The Radburn system*: It will be remembered that, in addition to suggesting a number of different layout-systems, the addendum to the Dudley Report had mentioned the 'striking advantages' to be obtained from the system employed 'in the well-known example of Radburn in the USA'. The layout of Radburn was based on the principle that in order to achieve road-safety, vehicular and pedestrian traffic must be segregated. To obtain such segregation, the housing was arranged in 'superblocks' surrounded by vehicular-roads. Service to the housing was provided by short culs-de-sac which led off these peripheral roads and gave access to the back gardens. Within the superblock a system of footways provided a means of approach to the front doors. This footway system was linked to a small park in the centre of each superblock, and also (by bridges or underpasses across the vehicular roads) to the footways of adjoining superblocks. In a town built

98: A Radburn underpass, Pin Green, Stevenage.

166

on the Radburn system it would be possible to walk anywhere without crossing a vehicular-road.

Radburn was laid out by the American architects Clarence Stein and Henry Wright. Stein and Wright were inspired partly by Unwin's work at Hampstead Garden Suburb and partly by Central Park, New York, where Frederick Olmstead and Calvert Vaux, the landscape-designers who had laid out the park, had arranged a road-system which was independent of the park's footpaths. The project was killed by the depression of the 1930s, but two superblocks were completed before the scheme was abandoned, and 'in these there was enough to demonstrate a new form of town and community building: the Radburn idea'.[13]

The purpose of the Radburn system is road-safety, but this is not its only benefit. By keeping the motor-vehicle away from the fronts of the houses, the system enables the architect to design the space between the fronts without reference to the vehicle's needs. The floorscape of this area no longer has to incorporate an ugly waste of tarmac. Kerbs and garage-drives are unnecessary, spatial-design at junctions is not controlled by sight-splays, and the scene is not ruined by a litter of parked cars. Furthermore, the fact that there is no carriageway in this part of the estate means that gas mains and electricity cables do not have to be placed under the verge or the pavement, footpaths can wander where they will, and tall trees can be planted without fear that their branches will interfere with passing traffic. In addition, the Radburn system offers other advantages. The architect who uses it not only avoids the danger and ugliness of traffic roads, he can provide access to the back gardens of terraces without recourse to such expedients as the combined passage and store, or the terrace of mirrored pairs. He can also couple narrow-frontage two-storied terrace-housing with individual garages in the garden of each house—an arrangement which is more convenient than the garage-blocks of the traditional estate.

It will be seen that the use of the Radburn system does much to ease the task of an architect who may be called upon to design a housing-estate. It does not, of course, solve the problem of suburbia. In the first place, the problem is affected by such matters as social symbolism, law and, until recently, professional ethics, as well as by costs of public services, transport, architecture and landscape; and any solution to the problem must take into account all the factors which influence suburban design. Secondly, the success of any housing-layout depends primarily upon the skill of its architect and landscape-designer, and the most brilliant landscape-designer cannot work satisfactorily except within a system of land-ownership which makes coherent landscaping possible; and thirdly, the easing which the Radburn system provides occurs only on the pedestrian side of the estate.

Nevertheless, when a Radburn layout is combined with public ownership of land, the problem of suburbia is greatly simplified. In these circumstances, and on the pedestrian side of the estate, the system helps the architect to achieve that 'marriage between building and landscape setting' which is suburbia's proper aim.

On the pedestrian side of the estate, that is; on the vehicular side there is no marriage. Indeed the parties hardly seem to be aware of each other's existence. The gardens are hidden by bulky garages instead of being visible beyond a privet hedge or a low wooden fence. Trees are absent. The tarmac is far more arid, and the space between the houses wider and more fragmented than in any layout of Unwin or de Soissons. The vehicular side of a Radburn layout is as disagreeable as the pedestrian side is attractive. Use of the system simplifies the architect's task on one side of the houses. On the other side it makes that task even more difficult.

99: Pin Green, Stevenage—a Radburn estate.

These benefits and disadvantages can be seen in several estates which have been designed in accordance with the Radburn system. For example, much of the Pin Green neighbourhood at Stevenage consists, on the pedestrian side, of footways and squares whose admirable scale, skilful details and charmingly-arranged planting make it one of the most attractive estates to have been built in this country since the death of the Georgian tradition. The garage culs-de-sac at Pin Green are however less happy in their design. The architects have done their best to create an agreeable environment from these bare stretches of concrete and ugly garage-doors, but the task has proved too much for them. Pin Green's culs-de-sac are barren places; their only relief comes from children, who in defiance of Radburn principles, use them as playgrounds.

If the difficulty of designing satisfactory culs-de-sac were the only objection to the Radburn system, we might perhaps recommend it as the best approach which has yet been found to the problem of suburbia. The safety of its footpaths and the opportunities which it offers for successful landscaping within the superblocks would do something to compensate for the system's ugliness on the vehicular side. Unfortunately, however, economy,

168

100: A view on the pedestrian side at Pin Green, Stevenage.

101: Garage culs-de-sac at Pin Green, Stevenage.

road-safety and appearance are not the only criteria for a housing-layout. Suburbia must not only look well, cost as little as possible and be safe, it must also function satisfactorily from a social standpoint, and socially the Radburn system possesses certain disadvantages.

The fact that vehicular-access leads to the backs of the houses rather than to their fronts is hardly an inconvenience to the house-holder. He may well be in the habit of entering his home by the back door. It is, however, awkward for his guests. A guest coming by car to visit a house on a Radburn estate must either go to the back door or leave his car in a nearby cul-de-sac and walk around to the front of the house. The one is socially unacceptable, the other is inconvenient. Such inconvenience and social disadvantage may be minimized by designing houses with two fronts, one to the cul-de-sac and

102: Back gardens at Broadwater, Stevenage.

one to the footway, but such an arrangement can have unexpected consequences. The fact that the doctor or the vicar may walk up the garden and knock on the garden door can influence the way in which a family uses its home. In particular it can affect the garden. We have noted the contrast between the tidiness of municipal suburbia's street-frontage and the chaos of its backs, and have seen how this chaos results from the multifarious uses which people make of their gardens. Such a combination of tidiness at the front and variety of garden-use is surely desirable. It is right that a family should have a piece of ground which they can use as they will, while at the same time they present a neat front to the world; we all have a suit to go out in, and a pair of dungarees in which to pursue our hobbies. The Radburn system impels a man to wear a suit all the time, to be neat at the back of his house as well as at the front. It is not easy to incorporate such things as washing-lines, greenhouses or motor-cycle sheds in a tidy garden, and a Radburn layout can lead to their suppression. Anything which limits the active use of leisure is surely to be deplored, and a Radburn layout can have this effect. This is perhaps its most serious disadvantage.

The Radburn system has much against it, as well as much in its favour. It produces estates which are safe from traffic, but which set a dilemma to their visitors, which are attractive in appearance in one place, but which are ugly elsewhere, which have houses and garages in close proximity, but which can limit the leisure activities of their inhabitants. In these circumstances it seems difficult to follow the Parker Morris Committee and 'be sure' that the system 'represents the right general direction for the future'.[14]

12 *Garage arrangements—the Hook Project*: The problems inherent in the Radburn system were discussed by the authors of the Hook Project, a scheme for a new town at Hook in Hampshire, which was prepared by the

170

architect's department of the London County Council, and which was later abandoned as a result of political pressure. They declared (*The planning of a new town*, p42) that the courts of most Radburn layouts 'often present the visitor with a scene so dreary as to discredit the whole Radburn idea', and added that at Hook garages would be supplemented by other systems of car-storage, including parking-spaces and semi-open car-ports. They went on as follows (p50): 'Skill and care in the design of the landscape as a whole—screen and retaining walls, planting, paving and the use of slight changes of level to drop the roofs of parked cars below pedestrian eye level—are as important in solving the problem of parked cars as the design of the grouped garages and semi-open car-ports themselves'. The solution shown in their layout consists of blocks of garages set back-to-back in the centre of large courts—courts which are linked to footpaths serving the fronts of one group of houses and the back gardens of others.

The Hook project was abandoned but the system which it described was put into effect a few years later in the Oakridge estate at Basingstoke. The idea of designing a housing-layout around several blocks of garages seems hardly more satisfactory than the orthodox practice of designing it around the dustbins, but the system does have certain advantages. The garage-courts

103: Oakridge Estate, Basingstoke.

171

are used as playgrounds by the children, as well as being (as the Hook Report declared) 'fathers' play-areas', and there is much to be said for arranging housing about a system of playgrounds, especially when they are used by the adult as well as the child. Oakridge's garage-courts are not the most attractive of environments, but they show that the culs-de-sac of a Radburn estate do not have to be as bleak as those at Pin Green.

13 *Post-war speculative suburbia*: The Radburn system was too unconventional for the speculative developer. He was hardly less conservative in the fifties and sixties than he had been in the twenties, and thus the great bulk of post-war speculative suburbia followed closely upon the well-tried precedents of the inter-war years.

There were differences. The most important was a negative rather than a positive change. The Act of 1947 caused the town to be held within specific boundaries which were defined by the town map. Ribbon-development was stopped, suburbia could not vomit over the countryside like its inter-war prototype, and post-war speculative building was, therefore, less overwhelmingly pervasive than its predecessor. In addition, the system of development-control embodied in the Act enabled local planning-authorities to veto the very worst projects, and gave their officers an opportunity to persuade or bamboozle developers into improving the design of their schemes. Road-layouts were better than before, house-designs were less ugly, and there were no more shacklands like Peacehaven, Jaywick or Billericay.

Within the estate the most obvious difference was stylistic. The hipped roofs, leaded lights, bay-windows and fake half-timbering of speculative-tudor gave way to the straight ridges, undivided casements, smooth facades and tile-hung panels of anglo-scandinavian. This metamorphosis caused the silhouette of the post-war estate to be less jagged and its use of materials less restless than that of its predecessor. The semi-detached pair remained the typical unit of design, partly on account of its practical convenience, partly so that a garage-space could be provided beside each house, and partly in order to maintain the middle-class character of the speculative suburb. The fact that anglo-scandinavian was a universal vernacular employed for council-housing as well as for speculative development prevented the speculator of the fifties and sixties from following his father's example and using a distinctive architectural style as a status-symbol. Instead he employed the same style as the municipal developers, but used it in a coarser, less sophisticated manner. Details were more crudely designed than in the municipal estates; terraces were less frequently employed, and instead of using his houses to form defined spaces of varied and interesting pattern, the post-war speculator usually allowed his semi-detached pairs to follow the building-line with the same dreary precision as those of his father.

By the late sixties, some speculators had decided that a coarse version of anglo-scandinavian did not meet the demands of their customers. Something more special was required. It could hardly be tudor or mievre, for these

172

104: *The speculator's misinterpretation of Corbusian functionalism—the Howard Estate, West Molesey, built 1934.*

had long ceased to be fashionable. The other available styles were Corbusian functionalism, (a manner of building which had never been favoured by the general public,[15] and was by this time becoming somewhat démodé, even among the architects), and neo-georgian (a style which, because it was not used for speculative building between the wars, had not had the opportunity to become unfashionable for this purpose). They adopted neo-georgian,

105: *Neo-georgian of the 1970s.*

106: Speculative suburbia at Saffron Walden, c1964.

but handled it more crudely than the architects of the inter-war period, using casements instead of sashes, and including, as one of their motives, the low-pitched pantile roofs of the anglo-scandinavian mode.[16]

There was another change, less obvious than the change in style, but perhaps more important in its effect on the environment of suburbia. This was an alteration in the treatment of the front fence. Fences were either omitted entirely or the boundary between private land and public road was marked by a dwarf wall of brick or artificial stone, rather than by a three-foot barrier of thorn or privet. Thus, though the floorscape was still fragmented, the space between the houses on one side of the road and those on the other was less sharply broken up than in the estates of the inter-war period.

107: Rylstone Way, Saffron Walden.

174

108: Post-war individualistic suburbia—Poyntell Crescent, Chislehurst.

It will be seen that post-war speculative suburbia was an improvement on its inter-war prototype, but that the improvement lay more in the field of land-use planning than of environmental design. Ribbon-building was halted, the countryside was no longer peppered with flimsy shacks, but the typical speculative estate remained much as it had been before the war. Changes were concerned with superficialities of style rather than with fundamentals of layout. Monotony, restlessness and poor spatial-design were still suburbia's most noticeable characteristics. Terraces were employed more frequently than between the wars, but the speculator's favourite housing-units were still the semi-detached pair, the narrow house, the L-planned house and the five-roomed and squared bungalows; the floorscape was still fragmented by lawns, flower-beds, garden-paths, boundary-walls, garage-drives, pavements,

109: A bungalow and L-plan house at Poyntell Crescent, Chislehurst.

verges, kerbs and carriageways; roadsides were still lined with flowering cherries and spatial-design was still controlled by the seventy-foot rule.

The unadventurous character of post-war speculative suburbia was due, at least in part, to the conservative standpoint of the building societies. Their blinkered attitude has frequently stultified originality of design.[17] It might seem that such behaviour is due to simple pigheadedness, but the problem is more complex than appears at first sight. A building society is a trustee for its investors. It lends their money to house-purchasers against the security of the purchasers' houses, and, like any other body concerned with lending money, it has to be sure that it can dispose of its security quickly in the event of trouble. This means that a building society is concerned, not with the architectural quality of its customers' houses, but with their saleability in the event of foreclosure.[18] Saleability depends on public taste, public taste is generally poor, and this poverty is reflected in the designs upon which building societies are prepared to advance money. The rare work of genius is, by the very fact of its originality, likely to be a poor security for a building-society loan.

14 *The Span estates*: The conservatism of building societies was a problem which faced Span Developments Ltd, a firm whose excellently-designed estates demonstrate both the benefits and dangers of architects' speculation. It might seem that speculation of this kind was impossible since forbidden by the code of practice of the RIBA. Ingenuity can, however, find a way around such rules. There was nothing in the code to prevent one partner in a firm of architects from resigning his memberships of the Institute and the Registration Councils from forming, perhaps in association with a building-contractor, a development company, and from employing his ex-colleague as his architect. This was the means by which G P Townsend (the founder of Span Developments Ltd) and Eric Lyons (their architect) overcame the restriction which made it impossible for them to practice together as speculative architects in the manner of John Wood or the Adam brothers.

Townsend resigned from the RIBA, joined forces with a building-contractor, Leslie Bilsby, and formed Span Developments Ltd. Span are the clients. They buy land, brief Lyons' firm, build the estate and sell the houses. The Span estates consist for the most part of two- and three-storied terraces at a density of about sixty-five persons to the acre, (though some of their estates include tower-blocks of flats and linked 'pavilion' houses). The style of their earlier schemes (an individual version of the anglo-scandinavian mode) is characterized by suppressed roofs, deep fascias, arrowhead tile-hanging and bold white-painted trim. Private gardens are omitted, or reduced to tiny patios, so that the landscaping flows around the buildings without the interruption of hedges or individual front gardens. This communal ownership of open space makes it possible for services to escape the restriction of a narrow verge along the kerbside. Paving is generous and trees and shrubs are lavish, well chosen and skilfully disposed. The terrace-blocks are well

176

110, 111: Two Span estates—The Priory, Blackheath (above) and Templemere, Weybridge.

designed and are grouped in such a way as to combine sufficient privacy for the rooms with an intimate scale for the open spaces. The Span estates are not only the best instances of speculative housing since Nash, they are probably the best pieces of suburbia anywhere in Britain.

To achieve these results Lyons, Townsend and Bilsby had to struggle against the conservatism of building societies (which were chary of lending money for the purchase of such unorthodox housing), the narrow-mindedness of planning authorities (who objected to terrace-houses with flat or mono-pitched roofs, and layouts which did not accord with the seventy-foot rule), and the limited outlook of road engineers (who could not understand why verges should be omitted or why footpaths should depart from the line of the road). The excellence of the Span estates is due in large part to Lyons' admirable pertinacity and diplomatic skill. Had he lacked these qualities his ideas would have been diluted in execution and his projects lost in the quag-mires of bureaucracy.

112: Punch Croft, part of the Span estate at New Ash Green.

We have noted that to achieve their results Lyons, Townsend and Bilsby adopted the georgian technique of architects' speculation. This, however, was not the only classical device which they employed in the administration of their projects. They also made use of leasehold tenure and of the communal maintenance of open spaces. Span remained the ground-landlords, selling accommodation (whether houses or flats) on long leases. Each estate had its own residents' association which was responsible for looking after the open spaces. One of the conditions attached to the purchase of a lease was that the purchaser should join his local residents' association. The system was a refined, twentieth-century version of that which was laid down in the Russell Square Act of 1800.

It must be recognized that if Span achieved their results by the same devices as the georgian developers, their estates were, like those of Nash and the Adam brothers, designed for a limited sector of the community. Their resident is a person of urban tastes, a professional man or young executive who has a small young family, who prefers to buy roses from the florist rather than to grow them himself, and who does not require a greenhouse, a

113, 114: Views of Punch Croft, New Ash Green.

178

workshop or an outdoor run for a boxer dog. There are many such people, and Span did an excellent job in providing for them; but while we admire the success of Lyons and Townsend, we should also recognise what Lyons himself admitted—that he 'had been intentionally building for one stratum of society and was not attempting to solve a national problem'.[19]

Span were not, however, satisfied with the limitations inherent in such an approach to estate-development, and in 1961 they launched a fresh and ambitious project. This was the creation at New Ash Green, between Rochester

115: Over Minnis, New Ash Green.

and Sevenoaks, of a new village. To it they hoped 'to attract people of all ages and all walks of life and enable them to identify with the place, participate in the activities within it, form local ties and live there permanently or, at least, for a long time'.[20] To this end they not only proposed to build a variety of house-types, they also sought to include, within the estate, a large proportion of houses which would be purchased by the Greater London Council and made available to people on that authority's housing list.

The implementation of the project was dogged by a series of misfortunes. First it was refused planning permission by the Kent County Council (a decision which was later reversed by the Minister on appeal); next Span found themselves faced with the same difficulties of conservatism on the part of building societies and narrow-mindedness on the part of local councils and their officers which had beset the company's earlier developments; then, in 1967, at a crucial stage in the development of the village they were smitten by a credit squeeze;[21] and finally, in 1969, the Greater London Council pulled out leaving Span with a debt of £2,000,000 and no evident source of funds to repay the loan. Span withdrew, management of the estate was taken over by a firm of surveyors, and the undeveloped portion of the site was sold to another development company, Bovis Holdings, who proceeded to complete Span's scheme but with certain modifications.

One of the most important of Bovis' changes concerned the design of the houses—yellow stock-bricks, slate-hanging, vertical weatherboards, and mono-pitched roofs had taken the place of the suppressed roofs, arrowhead tile-hanging and bold, white-painted trim of Span's earlier estates. Bovis ceased to employ Lyons and gave up this architectural mannerism, using instead the conventional gables of the anglo-scandinavian mode. On the other hand, Bovis continued Span's policy of small private gardens and communal open spaces, and their part of the estate, though less well landscaped and architecturally less exciting than Span's, is far more attractive in appearance than the conventional speculative estate with its dwarf walls defending patches of front garden.

The GLC's withdrawal triggered-off the debacle of New Ash Green, but the project's failure was due to other factors also. Some, such as the conservative attitude of building societies, have been mentioned, but Span and Lyons cannot be exonerated entirely from blame. Hessie Sachs, in her account of the project, reported (p12, para 3.1) that 'although Lyons and Span frequently referred to the need to take account of economic reality, they believed that artistic standards would be more important to the eventual success of the project than any short-term considerations . . . so in practice decision-making was dominated by design-considerations and this emphasis led to difficulties in production and to some extent in marketing.'

Sachs also notes that 'Span's relationship with Eric Lyons and their builders had always been more characteristic of a "one-off" situation than that of a 19th or 20th-century "spec" development.' Lyons in fact acted at first in the usual professional manner of an architect taking a brief from the client, preparing the design, instructing the builder and supervising the works, 'but as the village progressed, a more rational approach was evolved and the architect began to lessen his control over production and to delegate more functions to the builders. Whereas while the first neighbourhoods were being built he had provided full architectural service, by the time the fifth neighbourhood . . . was begun he was leaving the supervision, after completion of the prototypes to the production team,' though he did 'continue to supervise the exterior works, the layout of the buildings and the landscaping'. (pp12-13.)

It seems that the traditional relationship of architect and builder has to be modified if speculative development is to be financially successful, and there could well be a loss of design quality in the process. Bilsby has indeed declared (Sachs, p8, para 2) 'that it is not possible to build good housing and make money'. The view is one which would surely have been shared by Johnathan Carr, who got into serious financial troubles over Bedford Park, and by the Adam brothers who were reduced to running a lottery in order to clear their losses on the Adelphi. Experimental speculative building is a chancy business, but it would be tragedy if for that reason no such experiments were to take place. Heikki von Hertson (President and Planning Director of the Finnish Housing Foundation) has suggested that 'at least

5% or perhaps even 10% of the total investment in building activity should be devoted to unprejudiced experimental building of new communities'.[22] Such experiments have been carried out in Britain (several of them are discussed later in this book), but they have almost always taken place in the municipal field. The private developer can hardly be expected to chance his company's profits on such ventures, but it does not seem unreasonable to suggest that the taxpayer should support an occasional experiment in speculative house-building. The risks would not be very great, the benefits could be substantial.

As an example of such benefits it may be worth citing the findings of B R Gates, a graduate student at the Polytechnic of Central London, who wrote a thesis on the relationships between the layout of speculative estates, the management systems of their open spaces and the social interactions of their residents. Gates studied four recently-completed estates in Kent, in two of which the open spaces were managed communally (one of this pair was a part of New Ash Green). He concluded that 'The level of communal activity and social interaction was without doubt very much higher on those estates that exhibited a system of communal management of common open spaces,'[23] and he added that the satisfaction of residents related both to a high level of social interaction and to participation in communal activity.

The re-introduction of communal management of open space could well prove to be Span's most important contribution to suburbia's design. Its benefits are both social and aesthetic. Whether at New Ash Green or at Kensington Park, the presence of a communal open space next to the home provides an area where children can ride their tricycles in safety, where tall trees can grow amid shrubberies of bamboo and rhododendron, where there is space for infants' play equipment, where friendships can be struck easily, and where adults can meet in a more agreeable environment than the tarmac roads of conventional suburbia.

It will be for future historians to decide whether this assessment of Span's influence is correct. In the meantime, however, we can declare with confidence that the work of Lyons, Townsend and Bilsby has been a great achievement. They have shown us how small-scale, two- or three-storied housing can be related to open space; they have reminded us of the machinery by which communal gardens can be maintained in speculative development; they have demonstrated that the restrictive codes of the sanitarians and statutory undertakers can be circumvented; they have created environments in which people strike friendships more quickly than in traditional suburbia; they devised means by which architects' speculation could take place despite the code of practice of the RIBA, they have built the best speculative housing since Nash. But for all this they have not sought to solve the real problem of speculative suburbia. They have not shown how to create a decent environment from tens of thousands of those detached rose-covered cottages which are the dream of the vast majority of the developers' customers.[24]

15 *Design-control under the Planning Acts*: A speculative project is, of course, subject to the checks of planning legislation. We have noted that the system of development-control embodied in the Town and Country Planning Act of 1947 gave the officers of planning-authorities an opportunity to persuade developers to improve their designs, and that the philistinism of these authorities was one of the factors which impeded the admirable work of Lyons, Townsend and Bilsby. It may be worth considering the system in some detail, in order to discover why the development-control system has not been more effective in improving the appearance of suburbia, and how it could be thus beneficial and maleficent at the same time.

We must first realize that design control did not start with the Act of 1947, nor even with its predecessors, the Acts of 1909, 1919 and 1932. I have no idea where or when the system originated, but it seems to have existed in regard to parts of London's growing edge during the seventeenth century, for Summerson, in discussing the origins of georgian street-architecture implies that it was in operation during the reign of Charles I and, surprisingly, that one of the officials who administered it was Inigo Jones. Summerson declares (*Georgian London*) that a group of houses in Great Queen Street and Lincoln's Inn Fields which were built by a certain William Newton, 'laid down a canon of street-design which put an end to gabled individualism and provided a discipline for London's streets which was accepted for more than two hundred years'. He suggests (pp17-18) that Newton's activities must have been 'sedulously controlled by the Commissioners on Buildings, for in every case his houses are fronted in the Italian taste, while in almost every case tradition (but only tradition) associates Newton's buildings with the name of Inigo Jones . . . but the "authorship" of all these houses, which has been much debated, is an unprofitable quest: for the excellent reason that in Jones' time the present-day conception of an architect's entire responsibility for a building simply did not exist. To provide a row of houses with a proper Italian character might very well be merely a matter of verbal instructions to the mason or bricklayer together with the loan of an Italian engraving or two and the correction of the "plat-forme" or draft. Jones' part in getting such things done was probably far more that of a civil servant than a professional architect.

Secondly we must realize not only that the context of such control has changed since Jones' time (he was the servant of an autocratic monarch, not of a democratically-elected local authority), but also that there are some matters of great importance to the design of suburbia about which the law can do nothing. The architectural profession's code of practice is a matter for the profession itself, not for Parliament, and the Englishman's class-consciousness is hardly amenable to legislation. Furthermore, the planning Acts seek to control the use of land and the preservation of amenities, but do not (except in cases of compulsory purchase) affect land-ownership. The control of land-use is exercised by requiring permission for 'development', an activity which was defined in the 1947 Act (section 12, subsection

2) as the 'carrying out of building, engineering, mining or other operations in, on, over, or under land or the making of any material change in the use of any buildings or other land'.

Many forms of development, such as the wall-papering of a living-room, the building of a dog-kennel in the back garden, or the change from a butcher's shop to a greengrocer's shop are permitted either under the Act or under orders issued by the Secretary of State for the Environment, but for the rest, the consent of the local planning-authority is required.

An intending developer seeks permission for his project by answering a questionnaire upon it, and submitting a set of drawings showing what he proposes. The officers of the planning-authority study the drawings and questionnaire, obtain the opinions of other interested parties upon them, and issue a recommendation to their planning-committee. The committee studies the project, considers its officer's recommendations and makes its decision. This can take the form of a consent, a consent subject to certain conditions, or a refusal. An applicant can appeal to the Secretary of State against a refusal, or against conditions which he considers unreasonable. On receipt of an appeal, the Secretary of State instructs one of his inspectors to hold a local enquiry. This can take the form of an oral hearing or, in a simple case, can be dealt with by written representation. In the case of an oral hearing both parties can call and cross-examine witnesses. The inspector considers the evidence and visits the site. In a simple case he decides the issue himself. In a more complex situation he reports his findings to the Secretary of State. The Secretary of State considers his inspector's report and decides the case in the light of its findings.

One might imagine that such a system would make it possible to prevent poor design. A planning-authority can obtain expert advice on a proposal of doubtful architectural merit, its officers can meet an applicant and suggest ways in which he can improve his proposals, and if all else fails it can reject an unsatisfactory scheme. Design-control is, however, a matter in which practice does not correspond with theory. There are a number of reasons for this situation, but they can all be categorized either as problems of negotiation and diplomacy, or as problems of the mechanism of local government. Britain is a democracy. Our local authorities consist of councillors who are laymen elected by the general public. The bulk of an authority's work is carried out by committees made up of such councillors. Public taste is generally poor and this poverty is often reflected in the taste of the committees. Usually this is not important. A public-health committee, for example, deals with affairs in which taste is of little consequence. A planning-committee, on the other hand, is concerned with questions of aesthetics, and its taste matters. Local government officers spend much time educating their committees in the nature of their work, and a planning-officer will always seek to improve his committee's taste, but the job is slow. Moreover, councillors retire, new men are elected, committees change their membership and the planning-officer's educational task is never complete. There seems to be little prospect of an amelioration in this field until public taste as a whole has improved.

Planning-committees are subject to the educative influence of their officers, but the advice which a committee receives is often less felicitous than one might expect. The source of advice on design varies; some authorities call upon panels made up of architects living in the locality, others have their own architectural staffs, district councils sometimes seek assistance from a specialist design-group in the county planning-office, and many authorities leave the matter to the judgement of their own planning-officer, whether or not he possesses a special qualification in this field.[25]

Before recommending the rejection of a scheme the panel, or the planning-authority's officer, will usually seek to persuade the developer to improve his project. It is, however, not easy to carry out such persuasion successfully; suitable staff for the job are not easily found. Most projects about which there is doubt are designed as poorly and cheaply as possible, and in consequence the authority's officer has little leeway for improvement. He meets the applicant, perhaps offers an alternative sketch-elevation, talks as soothingly and persuasively as possible, and considers his job accomplished if the application passed to his committee with a recommendation for approval is somewhat less bad than it was when originally submitted.

There is no doubt that the operation of design-control, though much less effective than one might wish, has led many developers to improve the appearance of their projects. It has caused industrialists to employ architects, extractors of gravel to landscape their workings, and garage-proprietors to limit the number of their advertisements. It has led those who build homes for themselves to seek more agreeable forms than the narrow house and the square bungalow. It has caused speculative builders to arrange their houses in groups in the manner of Raymond Unwin, while some have even learnt to plan their streets to be seen, like those of the Well Hall Estate, in acute perspective. But for all this its results have not been wholly beneficial. It has led some developers to play for safety, and it has occasionally blocked or impeded a new or creative project.

This rejection of originality is a consequence of control by lay committees. We are all suspicious of change in matters about which we know little, and a lay committee is naturally conservative in its tastes. However good it may be, a project which is new, original and different is unlikely to be well received by a committee of laymen; the work of genius is the one which the planning-committee is most likely to reject. Design-control has improved the appearance of many bad buildings, but in doing so it has prevented a few good ones from being built.

During the 1950s this occurred most frequently in the architectural wastelands of individualistic suburbia. These are the places where the young, enthusiastic, newly-qualified architect often obtains his first commission, a house for some friend or relative. Too often he conceives his building as a jewel isolated from its surroundings. He designs it according to his personal

184

whim, devoting himself to the execution of those exciting ideas with which he experimented in his theoretical, student projects. For weeks he works late into the night preparing sketch-designs, discussing them with his client, amending them, discussing them again and finally producing an acceptable scheme. Drawings are prepared, the application is completed, and the project submitted to the local authority. A few weeks later the drawings come back accompanied by a formal note stating that the project has been rejected on the grounds that it would be 'detrimental to the amenities of the surrounding area'. Angry and embittered the young man sits down at his desk and writes to the *Architects' journal*. He points out that planning-committees are made up of laymen unqualified to judge the virtues of a scheme submitted to them, that such committees are either advised by planning-officers who are as ignorant of architecture as the committee itself, or by architects who are acting unethically if they make adverse criticisms of the work of their professional colleagues, and that to complain that a project is detrimental to the amenities of the surrounding area is often absurd. In his case the surrounding area has no amenities anyway.

At this period it was hardly possible to open an architectural magazine without seeing a letter from some unfortunate member of the profession whose design had been rejected by a planning-committee on aesthetic grounds. The journals of the time suggest that most architects regarded this part of planning as wasteful in effort, unfair in practice, ineffective in operation, contrary to professional ethics, artistically stultifying and a disgraceful interference with their liberty to design as they chose. These views were expressed by Theo Crosby in an article 'Notes on a domestic style', in the *Architects' year book* for 1957. He declared (p73) that the present situation is really fantastic. 'Here is a country that builds several hundred thousand houses a year, with over twenty thousand qualified architects almost all of whom are thoroughly at home in the modern movement; and a dozen or so houses of any architectural value or interest produced in ten years. That such a censorship should exist and be accepted as inevitable is incredible. That one architect should be in a position to destroy the work and livelihood of another is criminal. The present sterility in house-building is the result of our lack of freedom. Until the freedom to build is restored we shall not have a healthy domestic architecture, or indeed much of an architecture at all.'

Crosby's complaint was reiterated in the following year by Sir Basil Spence in his inaugural address as President of the RIBA. Spence declared that planning-committees are 'the lowest common denominator of ignorance and bad architecture'[26] and went on to suggest that they should be abolished for a trial period, a wild proposal which was probably intended to draw attention to the problem, rather than as a thoughtful contribution to its solution. In any case, Spence's comments were very properly ignored by government. The subject, indeed, dropped out of the public press during the sixties and early seventies, partly perhaps because by this time society had begun to become accustomed to the aesthetic of functionalism, and partly because the prosperity of those years kept the architects so busy that they had little time to complain about the operation of bureaucracy. Nevertheless, the profession's frustration remained below the surface, and in 1976 the RIBA itself declared its opposition to design-control except in certain limited and defined circumstances.

The Institute expressed this opinion in evidence which it submitted to the Environmental Sub-Committee of the House of Commons Expenditure Committee, a body whose terms of reference were concerned with identifying both the reasons for delays in the planning system and the resource-costs which such delays created. In its evidence the Institute declared that control of the external appearance of buildings 'has not been a successful part of development control. At best it has conduced to acceptable mediocrity and has not prevented some bad building or the destruction of many pleasant places.' The Institute went on to say that 'the role of censor into which planners have perforce been cast on matters for which few are qualified has frustrated the constructive professional collaboration which should exist between those who administer the system and the trained design-professional who should be responsible for the appearance of built form,' adding the opinion that 'for every case in which a planning-authority has helped an architect to achieve a better design than his client wanted, or improve on a design in which no architect had been employed at all, there must be many more cases of architects having to "design down" to planning requirements of an aesthetic kind, and of the employment by clients of architects who are felt to be more notable for their skill in "getting schemes through planning" than for their skill as designers.' They added that 'the opportunity to exercise judgment in matters of external appearance has generally proved irresistible, consequently lengthening the time taken to reach decisions and increasing the cost of building', and that 'therefore . . . in the interest of cost and effectiveness detailed control of external appearance should be greatly reduced, applying in the main to conservation areas and other areas of special interest where collaboration between planners and designers can be encouraged by shared study of problems and by general planning briefs.'[27]

In view of the sub-committee's terms of reference it was natural that the Institute's evidence should be directed towards cost and effectiveness, but it is difficult to escape the conclusion that their real concern was not so much the costs and delays of the control-system, as the fact that it can, and occasionally does, inhibit creative design. Other aspects of planning cause costs and delays, and though some of these were mentioned, they occupied a smaller proportion of the memorandum than that devoted to design-control.

As to the evidence itself we may agree that design-control has sometimes 'conduced to acceptable mediocrity', (adding, however, that there are times when acceptable mediocrity is a desirable quality. No-one would wish a corps-de-ballet to behave like an undisciplined assembly of Margot Fonteyns)

186

that it 'has not prevented some bad building or the destruction of many pleasant places', and that the planners' role of censor has frequently 'frustrated the constructive professional collaboration' which should exist between planner and architect'. But for all this the Institute's paper was a somewhat tendentious document. It made sweeping statements about the effects of the design-control system, but offered no statistics to support its opinions; it complained that 'the opportunity to exercise judgment on matters of external appearance has generally proved irresistible', thus implying that such judgments are usually damnatory, whereas in fact they are far more commonly favourable to the applicant; and it said nothing about the proportion of applications which are the subject of complaint on grounds of design, their characteristics, or how they are processed within the planning office. We should, perhaps try to make good this deficiency.

Perhaps ten percent—there is no nationwide statistic available—of submitted applications are sufficiently contentious to be the subject of negotiation on aesthetic grounds, and only a small proportion of those in this category are submitted by architects. (An application from an architect is far less likely to be the subject of complaint than one from a layman). Of the remainder, most are just incompetent, while some, though not incompetent, are poor by any standards even when allowance has been made for subjective preferences.

Of those which do come from architects, a few are weak efforts—in this, as in every other field, there are bad practitioners as well as good ones—while occasionally a project is received which, though well-designed in itself, would not fit happily into the local scene. These are probably the most controversial cases, particularly as a few of the more eminent members of the profession are prone to adopt a primadonna attitude to the environment in which their clients propose to build.

The first piece of advice which a planning-officer gives to an applicant who submits a poor or incompetent proposal is that he should employ an architect. Design-control does not necessarily inhibit, and indeed may sometimes promote the 'constructive professional collaboration' which the Institute mentioned in its evidence. If negotiations fail, it is rare, outside conservation areas, national parks etc, for a proposal to be rejected on design-grounds alone. Subjective aesthetic preferences do not provide a good basis on which to fight an appeal.

The RIBA's proposed solution to the problem of design-control included two suggestions apart from that already mentioned, that such control should apply only in certain specified areas. First, they proposed that all applications for development still coming within control should be submitted by architects, (adding that if this were done, the Institute would require its members to sign their buildings, a device designed to increase the architect's public accountability); secondly, they suggested that when an authority grants an outline permission it should append, to the consent, a schedule of detailed matters of special significance in the particular case, that the subsequent detailed application should relate only to the items listed in the schedule, and that this second application should receive a deemed consent unless a refusal had been issued within a specified time. The Expenditure Committee ignored these two aspects of the Institute's evidence. They accepted the principle that planning authorities should be able to exercise a degree of aesthetic control, but added, 'We think they must exercise restraint in this regard since it would be most undesirable to stifle creativity and innovation. They should therefore reject applications solely on ground of aesthetic detail only when they affect national parks, areas of outstanding natural beauty, conservation areas, listed buildings or other particularly sensitive cases'. They added that recommendations relating to aesthetic aspects of development-control should be handled only by appropriately qualified officers, and they recommended that the Department should issue revised guidelines on this subject as soon as possible.[28]

The government responded to the committee's report in a paper, *Planning procedures*, which included a brief paragraph on design-control. This declared (para 31) that the secretaries of state were considering how far local planning-authorities should become involved in the subject, and added that they would issue further guidance on the matter. Two years later, in 1980, a draft circular, *Development control-policy and practice*, was issued for limited distribution; ministerial decisions following this were still awaited at the time of going to press with this book.

Design-control is, perhaps unavoidably, a controversial subject. It may, however, become less controversial if it is seen in the perspective of history. The system does no more than provide machinery by which the planning-authorities of today try to do what others have done before. We have seen how the Commissioners on Buildings took care that William Newton's houses were fronted in the Italian taste, how the surveyors who laid out the georgian squares used building-agreements to ensure order in the development of their estates, how the terminating-benefit societies sought it by the rules which they imposed on their members, how the speculative architects of North Oxford achieved it by their own self-discipline; and how the inter-war land speculators sometimes imposed restrictive covenants which controlled the design of houses built on the land which they sold. The system has certainly failed to achieve a satisfactory suburban environment, but before damning it on this account we must consider the reasons for this failure.

There are many. One of them is the difficulty of creating an attractive scene from a series of box-like houses on plots thirty-five feet wide. Another is the difficulty of finding suitable staff to administer the system. A third is the inexpert nature of the committees which carry it out. But perhaps the most important is the fact that, unlike the earlier systems which we have described, the administrative mechanism of design-control is negative rather than positive. Just as schemes prepared under the Act of 1932 could (with great difficulty) prevent bad development but could not promote good development, so design-control can (with great difficulty) prevent bad design

188

but cannot promote good design. Later in this book we shall discuss the two devices, planning-briefs and design-guides, by which planning-authorities sought, during the 1970s to set up positive systems of control. In the meantime, however, we should perhaps note that the establishment of a decent environment in the circumstances of individualistic suburbia is made much easier if a single architect can be entrusted with the design of a group of adjoining houses. We have seen that the RIBA's code of practice created difficulties for the architect who wished to prepare such a group-scheme.

These difficulties were not, however, insuperable. This is shown by the work of Paul Mauger, an architect who built during the 1950s and 1960s a number of such schemes in Welwyn Garden City, despite the restriction of the code.

16   *Individualistic suburbia: grouped houses:* Mauger could not take the initiative, as Wilkinson seems to have done at North Oxford, and sell land to prospective clients on the understanding that he should be the architect of any house built upon it. He had to be commissioned first, and then persuade his clients to participate in a group-project. For this reason his house-groups were less frequent than Wilkinson's. He was only able to design them when he had several clients who happened to own adjoining sites.

One of his most successful projects is situated in a part of Welwyn Garden City known as 'The Reddings'. In this case he began by persuading three or four clients to join in a group-scheme. He then approached the officers of the Welwyn Garden City Development Corporation, obtained their support for the idea, explained that he expected to receive a few more commissions in the near future, and arranged that the people concerned should be allocated sites adjoining those of his existing clients. When he had obtained commissions from some six clients, all of whom had leased adjoining sites, he approached two other architects who were building on the other side of the road and persuaded them to use the same kind of bricks and roofing tiles as he was using in his own houses. In this way Mauger arranged for nine houses to be built together in the same architectural idiom and using the same facing materials. The effectiveness of the scheme has been diminished by the needless felling of forest trees and the subsequent planting of flowering prunus (it was laid out on a woodland site), and it suffers from the inevitable wide spaces and fragmented floorscape of the suburban estate, but the coherence of its design, and the skilful manner in which the houses are accommodated to the curve of the road, make it one of the best pieces of individualistic suburbia to have been erected since 1945. It is an admirable, if unadventurous, essay in the tradition of William Wilkinson's work at North Oxford, and of Mary Crowley's and Cecil Kemp's houses at Tewin.

Mauger's unadventurousness was typical of his time. Apart from the Span estates, the character of suburbia during the earlier post-war years was unadventurous. It had developed naturally from the experience of the previous century and a half. The municipal suburbia of the new towns was an improved

116: The Reddings, Welwyn Garden City. Paul Mauger's houses are in the foreground on the inside of the bend.

picturesque version of inter-war housing, while the speculative builder followed the same pattern as his predecessors, but dressed it up in a more fashionable architectural style. He could hardly do anything else, for, as we have seen, much of suburbia's deplorable appearance has been the secondary and unintended consequence of legal constraints, of quasi-legal codes of practice, or of the employment, in roles where design-skill is important, of people unqualified in this field.

REFERENCES

1 *Report of the Royal Commission on the Distribution of the Industrial Population* (the Barlow Report), Command 6153, 1940.
2 *Greater London Plan 1944*, HMSO, 1945.
3 This refers to the county boundaries as they existed at the time. These counties have since been reorganized. Middlesex and the County of London have disappeared, and parts of the Home Counties have been incorporated in the area of the Greater London Council. The City of London was excluded from the areas of the two plans. It had its own planning powers and was in consequence not discussed in the County of London Plan. It could not be considered in the Greater London Plan because that document dealt only with the suburbs and the surrounding countryside.
4 'Net residential density' was defined as 'the average number of persons per acre of housing area which comprises the curtilages of the dwellings, access or internal roads, and half the main roads up to a maximum of twenty feet where these give access to residential property' (p114, para 282). In order to convert houses per acre into persons per acre, a ratio for persons per house has to be used. This number varies from time to time in accordance with demographic changes. At the time that Abercrombie was writing, a reasonable figure for this ratio was 3.25. On this basis, a figure of 12 houses per acre is equivalent to one of 39 persons per acre.

5 More strictly a sub-committee. The full title of this body was the 'Design of Dwellings Sub-Committee of the Central Housing Advisory Committee'. Its report was published by HMSO in 1944.

6 'Within this total (of 10,000 people) there would be variety in types of accommodation corresponding to variations in rents, income-group requirements and size of family' (p61, para 22).

7 'For terrace-houses backing on to one another this approach has to be made either by a passage running along the end of the rear gardens (which is neither entirely satisfactory nor economical) or by ground-floor passages between the houses (p69, para 54). It is curious that the report did not mention the Radburn system as a means of providing rear-access.

8 In an article entitled 'Interior and exterior furnishing' which appeared in the issue for January 1944 (vol 95, p3). The editor was Sir James Richards.

9 The editor of the *Architectural review* seems to have been unaware of Geddes' teaching or of Sitte's book, for neither of their names was mentioned in the article.

10 'Privacy in housing layouts can only be secured by attention to a number of points. The windows of one dwelling should not directly face those of another unless there is a reasonable distance between them. A dimension of 70ft seems to be generally agreed as the minimum between houses to secure privacy in this respect.' Ministry of Housing & Local Government: *The density of residential areas*, HMSO, 1952, p7, para 25.

11 Strictly speaking, housing in the New Towns is not council-housing. The new towns are built, not by the local councils, but by development corporations, which are quasi-independent agencies of the central government. The character of their housing is, however, similar to that of council-housing, and for that reason I have grouped the two types together under the general heading of municipal suburbia.

12 This matter is discussed in detail by Peter Willmott in his book *The evolution of a community*, Routledge & Kegan Paul, 1963.

13 Clarence Stein: *Toward new towns for America*, Liverpool University Press, 1958, p37. This book includes a detailed description of the history of Radburn. It may be worth noting that the basis of the Radburn system (vehicular-access to the rear of the housing, and footpath-access to the front) was anticipated in an unfulfilled design of Raymond Unwin's for part of Hampstead Garden Suburb, and that Ironville was also in some way a Radburn prototype. The layout of Ironville is not strictly in accordance with the system, since the houses have vehicular-access to both sides. Nevertheless, it works as a Radburn plan, for the drive to the front doors is used only as a footpath. Unwin's scheme was illustrated in his book *Town planning in practice* (T Fisher Unwin, 1909, pp330, 331 illustrations 241 and 242). The caption to the illustrations states that the scheme shown was being built by the Garden Suburb Development Company. The garden suburb does not however contain a layout of this kind. My friend Leslie Ginsburg has suggested that the drawing represents an abandoned project for Turner Close and Meadway Close.

14 *Homes for today & tomorrow*, Report of The Sub-Committee of a Central Housing Advisory Committee (Parker-Morris Report) p44, para 201. For very useful studies of several different systems of pedestrian and vehicle segregation see *Cars in housing, some medium-density layouts*, Ministry of Housing & Local Government Design Bulletin 10, HMSO 1966; also *Land use and densities in traffic-separated housing layouts*, Ministry of Housing and Local Government Urban Planning Directorate Technical Study, 1968.

15 During the 1930s a few developers built estates with white-rendered walls, flat roofs and horizontal barred windows: a gross misinterpretation of the functionalist aesthetic. The public, however, did not take to them, and at least one such scheme led its creator to bankruptcy. See Jackson, op cit, pp139-140 and 208.

16 'The trend is definitely towards graceful houses, particularly of the georgian type'— Victor Matthews, Chairman of New Ideal Homesteads Ltd, quoted in *The housebuilder and estate developer*, July 1969.

17 'I am convinced that the building societies are the biggest enemies of progress in design in the country . . . We are still restricted in our design by the ideas upon which the building societies have been working for the past 25 years. We are trying to produce better designs, but we find it almost impossible to vary our methods because the systems and standards of construction which we know will work will not be accepted by the building societies'—P R Hodgkinson, ARIBA. The statement was made in the course of a symposium on the private-enterprise house and its setting held at the RIBA on May 2 1958. The proceedings of the symposium were published by the Institute under the title *Design pays*.

18 'At the moment, thanks to high wages, full employment and so on, there is a demand which is difficult to satisfy, but if there was a recession I should probably be down there at week-ends trying to sell some of the houses if I had lent on them. That is the problem. Whether you like it or not, we have to satisfy ourselves as to the adequacy of the security. That is the absolute law of the point.' Hubert Newton representing the Building Societies Association at the same symposium.

19 The sentence is taken from Lyons' answer to a question following a paper on urban housing which he read at the Town and Country Planning Summer School, September 1961. (See proceedings, p72.)

20 H Sachs: *A study of New Ash Green*, Social Research Unit, Bedford College London: Centre for Environmental Studies, unpublished, p29, para 4.0.

21 'Building societies had always regarded Span as a marginal investment . . . As the squeeze tightened, Span found itself almost squeezed out of the mortgage market. Further, in common with other developers, Span lost sales because prospective purchasers could not dispose of their homes in the second-hand market. In all, because of mortgage difficulties or failure to sell their own homes, 226 people who put down deposits at New Ash Green had to withdraw.' Ibid, pp27, 28, para 3.2(ii).

22 'New Ash Green: self-contained and self-controlled community', *The brick bulletin*, vol 8, no 4, May 1970, p10.

23 B R Gates: *The planner and communal management of open space in new housing estates*, unpublished thesis, The Polytechnic of Central London 1972, p103.

24 It has been difficult to decide whether to refer to Span's activities in the past tense or the present. Following the débâcle of New Ash Green the company ceased operations for six or seven years. In the late seventies it started again with a small estate at Blackheath; and at the time of writing another, larger, project is being built. Lyons died earlier in 1980. The practice, and in particular its work with Span, is carried on by Lyons' son Richard and his partner Ivor Cunningham.

25 'Investigations show that the sort of officer who often sits in the seat of aesthetic judgement over his betters is just as likely to be someone whose qualification for the job is twenty years in the Sanitation Department or who has taken a planning diploma after a geography or mathematics degree.' *Design guidance—a critical revue*: seminar introduced by Ian Davison, chief Architect Planner, Whelmer Ltd, and formerly Principal Planning Officer, Cheshire County Council. Town and Country Planning Summer School, *Report of proceedings*, 1979, p52. For an account of various philosophies in regard to design-control, and hence of various approaches to its administration, see Jo Hazan: *The treatment of aesthetics in urban planning*. Polytechnic of Central London, School of Environment Planning Unit, 1979, pp39-40.

26 Sir Basil Spence: Inaugural address as President of the RIBA, *RIBA journal*, third series, vol LXVI, 1958-59, p48.

27 *The resource-costs of planning*- Memorandum submitted by the Royal Institute of British Architects to the Environmental Sub-Committee of the Expenditure Committee of the House of Commons, Sessional Papers no 395, 1-2, 1976-77, p440, paras 18-20.

28 House of Commons: Sessional Papers no 395 1-2. *Eighth report from the Expenditure Committee Session 1976-77*, vol 1, report pxiii, para 92.

5 SOME LEGAL,
ADMINISTRATIVE
AND TECHNICAL REFORMS

1 *The new local-government system outside London:* The legal constraints and quasi-legal codes affecting suburbia's design did, in fact, change significantly during the sixties and seventies. The most important alteration concerned the structure of local government. The following paragraphs are an attempt to describe briefly these changes as they occurred outside London. The capital is ignored, not because it is unimportant, but because, apart from Dockland, which seems unlikely to be redeveloped at the densities of suburbia, it is full. Any future suburbias will have to be built beyond the metropolis. The reforms instituted by the London Government Act are not, therefore, germane to our subject.

Beyond the area of the London County Council the system of local government had remained substantially unaltered since the reforms incorporated in the Local Government Act of 1888. This had established four types of authority—the county councils, which by the 1960s were responsible for such subjects as education, police, most highways, fire and ambulance services and, as we have seen, town and country planning; the county districts (a generic term which included the municipal boroughs and the urban and rural district councils) which were responsible, inter alia, for housing, sewerage, refuse-disposal, street-lighting, building-regulations and (in some areas) local roads; the county boroughs, which were all-purpose authorities; and the parish councils, which existed only in rural areas and whose powers were confined to such matters as the maintenance of village greens.

Circumstances changed during the period between the passing of the 1888 Act and the early 1960s. The transport revolution made town and country far more interdependent than during the late nineteenth century; the built-up areas of many county boroughs overflowed their legal boundaries, with the result that a city's suburbs frequently formed a ring of urban districts, authorities which were administratively independent of the county borough at their centre; cities and adjacent towns often joined up to form continuous conurbations, yet remained administratively distinct; while many authorities, especially in rural areas, did not obtain enough income from the rates to enable them to discharge their responsibilities properly. The system was confused, anomalous, inefficient, out-of-date and a cause of constant friction between neighbouring authorities. New machinery was needed, and in 1966 a Royal Commission under Lord Redcliffe-Maud was appointed to investigate the problem and make recommendations for change.

The commission proposed a set of all-purpose authorities outside the three metropolitan regions of Manchester, Liverpool and Birmingham (places in which a two-tier structure of government was suggested). The concept of such unitary authorities was, however, rejected by the Conservative administration which came to power following the elections of 1970. Instead a two-tier system was introduced everywhere. The upper-tier—metropolitan counties in the great conurbations, shire counties elsewhere (the phrase 'shire county' is used in common parlance; it does not appear in the legislation)—became responsible for strategic issues, the lower tier (metropolitan

Your at-a-glance guide to who looks after what	If you live in a metropolitan county Greater Manchester (1) Merseyside (2) South Yorkshire (3) Tyne and Wear (4) West Midlands (5) West Yorkshire (6)		If you live in a non-metropolitan county	
	DISTRICT COUNCIL	COUNTY COUNCIL	DISTRICT COUNCIL	COUNTY COUNCIL
Large-scale planning Roads and traffic Road safety Parking Highway lighting Police* Fire service		●		●
Education Personal social services Youth employment Libraries	●			●

Local plans
Planning applications
Housing
Housing improvement grants
Slum clearance
Environmental health
  eg. Dangerous structures
    Rodent control
    Food safety and hygiene
    Street cleansing
    Shops
    Home safety
    Communicable diseases
Refuse collection
Rental rebates
Rates and rate rebates
	●		●	

Off-street parking Parks, playing fields and open spaces Museums and art galleries Swimming baths	These are facilities which may be provided by either county or district according to local decision			

*Controlled by a special authority of the County Council and the magistrates

Figure 1: The responsibilities of country & district councils (diagram from Neal Alison Roberts: The reform of planning law, Macmillan, 1976, p38).

196

districts in the great conurbations, district councils elsewhere) became responsible for tactical matters. Parishes were retained, were no longer limited to rural areas, and were given the new task of representing local opinion to other authorities. In addition to these changes, two vitally important activities, sewerage and water-supply, were removed from the ambit of local government and were entrusted to regional water authorities, organizations whose boundaries derive from the practical requirements of river-catchment, not from the interests and jealousies of political geography.

The new system included six 'metropolitan counties'—Tyne and Wear, West Yorkshire and South Yorkshire being added to the three 'metropolitan regions' proposed by the Maud Committee. As for the district councils, these were made large enough to ensure a reasonable rate-income, and their boundaries were drawn in such a way as to encompass not only cities and towns, but also any related rural hinterlands. The effect of the two-tier structure is illustrated by the fact that a county council, as an upper-tier authority responsible for planning-strategies, may properly define a general policy in regard to the design of new suburban developments in its area, but the implementation of this policy, including the building of new council-estates or the approval of speculative projects, are tasks for the second-tier authorities, the district councils. The quality of staff whom these bodies employ is, therefore, of the greatest importance. It is the district councils' officers who will make or mar our future environments.

We have noted, in an earlier chapter, the baleful influence of that local-authority Pooh Bah, the municipal surveyor. The fact that housing and local-planning are tasks for the kind of authority in which he held, historically, a most powerful role would give us cause for much alarm, were it not that the duties allocated to the districts under the new system have caused his influence to decline. He is now much smaller beer than before. The administration of water-supply and sewerage, the most fundamental of his duties, have passed to the regional water authorities; bridges, roads and highway-lighting are tasks for the counties; local-planning and housing remain with the lower tier, but are almost always established as separate departments under their own chief officers.

The new system does, of course, have weaknesses. County councils do not always possess the same interests as the districts of which they are composed, and such differences often result in conflict, frustration and waste of time. The arrangements are certainly not ideal, but they do make it easier than before for 'considerations of architectural effect' to 'enter the legal or official mind'.

2 *The Town and Country Planning Acts of 1968 and 1971:* By the early 1960s the planning system which had been established by the Act of 1947 had been in existence for some fifteen years. Certain weaknesses, particularly in the field of compensation and betterment, had been recognized, and efforts had been made to correct them, but very little had been done to

overhaul the machinery of plan-preparation or of development-control. This machinery was, however, beginning to creak badly. Plans prepared under the Act were complicated and all-but-incomprehensible documents, which when studied carefully showed very little that was different from the existing situation. Administrative delays were causing frustration at the system's apparent inefficiency, while some complained because certain types of development were not subject to control. It was evident that the system was in need of reform, and accordingly a technical committee, the Planning Advisory Group, was set up in 1964 with a brief 'to assist the departments concerned in a general review of the planning system'.[1]

The Group pointed out that the original intention of those who framed the Act of 1947 was that development plans should 'indicate the general principles upon which development in the area will be permitted and controlled'.[2] In practice, however, this had not happened. Instead the Act had defined the development-plan as a document 'indicating the manner in which the local planning authority propose that land in their area should be used'. This approach, together with the notations employed in the maps which illustrated the development-plans, had made it impossible for the plans to express their authority's policy in such critical matters as the interaction between land-use and transport systems, the detailed redevelopment of town-centres, or the social and economic relationships between town and country. The development-plans had thus lost touch both with the problems of their areas and with regional policies, while at the same time their maps, instead of being concerned with simple statements of general principle, had become documents which often showed little more than the land-uses of the areas which they illustrated.

The Group discovered other weaknesses in the existing system. In particular they noted that the need for every plan to go through the complex machinery of local public enquiry and ministerial approval caused serious delays (some sixty town-map submissions had been with the Ministry for more than three years), and (from our point of view most important of all) that the development-plan did not provide an adequate instrument for detailed planning at the local level. Indeed the Group recognized the circumstance, which we have already noted, that the machinery of design-control was negative rather than positive. In *The future of development plans* they declared (p7, para 1.28) that while town-maps may present a reasonably clear picture of land-use, they 'give little guidance to developers beyond the primary use zoning' and 'make no contribution to the quality of urban design'.

To rectify these faults the Group proposed, *inter alia*, that the Minister's approval should be concerned with matters of policy rather than of detail, that plans should be kept under continuous review, and should be capable of substantial amendment or revision whenever necessary, that they should take the form of surveys, analyses and proposals set out in writing, supplemented by sketch-maps or diagrams in the text, and that these should include (in the case of plans for urban areas with a population of over fifty thousand) a diagram to be called the 'urban-structure map'. They proposed that this document should be drawn to a relatively small scale, and that it should aim only to give a broad picture of the town's structure and of its future development. Among the items to be indicated on the urban-structure map would be those parts of the town and its surroundings, christened 'action-areas', where large-scale development, redevelopment or improvement was to be expected during the next few years, and which should, therefore, be planned as a whole and in detail.

The Group proposes (p28, para 4.12) that once an action-area had been approved by the Minister, the planning-authority should be under a statutory obligation to prepare an 'action-area plan' in respect of it.

The Group were optimistic about the opportunities which the action-area system offered. They declared (p33, para 5.11) that an action-area was 'potentially the means for developing an entirely new approach to what is often regarded as the negative aspect of planning, development-control,' and (p33, para 5.14) that 'it offers great scope for the development of new ideas and new methods in the field of large-scale planning'. They were, however, carefully vague about the form which an action-area plan should take, saying only that it should provide a framework of objectives, standards and layout, including public development and public services and the pattern of vehicular and pedestrian movement throughout the area, and that within this framework there should be the maximum freedom for the individual designer (p33, para 5.12).

The Group's ideas were accepted by the government and formed the basis of much of the Town and Country Planning Act of 1968. This Act was combined with sundry items of planning legislation which had been enacted previously to form a consolidating measure, the Town and Country Planning Act 1971.

The Act of 1971 provides, at the time of writing, the basic legislative framework for operative-planning.[3] Section 11, paragraph 6, confirmed the Planning Advisory Group's recommendation that once an action-area had been approved by the Minister, the planning-authority should be required to prepare a local plan in respect of it.

The Group could be, as we have seen, carefully vague about the form that such a plan should take. Government had to be more specific. Following the Act of 1968 the Ministry of Housing and Local Government and the Welsh Office published *Development plans, a manual of form and content*. This volume included, as one of a set of notes and accompanying diagrams describing and illustrating various kinds of plan, a section on an action-area plan for new development.

This consisted of a 'proposals-map' and some accompanying notes. The proposals-map was no more than a schematic diagram. It indicated, not the layout of the housing, but such matters as views to be retained and access-points from local distributor-roads, and it referred to policies, such as

199

the planning-authority's ideas about high buildings, which were incorporated in the written statement. The accompanying notes indicated that it was 'intended that the housing should be carried out by private builders' and that in consequence the plan had been designed 'as a brief for developers showing the authority's own proposals and the requirements that developers will need to satisfy'. The notes added that 'the written statement and the proposals-map together provide a framework within which details of layout and design can be worked out by the authority and the developers in co-operation'. The notes went on to discuss the form which such co-operation might take. They suggested that 'if the site were in the ownership of one or two major developers, it might well be that they would design the layout themselves in consultation with the authority. If, however, the site were owned by the authority and they intended to dispose of it in relatively small parcels to private developers, or if it were already in the hands of several developers, the authority might wish to take the initiative themselves in designing an advisory layout in order to secure a coherent and orderly development and an acceptable standard of design.'

'The authority might wish to take the initiative themselves'—positive control of new suburban development might not have arrived, but it was at last on the horizon.

Valuable though they were, the manual's recommendations seem only to have been used occasionally as a means to control suburban growth. Planning-authorities have preferred to use their limited staffs in other ways. In the great cities priority has been given either to the redevelopment of slums and of outworn industrial areas, or to the rehabilitation of areas of bye-law housing; while in the shire counties a district council has often preferred to prepare a structure-plan for the whole of its district, rather than local plans for particular places within it. Nevertheless the idea that a planning-authority should undertake the preparation of briefs for developers has begun to take root. It formed a most important part of the concepts which underlay the Community Land Act of 1975, a statute which was passed by the Labour government of the time and which was repealed by the Conservative adminis-tration which came to power in 1979. It should be added that Wales, where the Act has been a success, was exempted from the repeal legislation.

3 *The Community Land Act 1975:* The reader will remember that we referred in an earlier chapter to the tedious ping-pong game played by suc-cessive Labour and Conservative administrations in their efforts on the one hand to enable betterment to be collected, and on the other to dispense with the bureaucratic meddling which results from governmental interference in the land-market. The Community Land Act was a stroke in this game.

The game is tedious and, as we have said, the Act has been repealed. In these circumstances the reader may well wonder why we pay any attention to it. There are two reasons. In the first place the Act included as part of its machinery means by which a contemporary equivalent of the georgian system of development under leasehold-tenure might be established: secondly, the Act's failure provides us with a most valuable lesson about the limits which beset any system of planning-control.

The idea which underlay the Act was that 'betterment' should be collected by the local authority of the area concerned, and that to this end local authorities should operate as monopoly dealers in land, acquiring development sites at existing use-value and selling them to developers at market-value.[4] The profit on such transactions would, of course, constitute 'betterment'.

It is evident that a system such as this would not only have made it possible for the authorities to collect betterment, it would also have enabled them to practise a positive, rather than only a negative process of development-control. Under such a system they could offer development-land to builders on licence, imposing in the process whatever conditions they considered appropriate, and, when the houses were built they could convey them direct to the purchasers.

The Act was passed. It was, however, like all land-law, a very complex statute and it could not be brought into effect forthwith. Authorities required time to plan their sequence of operations and to appoint specialist staff. The Act therefore included machinery enabling it to be brought into operation in stages. The requirement caused it to be still-born. Some councils did not wish to undertake these new, onerous responsibilities. Some, in particular those with Conservative majorities, were dilatory about preparing to implement a statute which would involve them in much initial expense, whose spirit might well be contrary to their political ideologies, and which would probably be repealed at the next change of government. They were right to be cautious. Heaven knows how long the Act's transitional arrangements might have lasted, but they were still in operation in 1979 when the Labour government fell.

The Act's failure was almost certainly inevitable. Any system of planning-control involves three things: a certain degree of refinement in the legislation; employment by the authorities concerned of people capable of administering the system; and the readiness of society, or at least of its active and influential members, to endure whatever bureaucracy the system may involve. These three factors must be kept in balance. A highly refined statute will not work if the authorities who have the task of administering it cannot find suitable staff, nor will it succeed if society considers that the system's bureaucracy is so clumsy or so unfair as to be unacceptable.

The Community Land Act did not achieve the necessary balance. The skilled men were there, Britain has a large and highly efficient surveying profession. The surveyors, however, thought it a safe bet that the Act would be repealed by the next Conservative administration, and in these circumstances few of them relished the idea of exchanging the exciting freedom of independent consultancy for the more tedious role of a local government official. As for the rest, even the lawyers found difficulty in interpreting the

Act, while for the layman, such of it as he could understand he regarded as intolerably bureaucratic (it would certainly have demanded more local government staff, more completion of buff forms and more delay in dealing with applications), unnecessary (development gains had been subject to tax since 1974), and grossly unfair.

It is possible, though unlikely, that the Act would have gained public acceptance if it had been offered less as a stroke in the betterment ping-pong game and more as a means by which our cities might achieve something of the grace possessed by Bath or Bloomsbury. This however was not done. The opportunity for positive control which the Act offered was lost. The ping-pong game will no doubt continue.

4 *The development-brief:* The Community Land Act provided planning-authorites with an opportunity to exercise positive control, but few of them possessed the experience which they needed to execute the task properly. In order to assist them in this matter, the Department of the Environment issued a number of 'Development advice notes'.

The first of these, *The development-brief: private residential development* (1976), was concerned with the preparation of briefs for private residential development. The most significant feature of the note was its cautious, unambitious tone. It offered three general principles for writing that part of the brief which dealt with the proposed development, stating (p5, para 18) that 'it should be *realistic, clear* and leave *scope for the developer to exercise his skills'.* The section on design declared (para 17) that 'where an authority wishes to influence the appearance of the development it would be better to do this by indicating the design objectives rather than by offering specific solutions', adding that 'it may often be better to give the developer freedom in these aspects', (though this was qualified by the remark that 'they will be of particular importance in certain circumstances including development in or near conservation areas or countryside of scenic attraction'). The note went on to warn the authority against requirements which might lessen the ability of the prospective house-purchaser to obtain adequate mortgage-finance, and declared (para 23) that 'to enable developers to make full use of their skills and experience in designing, building and then selling a product at a price to meet market-demand, the requirements of the brief should be kept to a minimum'.

The implications of such advice are exemplified by the brief issued by the Milton Keynes Development Corporation for the building of part of Downs Barn, a district to the north-east of the new city's central area. The brief was in four parts: a contoured site plan; a 'design and materials handbook' (most of which consisted of details of such things as screens, arbours and pavings, though it also included suggestions about suitable materials for walls and roofs as well as a subdivision entitled 'open space structure', which showed road sections and photographs of attractive street scenes); a written document (most of which described the site conditions and defined the requirements of the project in terms of such matters as the number of dwellings to be provided, the proportion of dwellings in different price ranges, and arrangements for access and car parking, though the document also included, under the heading 'Materials and form', the statement that 'dwellings should be of traditional appearance with tile, brick and timber finishes sympathetic in colour and quality to adjacent development in central Milton Keynes'); and a drawing entitled 'indicative layout and opportunities' (which showed, in a highly diagrammatic manner, such things as the possible arrangement of houses, the positions of existing and advance tree-planting, and the location of roads and foot paths).[5]

A planning-brief, such as that for Downs Barn, is certainly a less restrictive method of control than was used by the surveyors to the georgian estates. The limitations on design which were defined in the Bedford Estate's building-agreements were more detailed than those required by the Milton Keynes Development Corporation, and the 'rates' of the 1774 Building Act were more constraining than today's bye-laws and codes of practice. We should realize, however, that the development corporation's planning-brief, and the georgian surveyor's building-agreement are not strictly comparable documents. The building-agreement was often the result of a set of negotiations, while the planning-brief is the first stage in such a process. The Downs Barn Project is still being discussed at the time of writing. There can be little doubt that whatever scheme is finally agreed will involve a more precise statement than is contained in the present paper.

The planning-brief, as a positive system of design-control, is a far more satisfactory device than the negative machinery of the development-control process. Such briefs have, however, certain limitations. In the first place they can hardly be used other than on relatively large sites; secondly, they are difficult to prepare—a nice balance has to be struck between giving the developer's architect freedom to evolve his ideas and directing him in such a way as to ensure that he makes an appropriate contribution to the environment as a whole; and finally, the constraints which a brief imposes are so complex that they cannot easily be applied unless they form part of the landowner's conditions of sale. This could, of course, have been done under the machinery of the Community Land Act, but since its demise the landowner is seldom anxious to impose such constraints.

An authority should, however, be able to circumvent the last of these difficulties. Section 52 of the Town and Country Planning Act of 1971 authorizes the planning-authority to enter into a 'planning-agreement' with a prospective developer. Such an agreement can include more complex conditions that can be attached to a planning-consent of the ordinary kind. Section 52 agreements are usually employed in situations where the authority seeks to obtain a 'planning gain' when it grants the consent. (The agreement may, for example, require the developer to provide the authority with land for a major road-improvement or the erection of some public building.) But section 52 agreements can be used in other ways also, and an authority could employ this machinery for agreeing with a developer the brief for a new suburban estate.

The negotiations which such agreements involve would provide opportunities for the 'constructive professional collaboration' between architect and planner which, in the RIBA's opinion, is frustrated by design-control. The Institute was indeed enthusiastic about the opportunities offered by the planning-brief system. In its memorandum to the Environmental sub-Committee, *The resource-costs of planning*, it discussed the two systems of positive control: planning-briefs and design-guides. It objected to design-guides, but declared (para 27) that the planning-brief required under the Community Land Act 'is a different matter altogether. If detailed control of appearance is abandoned, planners and architects could collaborate in a more positive way to establish a view in terms of urban design of the ways in which economic and functional needs could be met on particular sites, and within which individual developer's architects would be free from detailed constraint.'

5 *The end of leasehold-tenure:* Following the passing of the Community Land Act the Department of the Environment issued, in addition to the development advice notes, a circular to local authorities (no 26/76) which described the Department's recommended policies and procedures in regard to the acquisition and disposal of land for private development.[6] Part of this document was concerned with the machinery of building-agreements. It included (annexe E, section 13b) the statement that on completion of each house the house-plot should be conveyed 'freehold (or where appropriate a leasehold)' to the developer's nominee. The qualification was probably inserted to cover circumstances in which the development might consist of flats. Leasehold had not been mentioned in the White Paper which preceded the Act,[7] and since 1967 there have been hardly any leasehold sales except where flats are involved.

The leasehold system had, we have seen, begun to receive a bad name by the latter part of the nineteenth century. It was disliked by many, and between 1884 and 1967 eighteen abortive parliamentary bills for leasehold enfranchisement were introduced, as well as a number of others which never passed the 'dummy' stage. In addition, the subject was considered by three special committees, though only one of them, The Leasehold Committee under the chairmanship of Lord Justice Jenkins, was able by its terms of reference to report formally upon the subject. In their *Final report* (1950),[8] the majority of the Jenkins Committee followed the example of their predecessor, the Committee on Town Holdings, and concluded that enfranchisement would not be in the public interest. They gave, as their first reason for this belief, the opinion that 'the multiplication of small freeholds would hinder orderly planning and development and good estate-management'. A minority report reached the opposite conclusion. Its signatories, Mr A L Ungoed Thomas KC and Mr C Leslie Hale MP, considered that the landlord's interest is one of investment and finance, while the tenant's is one of use and occupation, an interest which they described (para 103) as a 'moral right'. They considered that the test of good estate-management was the interest of the landlord, and that this was not necessarily identical with the interests of the public at large, 'insofar as it is identical with the public interest it should be covered by an exception based expressly on that ground' (para 104).

During the next fifteen years the question of leasehold enfranchisement gradually came to a head once more. The change was due to the facts that the leases of many artisans' dwellings built during the latter part of the nineteenth century were coming close to expiry, and that purchasers of leasehold property with less than thirty years to run were finding it difficult to obtain mortgages. The politicians' attitudes reflected this new situation, and by 1966 all three parties had become convinced of the need for reform. In 1967 a Bill for this purpose was introduced.

The Leasehold Reform Act of 1967 was based on the principle (defined in the White Paper which preceded it) that 'the land belongs in equity to the landowner, and the house belongs in equity to the occupying leaseholder'.[9] The Act sought particularly to help the resident leaseholder who held his house at a low rent. Such people were given power either to acquire the freehold of their property, or to extend the period of their lease.

In regard to estate-management the Act followed the recommendations of the minority of the Jenkins Committee. It recognized the importance of the subject, and provided machinery by which a management scheme could be prepared by the landlord and approved in appropriate circumstances by the High Court.

Whatever one may think about the social propriety of leasehold tenure, there can be no doubt that it provided the machinery under which the best of our speculative housing has been carried out. The georgian squares, the Eyre Estate in St John's Wood, Bournville, Letchworth, much of Welwyn Garden City, most of the new towns and the earlier Span estates were all developed under leases. The Act of 1967 destroyed the system while at the same time ensuring that the management-standards of the best estates could be maintained. The destruction was probably justified. For all its excellence as a piece of estate-development machinery, leasehold-tenure does not accord with our present concepts of social justice. We reject the principle that the landlord should receive, at the termination of the lease, not only his land but also the house which someone else has built upon it. In any case, whatever the benefits and disadvantages of leasehold, it had long ceased to be the typical method by which speculative development was carried out. The Span estates, and even the new towns were exceptional projects. The Act emasculated a system which had been largely impotent for eighty years. We are fortunate that it existed, and fortunate that we now have other, and possibly even better, pieces of estate-development machinery. Among these is a system of freehold-tenure, combined with some form of management-trust or company responsible for the maintenance of the estate concerned.

This system, which is analogous to that established for the maintenance of Ladbroke Square, was revived by Messrs Wates in the late sixties and was also used by Span at New Ash Green.

6 *Freehold-tenure and open-space management:* Messrs Wates have devised a number of different systems for the continued management of the open spaces on their estates. The most satisfactory of these systems involves the establishment of a management-trust. The trust has a custodian trustee, such as a bank, as well as managing-trustees, who are likely to be a professional firm of surveyors. Each householder on the estate has an indivisible share in the trust by virtue of which he possesses rights over the estate's open spaces. He is committed to contribute to their upkeep and management, he has a share in the control of the expenses involved in maintaining the estate, and he has the power to appoint and change the managing-trustees. The system has two advantages: the developer avoids the need, implicit in leasehold-tenure, that he should preserve his interest in the estate after it is built—few speculative builders want the duties inherent in such continued ownership, and there are obvious advantages in a system which enables the developer to withdraw when his building task is complete—and the householders undertake the responsibility for maintenance of the open spaces of their estate, a responsibility which is in accord with our concept of democracy.

The system has not yet been used extensively, but there seems to be little reason why it should not become as typical of speculative building in the late twentieth century as was leasehold-tenure in the early nineteenth. All that is required is some additional condition to the normal consents for permission to develop. In granting such a consent to an 'application in principle'—ie, an application for permission to carry out a certain kind of development, without giving details of the form that such development is to take—a local planning-authority could require that the subsequent detailed application should include a scheme for the landscaping and open-space management of the estate concerned. This is already standard practice in regard to applications for permission to work minerals, and it could, surely, be applied also to housing-projects. Such an arrangement need not be unduly costly to the developer, and it could well be popular among his customers. A market-research survey carried out in 1979 by National Opinion Polls on behalf of the National House-Building Council found that 50 percent of respondents considered that there had not been enough efforts to landscape the estates on which their houses were situated. The House-Builders Federation could produce a set of model clauses for a management-scheme and the cost of landscaping and planting could be spread over the whole estate. The most serious impediment to the general establishment of such systems is probably that we do not have enough landscape-architects, but if this technique were to become normal practice, the demand for competent landscape-architects should generate a supply.

206

7 *The sale of council-houses:* The upkeep of communal open space is not the only maintenance problem which arises under conditions of freehold-tenure. There is also the matter of ensuring that any consistent pattern in the house-groups is not damaged by alteration to the houses themselves.

In normal circumstances the freeholder can not only plant what he likes in his garden, he can also (within certain limits) change the appearance of his home. He can construct a porch over his front door, substitute picture-windows for leaded lights, or hide brickwork behind a cosmetic layer of pink rendering. Much inter-war speculative suburbia has been modified in this way. Here it hardly matters. The appearance of the place is so restless that such changes are scarcely noticed in the jolting regularity of the scene. Modifications of this kind are, however out of place in the trim, symmetrical environments of inter-war municipal suburbia. Here a new porch or a rendered wall can destroy the carefully devised pattern of a group of houses.

For many years this did not occur. The houses of municipal suburbia were rented, and the local-authority, as landlord, maintained a strict control over what its tenants did to their homes. Circumstances changed, however, in the fifties, sixties and seventies. The one-class, municipal estate did not accord with the Conservative Party's concept of a property-owning democracy, and in 1952 the Ministry of Housing and Local Government issued a circular (no 64/52) to local authorities which stated that the Minister had 'decided to give a general consent' in relation to the sale of council-houses to sitting tenants. This was followed eighteen years later by another circular (no 54/70) which declared that the tenants of Council houses 'ought to have

117: 'Individualizing' of a house in a council terrace at Dagenham.

207

the opportunity of owning the houses in which they live', and went on to ask local authorities to 'do all they can consistent with their general housing responsibilities to make this possible'. Some local authorities were, however, unwilling to take the hint, so to force their hands the Housing Act 1980 gave all council tenants except those living in old-people's dwellings the legal right to buy their homes on generous terms.

Whatever may be the social, economic or political benefits of this policy, its effect on the environment of municipal suburbia has certainly been disruptive. The purchaser of a council-house may not be content to remain an anonymous occupant of a dwelling built originally for some member of the working-class. His social position has changed. He is now a freeholder. To signal this new status he frequently alters the appearance of his home by carrying out changes such as we have described, and the house-group in which he lives loses, in consequence, its pristine symmetry.

The effect of such changes in land-ownership may be seen by comparing two parts of the same estate, one which has been so modified, and one which has remained unchanged.

8 *Building-lines:* Management-trusts such as those established by Wates are pieces of administrative machinery. Their benefit, so far as suburbia is concerned, lies in the opportunities for open-space maintenance which they offer. We have seen that the existence of such machinery appears to be the sine qua non of any pleasing suburban environment at densities above that of arcadia. We should realize, however, that the effectiveness of a management-trust is limited. It can ensure that any greens or shrubberies on the estate are adequately maintained, but it can have no effect on the estate's design and layout, nor can it create the circumstances in which the developer's architect can contrive agreeable spaces between the buildings. For these purposes other devices are required. The local authority must establish means by which it can give a lead to the developer's architect, the seventy-foot rule must be forgotten, the road-engineer's code of practice must be revised, and building-line legislation must be revoked.

This last began to be achieved in 1959 when most building-line legislation was repealed by section 312 of the Highways Act of that year. Thirteen years later, what remained was repealed by sections 188 and 272 of the local Government Act of 1972, thus leaving building-alignment to be controlled under planning-legislation.

It was about time. Building-lines were certainly necessary in the seventeenth century when they were first introduced to control the rebuilding of London after the Great Fire; and we can appreciate the need for similar regulations in the various Metropolitan Improvement Acts of the eighteenth and nineteenth centuries, in the bye-laws established under the Public Health Act of 1875, and the Building in Streets Act of 1888, and in the Road Improvement Act of thirty-five years later. We should realize, however, that these statutes were all passed at a time when town-planning law was either

208

non-existent or rudimentary. The Act of 1947 changed this situation. It and the Act which followed made British planning-legislation as sophisticated as any in the world. The system which we have possessed since 1947 readily copes with far more complicated issues than the alignment of buildings. Building-line legislation was a crude weapon with which to attack the subtle and complex problems of street-design and the unpredictable needs of future traffic. The changes ordained in 1959 and 1972 should have been incorporated in the Act of 1947.

9 *Road systems:* But if the needs of future traffic were unpredictable in detail, they were, by the early 1960s, being predicted in general terms. Traffic congestion had, by this time, become a serious problem, and one which was expected to worsen. The Buchanan Report, *Traffic in towns*, revealed (p11) that the number of vehicles in Britain had grown from just under five millions in 1952 to ten and a half millions in 1962, and a figure of forty millions was predicted (p26,para 45) for the year 2010. Various ideas had been put forward for dealing with road traffic—one of them was the suggestion in the addendum to the Dudley Report that the boundaries of residential neighbourhoods should be delimited by barriers such as main highways and open-space features like parkways—but no-one had propounded a general theory of how to cope with the problem.

In these circumstances the Minister of Transport, Ernest Marples, appointed a group under the chairmanship of Sir Colin Buchanan to study the problem and propose measures for its solution. Their report *Traffic in towns* was published in 1963. It was a classic study. Its principal conclusion was that cities should be reorganized so that they might possess a cellular structure of 'environmental-areas' from which through-traffic would be excluded, and that these environmental areas should be served by a hierarchy of distributor roads whereby the important distributors might 'feed down through distributors of a lesser capacity to minor roads which give access to the buildings' (p44, para 108).

Buchanan's ideas were quickly accepted, and they now provide the principles upon which our planning and highway authorities attempt to resolve the problems of traffic in towns.

The definition of environmental-areas, and the establishment of an hierarchy of roads provided the town-planner with a theoretical system upon which to restructure his city, but it did nothing to modify the road-engineer's fundamental philosophy. This was defined in a government manual, *Roads in urban areas*, which was published in 1966 and which covered much the same ground as its predecessor, *The design and layout of roads in built-up areas*, a document whose shortcomings we discussed in chapter 4. The authors of the manual declared in their introduction (p1) that urban roads 'should be designed to be safe and to permit the free flow of traffic at reasonable speeds'.

This philosophy was questioned in an article, 'Straitjacket', which appeared in the *Architectural review* of October 1973. The authors, David Crawford and Melville Dunbar,[10] followed Richards in pressing for an increase in housing-densities, but their article, unlike 'The failure of the new towns', was more an analytical study than a polemical argument. Their central thesis was the same as that of the present book—that the dreary appearance of our housing-estates is due in large part to the straitjacket of laws and codes of practice which constrain the designer's activities; regulations which were devised with the best of intentions in order to prevent a repetition of the slums of the industrial revolution.

Crawford and Dunbar pointed out that the philosophy defined in *Roads in urban areas* sought to combine safety and convenience. 'The first is obviously crucial, but it is when safety is linked to convenience—for vehicles —that the trouble starts. For the underlying principle in regulating road and pavement dimensions seems to have been to assume the unlikeliest possible concatenation of hazards, coupled with the least possible likelihood of consideration for other road-users and the greatest possible need for uninterrupted driving' (p232). They went on to declare (p235) that there is no reason why we should expect people to drive around housing-estates at thirty miles an hour. 'Substantially reduced speed, even walking pace, could not possibly add more than five minutes to any journey.' Such slowing down would, however, involve a different approach to road-design: 'pinch-points where the roadway is deliberately narrowed, "sleeping policemen", tight corners, and "stop" rather than "slow" junctions are all feasible ways of ensuring that the motorist drives slower in his own interest and avoids accidents'.

Ideas such as these provided the basis of the road-system employed at the Brow estate at Runcorn, one of the third generation of new towns. The pattern which resulted is economical in cost (pavements are minimized), it

118: The Brow, Runcorn.

210

119: The Brow, Runcorn.

is safe (during the first ten years of the Brow's existence there have been no records of accidents involving personal injury)[11] and, significantly from our standpoint, it avoids both the traditional estate's fragmented floorscape and the Radburn system's ambiguous entrances and arid garage-courts.

The Radburn system achieves its effect by banishing the road to the rear of the houses. In the Runcorn system the informal drive which serves the houses is an essential, but not a dominant component of the floorscape. The Brow is not, perhaps, quite as attractive in appearance as the front approaches of Pin Green (the cars are an inevitable intrusion), but it runs the Stevenage estate a close second and it does not possess Pin Green's inherent disadvantages. We can, perhaps, recommend the Runcorn system as the best solution which has yet been devised to the problem of suburbia's roads.

This devaluation of the road-system enabled the team which designed the Brow to change the normal process by which housing-layouts are prepared. They did not design the road-pattern first, then fit the houses to the roads, and finally suggest that a few trees be planted on any patches of SLOAP.[12] Instead the architect-member of the team began by devising the spaces and the house-groups. When he was satisfied with these arrangements, the roads were roughed out as an engineer's solution to the requirements of parking, manoeuvring, passing, etc. The road-pattern was not, however, finalized until the landscape-architect had made his contribution. He not only suggested where trees and shrubs might be planted, he also modified the alignment of roads and parking-areas in such a way as to ensure that they not only met the engineer's requirements, but also formed part of an attractive and coherent scheme.

Runcorn is in Cheshire, and we may be certain that the county council's Planning and Highways Departments watched their local New Town Corporation's experiment with interest and concern. By 1976 it was evident that the experiment was a success, and in that year the county council defined its policy on roads in housing-estates in words which echoed the philosophy of Crawford and Dunbar. They declared, in a manual entitled *Housing: roads*, that a journey has three parts: leaving, travelling and arriving. 'It is only at the travelling stage that speed is a major consideration, and on "travelling" roads . . . vehicles should be dominant. On other roads, the roads where we live and where our journeys start and end, the pedestrian and the cyclist should be dominant. To achieve this there must be two distinct road-types: roads must be designed either to lead to places or as roads which *are* places' (p4).

To explain and illustrate the implications of this philosophy, the manual included typical layout-plans for municipal, speculative and individualistic estates, as well as written notes and diagrammatic perspectives. The notes which described 'accessways' (the informal culs-de-sac serving groups of about twenty dwellings and equipped with a joint pedestrian-vehicle surface upon which pedestrians enjoy priority) declared (p28) that it is essential that the joint-use surface be visually distinct from traditional vehicle-priority carriageways. To achieve this objective it suggested, inter alia, that the surface-finish of an accessway should contrast with that of the road which serves it, and also that at the junction between them the accessway's kerb should be carried across the road as a bumper-course backed with a device such as a shallow ramp.

The authors of this manual did not, however, limit themselves to technicalities of this kind. They also included a number of appendices dealing with such matters as landscaping, public utilities and the adoption, by the authorities concerned, of highways and open spaces. The appendix on landscaping declared (p48) that the first and perhaps the most lasting impression of any housing-area is created by the public and semi-private spaces between the houses. It added (in heavy type) a strong recommendation that developers should seek the advice of a qualified landscape-designer, it explained that local authorities have limited resources for the maintenance of planting, and suggested that for that reason the soft landscaping related to accessways and similar roads serving small groups of houses should be in private ownership. It went on to say that 'in accessways the soft landscaping will be the dominant feature and, although it should all be in private ownership, a comprehensive planning-strategy for the space can reinforce its identity as a group of houses and set a generally high standard for the residents'. The authors did not, regrettably, suggest that the strategy should include means, such as management-trust, by which the strategy could be implemented and the planting maintained: perhaps they thought that they had gone far enough in suggesting a strategy in the first place. They did, however, recognize, by implication rather than by direct statement, not only that such a strategy should provide for underground services, but also that it should not be constrained by the need to fence off a verge of public land for this purposes. To this end the appendix on the adoption of highways and public open spaces

1

120: A scheme for a speculative estate, from Cheshire County Council's Housing: roads.

declares (p46) that where a verge is contiguous with private gardens, 'much can be done by careful landscaping to indicate that such a verge is part of the highway, sett or cobble-patches to contain stop-cocks, hydrants, etc,' and they went on to suggest that householders should 'be encouraged to maintain to the edge of the joint-use surface, and whatever measures are taken to define the verges must not militate against this'. The wording is clumsy, but the implications are clear.

The Cheshire County Council document was published in 1976. A year later the Housing Development Directorate (a section of the Department of the Environment) published a manual, *Residential roads and footpaths*, which superseded those parts of *Roads in urban areas* which referred to residential access-roads. This document declared (p13) that where non-access traffic is excluded, vehicle-flows would normally be very light for most periods of the day, and that 'to provide a safe environment for pedestrian movement in this context it is necessary in design to ensure that drivers are aware on entry and throughout the layout that they are in part of the urban-road system where consideration of pedestrian movement should predominate over the free flow and convenience of vehicular movement', and that the design of the estate should be such as to 'encourage drivers to keep to speeds of well below 30 mph'.

The ideas of Crawford and Dunbar had received the final accolade—recommendation in a document issued by central government.

10 *The RIBA code of practice:* I have sought in the foregoing paragraphs to describe how some of the governmental influences which affect suburbia's design were modified during the 1960s and 70s. Such bureaucracy is not, however, confined to government. The professional institutes have their regulations also. We have noted how the RIBA's code of practice of May 1920 prevented the Institute's members from emulating the speculative enterprise of John Wood or the Adam brothers. It may be worthwhile to glance briefly at the code's origins and to describe the proposals for change which have been mooted in recent years.

The code, as it was defined in May 1920 was a formalisation of late victorian and edwardian architectural practice. This was the era of Norman Shaw, Voysey, Scott, and Lutyens; a time when the architect's commissions consisted of town halls, churches and large elegant homes for the wealthy. The code was based on the idea that the architect is an independent professional man who takes instructions from, and advises his client, and who himself gives instructions to the builder. Commercial association with the builder would clearly prejudice his ability to give impartial advice to the client, and the code therefore insisted on the establishment of the architect's professional status. This status did not prevent the architect from accepting employment in the office of one of the professions from which he was debarred, but it did mean that he must always remain an employee: he might not aspire to a seat on the board.

214

Circumstance, however, altered during the next half-century. The architect's typical commissions ceased to consist of town halls, churches and large elegant homes for the wealthy. Instead he was called upon to devise conversions of existing properties, or to design housing-estates, factories, office blocks or schools. This change was reflected in the structure of the profession, and by 1969 about half the nation's architects were salaried employees of official or commercial organizations, while the other half, those in private practice, obtained a large proportion of their commissions from public agencies. Furthermore the structure of the building industry altered as it developed from a craft industry to one which included prefabrication and system-building, and the architect had to adapt his thinking to these technological changes. These new circumstances led to much debate in the professions as to the wisdom of preserving that part of the code of practice which prevents the architect from acting as the director of a building firm or dealing in land or property.

Among the contributions to this discussion was a paper by Lords Esher and Llewellyn Davies entitled 'The architect in 1969'. It appeared in the RIBA *Journal* of October of that year, and was written at the request of the Institute's president, who hoped that it would help to provide the Institute's Policy and Finance Committee with a framework for their activities. The paper's authors pointed out that the historical process which took the architect out of building had begun in the 1830s, and added that if this process 'is to come full circle in the 1970s, as we believe it must, by putting him back again, two steps must be taken simultaneously. The first is to implant in *all* architects, so that it becomes second nature, their own version of the Hippocratic Oath, which is that the human environment take priority over their personal interests; the other is to forbid one person from working on both sides of the contractual fence, and to retain for the independent architect the present restrictions as to competition, remuneration and advertising.'

Such alterations, however desirable, were too radical for the profession to contemplate immediately, and it was not until October 1979 that the Council of the Institute decided to accept, subject to full consultation with the membership, a number of radical changes in the code of practice, including the removal of the ban on prescribed occupations. A draft version of the amended code appeared in the RIBA *Journal* for April 1980 (pp83/84) and shortly afterwards the Council balloted the membership on the proposals. The results of the ballot were inconclusive. The *Architects' journal* of August 9 reported that less than 25% had voted in favour of the removal of the ban on proscribed occupations, a figure too low for the vote to be binding. The report went on to declare that 'Council must now exercise its leadership in deciding what package of changes is consistent with the profession's image for the 1980s'.

In the event, the Council accepted the journal's advice. It decided, subject to a number of qualifications and safeguards, that its members might go back into building so long as, in doing so, they did not work simultaneously on both sides of the contractual fence. Thus, after a period of sixty years, the disastrous decision of May 1920 was rescinded, and a member of the institute is once more permitted to emulate the speculative enterprise of John Wood and the Adam brothers.

11 *The requirements of an effective control system:* This has been a lengthy account of the mechanisms of bureaucracy, both governmental and professional. The reader will, however, have realised that some understanding of these matters is essential if we are to consider how far our present resources (in terms of legislation, manpower etc) meet the requirements of an effective system of planning-control.

It will be remembered that in our account of the Community Land Act we pointed out that any such system requires that a balance be established between three factors: the refinement of the relevant legislation, the readiness of society, or at least of its most active and influential members, to endure whatever bureaucracy the system may involve, and the employment by the authorities concerned of people capable of administering the system.

As to the first factor—legislation—there can be no doubt that the legal and administrative machinery by which development is assisted and controlled is now more refined than ever before. Britain's structure of local government may not be ideal, but it is far less arbitrary than that which the nation endured for the first three-quarters of this century. The worst anomalies of our planning system were recognized by the Planning Advisory Group and were rectified by the Acts of 1968 and 1971. Leasehold-tenure has been emasculated, but the Section 52 agreement and the management trust provide means by which its most significant advantages (positive control of design and the maintenance of communal open space) can be obtained. Finally, and most important of all, the designer of a suburban estate has at last been released from the straitjacket of legislation and precept which he inherited from the nineteenth-century sanitarians and the twentieth-century road-engineers. Building-lines are things of the past, culs-de-sac no longer require verges and footways, and the seventy-foot rule is, praise God, on its way out.

As for the second factor—a sufficiently compliant society—nobody except perhaps the planners themselves likes the bureaucracy which planning involves. We have come to realize, however, that the red-tape of development-control is a disagreeable necessity, similar perhaps to paying taxes or going to the dentist. The architects may jostle, but the rest of us are prepared to endure the drawbacks of the system in return for its manifest advantages. Architects apart, society's degree of compliance seems to match the legislation's degree of refinement.

The third factor—personnel—is, however out of key with the others. We have seen that the development-control staffs of our district councils are seldom sufficiently skilled in design to enable the legislation to be implemented effectively. In these circumstances it is hardly surprising that

216

consent is sometimes granted to an eyesore, that architects press for reform of design-control, and that politicians look for ways in which the benefits of the process can be more closely related to its costs.

We should, perhaps, consider why our development control staffs so frequently lack design ability and what can be done to provide them with such skills.

12 *The urban-designer:* The scarcity of design-staff in district-authority offices is the result of two factors. In the first place, the new system of local government required, for its administration, many more planning officials than had existed previously, and they were not always as appropriately qualified as one might wish. Secondly, by the 1970s, skill in design was no longer central to the town-planner's professional expertise. This profession, which had originated so far as Britain was concerned as a specialism in the fields of architecture, surveying, civil engineering and law, had developed a new ethos during the 1950s and 1960s.

The 'divine inoculation' of Patrick Geddes had so affected the discipline of town-planning that it had come to be concerned less with the detailed design of streets and squares than with an appreciation of the machinery of politics, and an understanding of the complex interactions of forces (social, economic, geographical, technological, political, historic and administrative) which combine to give the environment its form. This change of attitude was accompanied by a change in the make-up of the profession. The graph on the next page shows how the number of architects joining the Town Planning Institute remained stable at the same time that 'direct-entry' town-planners [13] and graduates in other disciplines were joining it in increasing numbers. The planner was becoming less of a designer and more of a manager. As a result, a gap was created, a gap between the architect, concerned with the design of buildings, and the planner, concerned with the definition and implementation of environmental policies in the context of their social, economic and political determinants.

By the late 60s it was evident that the gap had to be filled; and in September 1967 an article advocating the establishment of a RIBA diploma in urban-planning appeared in the Institute's *Journal* under the authorship of William Kretchmer. The idea received general support in the profession, (though the phrase 'urban-planning' was amended to 'urban-design'), and in February 1969 the journals of the RIBA and the Town Planning Institute published a joint statement which declared inter alia that the RIBA Council had approved in principle the establishment of an urban-design diploma for architects. Academic institutions took the hint, and now eight universities and polytechnics offer urban-design courses of which five lead to the RIBA's diploma. We may hope that other academic bodies will soon do the same, and that the RTPI will not be long in following the lead of her sister institute. The alumni of such courses are the first people in Britain to hold a special qualification in the subtle, complex, frustrating art of environmental-choreography.

217

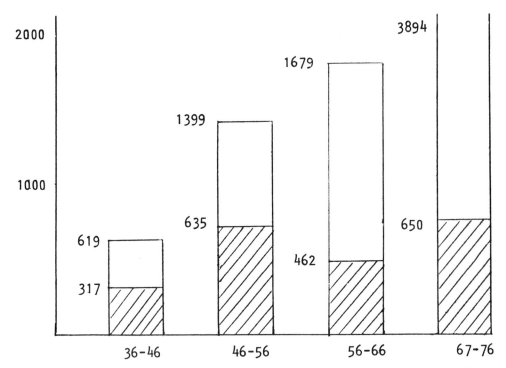

Figure 2: Applications for Associate Membership of RTPI with the number of architects applying—by decade—1936-1976. (Sources: Journal of the Town Planning Institute, *vol 53, 1967, p245, together with my own investigations. The number of architects in the final column is based on a 20 percent sample of applications for entry.)*

The output of these courses, perhaps one hundred a year, of whom half are overseas students, is quite inadequate to meet the need. The courses do, however, provide a nucleus of teaching-skills and they could be expanded rapidly, particularly if they were operated on a day, or block-release basis instead of being (as is the case in all but two of them) year-long and full-time.

If they were to expand in this way, our urban-design courses would certainly have to accept a large proportion of non-architects as students. It might be thought that this would not work, that urban-design is essentially a post-graduate study in architecture, and that the non-architect development-control officer is, by the nature of his background, unlikely to be a suitable candidate for an urban-design course.

This view is not shared by those who have studied the problem. Thus Joe Hazan declares in the conclusion to his essay *The treatment of aesthetics in urban planning*: that the officers who had not had special training in design 'seemed to have the potential to perform at the level of the other design-trained officers'. Earlier he had defined four different approaches to the practice of design-control and the preparation of planning-briefs. One of these, which he called the 'urban-design approach' was based on 'the belief

218

that control of how the physical environment evolves should be left in the hands of a knowledgeable few who have the capacity to envisage a desirable environment and orchestrate its realization. In practical terms this results in authorities engaging design staffs to prepare design-briefs, master-plans, and act as arbiters of proposed developments' (pp39-40). Hazan found that although the planning-authorities which practised the urban-designer approach were both more efficient and more sensitive in their design-control activities than the others, 'the difference between them and the remaining authorities in the study, though noticeable was not enormous' (p101). He concluded that 'although the use of architects and urban-designers by an authority raises their level of performance, it does not seem inconceivable to raise to the same level other authorities by simply increasing the basic design-training that their officers receive'.

We may, I think, conclude that the development-control staffs of our district councils are seldom as competent in design as we should wish, but that this is not an irremediable circumstance. It should be possible to modify and expand our urban design courses in such a way as to provide the people concerned with the opportunity to acquire the skills which they did not obtain in their town-planning studies.

If this were done, and employing-authorities enabled the staffs concerned to take advantage of the opportunities presented to them, the three requirements which we saw as necessary to an effective control-system will have been met. We should realize, however, that though an effective control system is a prerequisite of any general improvement in suburbia's design, good administrative machinery, skilled staff and an accepting society will not alone ensure that our future suburbias possess the quality of Park Village West or the Span estates.

Before this can be achieved, other changes will have to take place. Some have already been mentioned. We have discussed the low level of public taste and the anomalous nature of the RIBA's code of practice, but the most important is one which concerns suburbia's theoretical base. There is little purpose in seeking to improve suburbia's design if the ideal which inspired Nash, Carr, Cadbury and Unwin is itself invalid. And, as we shall see, many eminent men have doubted the validity of the suburban ideal. We must now consider their arguments.

REFERENCES

1 The Planning Advisory Group: *The future of development plans*, HMSO, 1965, p1.

2 Ibid, p6, para 1.22, quoting the first draft of the Parliamentary Bill which was later passed as the Act of 1947.

3 The other important piece of legislation, the Community Land Act 1975, was a comatose piece of legislation and was recently repealed. It is, nonetheless, discussed below, page 200.

4 'The net effect of . . . the scheme is that the landowner seeking to develop his own land will be obliged to sell it to the local authority less its development value and then acquire it back on terms reflecting the full development value before he can lay a brick, unless he falls within one of the exceptions laid down in regulations made from time to time or contained in the Act.' Hugh Rossi: *Shaw's guide to the Community Land Act 1975*, Shaw and Son 1976, p5.

5 I have to thank Mr Ken Gibbons of the Milton Keynes Development Corporation staff for information about this brief.

6 Department of the Environment: Circular 26/76. Community Land Circular 6. *Land for private development, acquisition, management and disposal*, HMSO, 1976.

7 The White Paper which preceded the Act declared that land for housing might be disposed of in a variety of ways. 'Local authorities will be encouraged to offer it to builders on licence with the plots being conveyed direct to the house purchasers. Plots for owner occupation will also be made available freehold.' Department of the Environment, Scottish Office, Welsh Office: *Land*, Command 5730, HMSO, 1974, para 56.

8 *Leasehold Committee, final report*, Command 7982, HMSO, 1950, para 100.

9 *Leasehold reform in England and Wales*, Command 2916, HMSO, 1966, para 4.

10 The article is credited to David Crawford 'in discussion with Melville Dunbar, Principal Planning Officer, Essex County Council'. *Architectural review*, vol 154, 1973, p228. This curious formula was presumably devised in order to enable Dunbar, as a local-government officer to deny responsibility for any controversial statements which the article might contain.

11 See Eddie Jenkins: 'Revisit part one', *Architects' journal*, vol 169, 1979, p586.

12 SLOAP: Space Left Over After Planning. This valuable acronym was coined by Leslie Ginsburg when teaching at the Birmingham School of Planning—Leslie B Ginsburg: 'Summing-up', *Architectural review*, vol 154, 1973, p264.

13 That is, people who obtained a town-planning qualification without obtaining one of the professional qualifications or academic degrees which exempt a candidate from the Institute's first professional examination.

6 THE VALIDITY OF THE
SUBURBAN IDEAL

1 *Theoretical objections to the suburban ideal:* Until the 1950s there had been no fundamental reassessment of the suburban ideal since it was first established.

This does not mean that suburbia itself had not been the subject of criticism. Indeed, adverse comments on suburbia had appeared as early as 1876, when a contributor to *The architect* had declared that the 'crowd of half-bred towns that belt about London and are known usually by the name *suburbs* has always been to me the occasion for distinct and unmitigated hatred. . . A modern suburb is a place which is neither one thing nor the other, which had neither the advantage of the town nor the open freedom of the country, but manages to combine in a nice equality of proportion the disadvantages of both.'[1]

A quarter of a century later, Raymond Unwin asserted, in a paper at the Garden City Conference at Bournville, that 'no weak compound of town and country composed of wandering suburban roads lined with semi-detached villas set each in a scrap of garden will ever deserve the name of garden city';[2] and in 1913, A T Edwards (who, like his contemporary E G Culpin, did not distinguish between the garden city and the garden suburb) published an article, 'A criticism of the Garden City Movement', in which he declared that low-density housing contravened mankind's desire for a close relationship with his fellows. 'We are,' he wrote, 'really just like bees that must huddle together. The working man is quite content to be in a row of houses, to stand outside his door and talk to neighbours on the other side of the street. All he asks for is better houses and a better street.'[3] As for the suburb, he continues, 'the very word suburban implies something that is second-rate, some narrow and pharisaical attitude of mind . . . but of all suburbs the most shoddy and depressing is the typical garden suburb. It has neither the crowded interest of the town, nor the quiet charm of the country, it gives us the advantages neither of solitude nor of society.'

Eighteen years later, the argument was taken up by Thomas Sharp who published in 1932 a book, *Town and countryside*, which contained a tirade against the suburban ideal, an ideal which he mistakenly attributed to Ebenezer Howard. According to Sharp (p143), 'Howard's new life, new civilization, town-country is a hermaphrodite; sterile, imbecile, a monster, abhorrent and loathsome to the nature which he worships'.[4] Sharp declared that the antithesis between town and country ought to be preserved. They are 'two fundamentally different things, capable of two fundamentally different types of beauty, each heightening the beauty of the other by the sharpness of their contrasts . . . We must strive for sheer urbanity in one place as we strive for sheer rusticity in the other' (p162).

At the time Sharp's was a lonely voice, but in July 1953 similar arguments appeared in the columns of the *Architectural review*. We have seen how in 1944 its editor had rejected the concepts of Unwin and Cadbury. Nine years afterwards it published an article by Sir James Richards entitled 'Failure of the new towns'.[5] Richards declared that a town is a 'sociable place, for people who want to live close together, and expresses itself as such through the compactness of its layout, through the sense of enclosure experienced within it, and through being composed of *streets*. The new towns, by and large, have none of these attributes. They consist for the most part of scattered two-storey dwellings separated by great spaces. Their inhabitants, instead of feeling themselves secure within an environment devoted to their convenience and pleasure, find themselves marooned in a desert of grass verges and concrete roadways.' Richards went on to say that the new towns are 'dominated by the same pretence of being in the country . . . that was characteristic of the nineteen-twenties', and added, 'they commit again every one of the faults committed then: eating up valuable acres of agricultural land, scattering houses along either side of draughty expanses of roadway; marooning the unhappy housewife on the distant rim of their sentimental green landscapes so that she has to tramp for miles with her shopping basket and is altogether cut off from the neighbourliness of closely built-up streets.' Richards held that the responsibility for this situation did not lie with the architects. It was the fault of the Reith Committee upon whose report the New Towns Act was based, and of government officials, planning-officers and local councillors. 'It is they who have fostered the garden-city bias in house-building; not the people who are going to live in the houses, who are not in a position to demand anything different because they are never shown anything different. They are told that they are being given what they want, and they therefore accept it, unknowingly accepting at the same time the burden of frustration that will inevitably accompany their translation from the compact sociability and the architectural solidity of the cities, where they belong, to these scattered insubstantial suburbs lacking form or focus.'

It is perhaps worth noting the difference in emphasis between Sharp's approach and that of Richards. The one held suburbia to be aesthetically impure, while the other contended that it is not only ugly, but also socially sterile, a thesis in support of which he brought no evidence.

Richards' complaints were, indeed, little more than supporting arguments to back up his chief objection to New Town suburbia. This was his proper distaste for its 'two-storey dwellings separated by great spaces', and its 'desert of grass verges and concrete roadways'. Here his strictures were fully justified; with rare exceptions suburbia is at best dull and at worst hideous, but the weak scale and dreary spatial design of the new towns was not the result of the whims of the Reith Committee, or even of the officials and councillors who briefed the towns' architects. It derived, as we have seen, from practical requirements—even if some of these requirements (such as the seventy-foot rule) possessed little justification in logic. It is a pity that Richards did not study these requirements, sad that he apparently forgot how, seven years earlier, he had declared (in *The castles on the ground*, p85) that 'for better of worse the English of this generation are becoming a nation of suburban dwellers', and regrettable that he should have used the authority of his position as editor of our foremost architectural magazine to lead the attack on the attempts of government to promote the very ideal of which he had previously written with such charm and sympathy. Had he done these things instead of firing a broadside at the suburban character of the new towns, his article would have been a more valuable, though perhaps less entertaining essay than it was.

During the following decade the fight against the suburban ideal was led by architects and architectural journalists. These men often argued their case on social as well as on visual grounds, but their social arguments were seldom based on careful scientific analysis. They were, rather, examples of 'architects' sociology', a curious, subjective pseudo-science which some architects employ in order to convince themselves of the social propriety of their aesthetic preferences. It should not be thought that the men and women who argued in this way were in any sense hypocritical. As creative artists they were not used to following the rigorous disciplines of scientific study; as conscientious citizens they were aware of the social importance of housing; as architects they were conscious of their special responsibilities in regard to it; while as busy men with their practices to run and their magazines to publish they had little time to investigate the scanty researches which sociologists and doctors had made in the field of suburbia.

The most influential of these studies, Michael (now Lord) Young and Peter Willmott's *Family and kinship in East London* was published in 1957, four years after Richards' article in the *Architectural review*. Young and Willmott compared the social patterns of Bethnal Green with those of 'Greenleigh' (a pseudonym for one of the London County Council's inter-war cottage housing estates). Their discoveries have already been summarized in chapter III. Their book has sometimes been construed as an attack on low-density housing. This is not so, indeed its authors discussed neither the social effects of housing at different densities nor the form that a new estate might take. They were concerned about other things, in particular about the destruction of social relationships which resulted from slum-clearance and suburban rehousing. They considered that most people prefer to remain where they were brought up, rather than move, as a consequence of redevelopment, to some distant suburban estate. 'They are attached to Mum and Dad, to the markets, to the pubs and settlements, to Club Row and the London Hospital' (p186).

Young and Willmott concluded with the following words (pp198-9): 'Even when the town-planners have set themselves to create communities anew as well as houses, they have still put their faith in buildings, sometimes speaking as though all that was needed for neighbourliness was a neighbourhood-unit, for community-spirit a community-centre. If this were so then there would be no harm in shifting people about the country, for what is lost could soon be repaired by skilful architecture and design. But there is surely more to a community than that. The sense of loyalty to each other amongst the inhabitants of a place like Bethnal Green is not due to buildings. It is due far more to the ties of kinship and friendship which connect the *people* of one household to the *people* of another. In such a district community-spirit does not have to be fostered. It is already there. If the authorities regard that spirit as a social asset worth preserving, they will not uproot more people, but build the new houses around the social groups to which they already belong.'

Young and Willmott were sociologists anxious to preserve existing social patterns. The Society for the Promotion of Urban Renewal, though it included engineers, sociologists and economists, was primarily an association of architects. It was dedicated to the principle that the decayed parts of our towns and cities should be redeveloped at relatively high densities in order to check the further extension of suburbia. Its chairman, Lionel Brett, now Lord Esher, declared (in an article in the *Architectural review*) that 'the space for redevelopment is there, inside the conurbations, inside the old towns, even inside the villages, but to use it needs courage of various kinds, courage above all to refuse the easy way out of grabbing cheap farm land and leaving outworn urban areas to rot. To stop the rot, to turn retreat into advance, and in the second half of this century to exorcise the escapism that nearly wrecked our environment in the first: that is the job.'[6]

The objections to the suburban ideal which were expressed by men such as Edwards, Richards and Sharp may perhaps be summarized under five headings: that suburbia is wasteful of land; that it is socially sterile; that it involves much cost, discomfort and waste of time in commuting for the bread-winner and in walking to and from shops and school for his wife and children; that town and country are opposites and an attempt to fuse them can therefore only produce results which are aesthetically impure; and that suburbia is both weak in scale and lamentably poor in its spatial design.

The first objection was a matter of density and the economics of land-usage, the second was concerned with sociology and mental-health, the third involved other matters as well as that of suburbia itself—the distribution of land-uses such as industry and offices, and their geographical relationship to areas of housing—the last two were concerned with aesthetics only. We shall consider these objections in turn, but before we do this it is worth glancing first at three estates which sought in their different ways to meet the objections of Richards and his associates, and then at the Parker—Morris Report, the document which has done for the sixties and seventies that which the Tudor Walters Report had done for the inter-war period, and the Dudley Report for the forties and fifties.

2 *Muirhead Four, Cumbernauld:* By the late fifties, the views of the anti-suburban lobby had begun to receive the support of Authority. This is exemplified by the brief which was issued to the Cumbernauld Development Corporation by the Secretary of State for Scotland. The area which was designated for the new town, the configuration of the site, the existence of local mineral deposits and the population which the corporation was required to house, together compelled the corporation to build at a density

which was twice as high as that which had been recommended in the adden-dum to the Dudley Report. The South-side housing-scheme at Cumbernauld has a density of 86 persons to the acre, the addendum to the Dudley Report recommended a figure of between 30 and 50. In order to achieve this density, Sir Hugh Wilson, the architect and planner of the new town, employed two devices: a larger proportion of flats than had been recom-mended in the Dudley Report (about forty per cent of Cumbernauld's housing takes this form), and a system of layout which was radically different from that of the traditional estate.

It will be remembered that the Dudley Report had suggested the use of the 'branch' system of layout, by which houses are approached by a short footpath leading from the carriageway-road. The branch footpaths of a traditional estate surround an open green which takes the place of the carriageway. The pattern is that of a road or cul-de-sac in which grass is substituted for tarmac. At Cumbernauld Wilson adopted the branch-system, but modified it drastically. He omitted both greens and front gardens, arranged the houses so that they all faced in the same direction, and planned the footpaths in the form of narrow alleys running between the front wall of one terrace and the back-garden fence of the next. This system causes the terrace-blocks to be much closer together than on the traditional estate (the normal distance is about 45 feet). Such close proximity of houses might be

121: Cumbernauld.

expected to cause a loss of privacy, but this problem has been overcome by an ingenious device. At Muirhead Four, Cumbernauld, bedrooms and living-rooms are placed on the garden side of the houses, while on the footpath side the roofs slope down to first floor level. This arrangement means that instead of facing each other the bedrooms overlook the roof of the next terrace block.

The narrow alleyways of Cumbernauld are an extreme example of the 'sense of enclosure' which had been recommended by the manual of 1944. Their narrowness is due partly to the fact that they do not have to provide carriageways for vehicular-traffic, and partly to the fact that since they were not vehicular-roads, they were not subject to building-line legislation. This absence of building-lines meant that front gardens could be omitted, space could be saved and a sense of enclosure achieved. The achievement of a sense of enclosure does not, however, depend only on the width of access-paths and the absence of front gardens. A narrow path would not give an impression of enclosure if it were bounded by low hedges on both sides. The footpaths of Cumbernauld are alleys with houses on one side and high paling fences on the other. This arrangement could easily produce an environment as depressing as that of a Yorkshire mill-town. That this has not occurred is due partly to the admirable manner in which details like fences, paving and door-surrounds have been designed, partly to the variety of space which results from the use of roads and squares as well as of alleys, and partly due to the skilful landscaping of the open spaces.

This landscaping does not take the form of the large greens which are a feature of the traditional estate. The open spaces of Cumbernauld are either parks, lawns surrounding blocks of flats, or small paved courtyards contain-ing one or two trees and a children's playground with a sandpit and perhaps a piece of play-sculpture. The scale of these open spaces relates to their surroundings. It is either small, like the houses and flats which surround a courtyard, or large, like the countryside which lies beyond the town. This relationship of the scale of the open space to the buildings could hardly have been achieved in a traditional layout. Sir Hugh Wilson's version of the branch-system makes it possible for him to design his spaces without the limitations of sight-splays, building-lines or the seventy-foot rule.

Cumbernauld differs from the traditional estate not only in the arrange-ment and design of terraces and open spaces, but also in the use of building-materials. We have seen how the architects of the traditional estate seek variety by changing the materials of walls or the silhouettes of terraces. Sir Hugh Wilson disdained such expedients. His houses are all faced in grey rendering, picked out with white window-surrounds and doors of mulberry-red or olive-green. It might be expected that these dour grey alleyways and courtyards, with their lack of grass, their few trees and their uniformity of outlook, would produce a sordid slum-like atmosphere. This has not hap-pened. Cumbernauld's housing is an excellent piece of design. Whether it can be recommended as an exemplar for future developers is more doubtful.

228

Not many architects and still fewer speculative builders possess the ability of Sir Hugh and his team. Their version of the branch-system of planning could easily fail if it were carried out by a developer without their skill and imagination.

Cumbernauld was not the only example of the experimental housing in the new towns. The Ministry of Housing and Local Government, under whose aegis the earlier new towns were erected, required a laboratory for such experiments, and with this in mind sought to ensure that the development corporations who built them would be more venturesome than the typical municipal housing-committee.

A number of experiments of this kind have been carried out. At Harlow Sir Frederick Gibberd introduced 'point-blocks' (tower-blocks of flats ten or twelve storeys high) in order to give a dramatic change of scale at certain key places in the layout. At Roe Green, Hatfield, Lord Esher designed an estate of terraces which undulate in sinuous curves like Lansdowne Crescent, Bath, or the walls of Borromini's churches; and at Ghyllgrove, Basildon, the same architect broke away completely from the suburban tradition and laid out an estate whose lack of planting and vigorous details are reminiscent of some aspects of Victorian industrial housing.

3 *The south-western area of Peterlee:* One of the most interesting of these experiments took place at Peterlee, in the south-western area of the town. To develop this site, the new town's General Manager called together a team consisting of two architects and an artist. Their brief was simple: 'Do what you like; but don't do what we have done before'. To this was added the proviso that the plans should be 'socially and economically acceptable to the community and to the corporation'.[7] (This was an odd request, since the

122: The south-western area of Peterlee.

community could not decide in advance whether the scheme was acceptable or not. Such a decision could only be made by the corporation and by the Minister of Housing.)

The team began by rejecting the theory of the picturesque which had been the basis of suburbia since the building of Park Village. Instead of winding roads, informal planting and ingeniously grouped houses, their townscape was to be a rectilinear construction of roads, courtyards and buildings whose rigid geometry would contrast with the free-flowing countryside beyond the town. To this theoretical principle was added a practical requirement. The fact that the site was subject to colliery-subsidence compelled them to devise a layout without long terraces or high buildings.

The need to avoid terraces caused the team to design the bulk of the housing in semi-detached units. They overcame the monotony inherent in the semi-detached plan by arranging their pairs of houses around small paved courtyards leading off the highway. The houses were designed with bold details, neutral colours and cubic forms. Eaves were suppressed; roofs were flat or very slightly pitched, while walls were of black or white flint-lime bricks relieved by panels of grey or creosote-stained timber. This cool, vigorous formality was reflected in the design of the floorscape. Front gardens were omitted. There were no verges beside the roads, hard surfaces (concrete slabs, gravel or tarmacadam) occupied all the area between the houses. Trees were used sparingly, and were planted in formal grids which echoed the rectilinear character of the layout. The team decided, apparently without any preliminary social survey, that the back garden is an undesirable feature. They therefore substituted tiny walled yards for the long narrow wire-enclosed gardens of the traditional estate. The land which was saved by this arrangement was formed into communal grassed areas whose flowing shapes and soft surfaces were designed to contrast pleasantly with the hard geometry of the roads and forecourts.

The south-western area of Peterlee is not of course a piece of suburbia in the sense that the word is used in this book. The team which designed it would have nothing to do with the romantic idea that landscape and houses should be fused into a new whole. Instead they created a classical scheme based upon the separation of planting and buildings, upon the right-angle and upon the mathematical unity of a five-foot planning grid. The place possesses something of the clear unalterable logic of a Bach fugue or a Euclidean theorem.

It is here that I begin to doubt the validity of their conception. The essence of classicism is that it is inviolable. It cannot be altered because alteration would destroy its purity. Any housing-estate, however, is subject to changes caused by climate and usage, while one which is situated on the brow of a hill within a few miles of the North-East coast is exceptionally liable to such deterioration. Painted-timber panels and formal grids of trees are peculiarly vulnerable to bleak winds and human wear-and-tear, and a classical project built with these materials and in this location requires

230

constant, unremitting maintenance if its character is to be preserved. Such maintenance has not taken place, and so, when I visited the estate a dozen years after its completion I found it sadly tattered and forlorn. Grass grew between the paving-slabs, paint peeled from the fascias, cars were parked in unsuitable places, windows were decked with garish curtains, and the trees, where they survived, were stunted and bent with the winter gales.

Aesthetically Peterlee's south-western area must be considered to be a brave experiment, but one which failed. It demonstrates the need to choose facing materials and planting which can survive both the rigours of climate and the batterings of humanity; and it shows that the purity of form which is the essence of classicism is likely to demand standards of maintenance and control of usage which are beyond the resources and powers of the municipal developer.

We should realise, however, that the application of classical principles demands more than rigorous maintenance. Classical purity is, as we have said, unalterable, and a classical estate should, therefore remain inviolate from the day of the completion to the time that it is demolished. To ask this, however, is to ask the impossible. Any estate is bound to be altered, as fashions vary, economic circumstances change, and technology develops. We live in a period when such changes occur more rapidly than ever before in history. In these circumstances it seems better to design such places with an eye to flexibility rather than to seek the unchangeable logic of classicism.

Classicism is not however the only, or indeed the most important among the disturbing features of this project. We have noted that the decision to dispense with the traditional back garden seems to have been made without any preliminary social survey. One of the team described this decision in the following terms: 'We decided that we would not tolerate the back-garden mania of the new town, with its chicken-wire fences. We decided that there would be no front and back in the normally accepted way' (p11).

The team recognised that such a decision implied profound social changes, for their spokesman went on to declare that the new planning-concept 'also required new ways of living'.

This attitude of airy contempt for the established social pattern of the estate's tenants is to me most shocking. It may be held that the scheme was an experiment; that fourteen different dwelling-types were provided; that it was designed in accordance both with housing manual standards and with the suggestion (in the addendum to the Dudley Report) that layouts might be arranged so that their houses should have small individual gardens abutting on to a communal garden; that the northeast has the smallest proportion of households with cultivated gardens of any region in England and Wales, and that the estate would never have been built if it had not been socially acceptable to the new town's development corporation and the Minister of Housing and Local Government.

All this is so, but nevertheless an unhappy impression remains. A housing-estate should be, above everything else, a place to live in, but for all its

231

originality Peterlee's south-western area seems to have been designed in a different spirit. It appears to have been conceived as a large piece of constructivist sculpture rather than as a carefully designed background for the varied, complex, ill-organised lives of human beings.

4 *Bishopsfield, Harlow:* A new pattern of layout requires a new design of house. Thus, throughout the first three-quarters of the nineteenth century, semi-detached villas were built, made up of pairs of georgian terrace-houses, but the semi-detached villa did not become the typical suburban dwelling until Godwin designed his houses at Bedford Park without basements. In the same way, the problem of back-door and garden access produced in the terrace of mirrored pairs a block which could hardly be more than six houses long.

This persisted for almost a hundred years as the standard unit of industrial housing, until the *Housing manual* of 1949 showed how such access could be provided through a store-room, and in so doing freed the architect to design his layouts with long terraces; while the narrow alleys and single-aspect terraces of Cumbernauld could not have been arranged as they were if it had not been for the use of a special house-type to accompany them.

The pressure to raise the densities during the 1960s led to the introduction of a kind of dwelling which could be packed together more tightly than the terrace-houses of the orthodox estate. This was the patio-house, a building which, despite its name, is usually single-storied. It has an L-shaped plan, arranged so that living-rooms and bedrooms all face into a small rectangular courtyard, two of whose sides are formed from the arms of the L, the other two being closed with walls to a few inches below eaves-level. The kitchen and front door usually face outwards and are situated close to the corner of the L, while dustbin and fuel store may be arranged in an ingeniously-designed cupboard beside the entrance. The system gives almost complete privacy. All rooms except the kitchen look inwards to the patio, which, because the houses are single-storied, gets some sunshine and, because it is enclosed, cannot in normal circumstances be overlooked. This freedom from overlooking makes it possible for houses to be packed very tightly together, since close proximity does not, in this situation involve any loss of privacy.

The system was used in the Bishopsfield estate at Harlow,[8] a project which was the subject of an open competition devised with the aim of re-thinking problems of housing-design without the restrictions of accepted regulations. Michael Neylan, the architect of the winning scheme, arranged his groups of patio-houses in a star-shaped pattern, radiating down a slope from a central 'citadel' of flats, garages and maisonettes. Neyland's houses are approached by alleyways which are even narrower and more enclosed than those of Cumbernauld (though, like those of Cumbernauld, some of them open out here and there into larger courtyards). There are, of course, no large windows facing these alleys, and the fact that the house-roofs all slope inwards to the patio means that the walls of the alleys are relatively high, and are not

123: Bishopsfield, Harlow.

crowned with eaves. This combination of narrow alleys sloping down a hill, rectangular building forms, plain brick walls perforated here and there with tiny windows and an occasional small courtyard, gives the place the air of a North African casbah rather than that of an English town.

Neylan, like the architects of Peterlee's south-western area, contrasts this tight congested atmosphere with the stretches of open landscape which lie between the arms of his radiating lines of building.

The effect is strange to the eye of one accustomed to the pattern of English municipal suburbia, but its strangeness should not blind us to its benefits. No other system of housing which we have discussed possesses the combination of convenience, economy of land-use and privacy which the patio-house affords. On the other hand, these very benefits are gained at the cost of certain disadvantages. The patio is too small to be used for any other

124, 125: Bishopsfield, Harlow.

purpose than that of an outdoor room. It has space for one or two flower-beds, a babe in a pram, a patch of lawn on which a family can eat outdoors on a sunny weekend, and a clothes-line, but it can hardly accommodate the play of a couple of schoolboys or a greenhouse in which their father can grow chrysanthemums. The patio-house is an inflexible form of dwelling, suited to a family whose children are too young to demand more play-space than a toddler requires, or to a couple whose joy is a small, closely-tended garden, but too restricting in its form for more than a minority of households.

Neylan's combination of the patio-system with the central citadel, pedestrian alleys, occasional courtyards and nearby open-space provides contrasts of spatial-design and creates a hierarchy of play-areas suited to the requirements of different age-groups. It is a scheme of great originality and considerable dramatic power, but it cannot overcome the problems which are inherent in the house-type which it employs.

5 *The Parker-Morris Report:* Apart from Cumbernauld, the first indication that government policy on housing densities was changing occurred in 1961 when the Ministry of Housing and Local Government published a report on housing, *Homes for today and tomorrow.*[9] This study was prepared by a subcommittee of the Central Housing Advisory Committee under the chairmanship of Sir Parker Morris, and, like its predecessors, is generally known by the name of its chairman.

The Parker-Morris Committee declared (p36, para 160) that they were 'given to understand' that advice would be welcomed as to the provision of accommodation for cars and of play-space in relation to blocks of flats. Their studies of the latter problem lie somewhat outside the subject of the present book. We may note, however, that, unlike their predecessors, they did not suggest that flats were unpopular. Instead they accepted the principle that flat-living would increase, recognized its disadvantages, and sought means by which these difficulties might be allayed.[10]

The committee felt that their primary task was to consider standards of internal design, and that layout was outside their terms of reference. Nevertheless, they were 'obliged to formulate views upon it' in connection with the two problems upon which their advice was specially sought. In addition, they discussed rear-access to terrace-housing, gardens and the general appearance of domestic building.

On the question of rear-access to terrace-housing they differed from the conclusions of their predecessors. They recognised the need to provide such access, and declared roundly (p39, para 171) that there was a requirement which 'should not be contravened in any circumstances—the refuse-collector should be able to reach the dustbin-store and the coalman the fuel-store without entering any part of the house'; but they preferred the Radburn system of providing rear-access to the terrace of mirrored-pairs which the Dudley Committee had recommended, and they objected to the combined passage and store, a device which had been proposed in the *Housing manual* of 1949.[11]

Like their predecessors, they stressed the need for architects to be employed in the design of houses,[12] but they did not stop there. They laid great stress on the necessity for good layout and on the need to employ landscape architects in the design team. 'Good layout and appearance . . . cannot be achieved without using professional people, architects and landscape-architects, to design not only the individual house and house-group, but, every bit as important, the layout as a whole and the landscaping . . . Good layout and landscaping together with the use of good and well-chosen external materials and colours throughout the estate go nine-tenths of the way towards creating beauty instead of ugliness . . . We therefore urge those developers who do not already do so to turn increasingly to qualified people for the difficult and indispensible work of designing the buildings, the layout and the landscaping' (p37, paras 162-3).

The committee went on to point out that landscaping has to be maintained, and that maintenance not only costs money, but involves an administrative mechanism to make it possible. 'With notable exceptions, most private development . . . lags far behind that of many local authorities who as landlords can maintain the whole of the estate. It must be admitted that many other European countries reach a far higher standard of private-estate layout than do we, very largely through the use of housing-associations which take full responsibility for both the initial landscaping and its maintenance. There are already in this country established ways of keeping owner-occupied property in good condition by the use of restrictive covenants governing repainting and the maintenance of the landscaping. Non-profit-making companies run by the occupiers can see that the work is carried out and these are proving successful' (p37, para 165).

On the subject of gardens the committee made two important findings: that the present-day garden is often lacking in privacy, and that improvements in the standard of living have changed the way in which gardens are used. They suggested that in all gardens arrangements should be made to ensure a reasonable degree of privacy for sitting out and for outdoor meals, they pointed out that few families now rely on the garden to keep them properly fed, and they warned against serious diminution in garden size. 'It is now used,' they wrote (p39, para 169), 'for outdoor living, for children's play and the baby's sleep: and it is cultivated either for the pleasure of gardening or only because it has to be kept tidy. With the tendency for densities to increase at the same time that space has to be provided for more cars to be kept, it will be a temptation to squeeze garden-sizes to a point where they will no longer cater for these things. The evidence we received suggests that any call for large gardens is declining as other interests, such as the car come to take up more of people's leisure time.'

In this the committee made a serious omission. They do not seem to have realized that gardening is not the only hobby for which gardens are used.

235

They forgot the shed for the teenager's motor-bike, and the cotes for his father's racing-pigeons, and though they mentioned (in the section on kitchen-planning) the need to provide space for a washing-machine, they said nothing (in the section on gardens) about somewhere for the washing to dry.

The most important difference between the Parker-Morris Report and the addendum to the Dudley Report lay in their attitudes to the motor-vehicle. The addendum to the Dudley Report noted that the use of cars was increasing at a very rapid rate before the war, that England had more cars per mile of road than any other country in the world, and that this condition was likely to continue; but its authors declared that they could not 'give any kind of formula to determine the amount of public parking space required. All that can be said is that reservations of space for the purpose should be on a generous scale' (Dudley Report, p68, para 49).

The Parker-Morris Committee were more precise. They pointed out that according to the Road Research Laboratory there will be, by 1980, an average of one car per household in Great Britain. 'Thus in less than twenty years' time, for every car now on the roads of this country there will be three' (p43, para 197). They went on to say, 'Each of these ten-and-a-half-million extra cars will need about two hundred and fifty square feet of scarce residential land or building-space for overnight parking and for access to the place where it is kept . . . in the face of these figures, even if it turned out that the increase was slower than the Laboratory believe it will be, it is impossible to do less than recommend that for every new home built in the future there should be space for a car' (p43, para 198).

The committee went on to discuss the economic effects of this recommendation and its influence on housing layout. They declared that the costs would be considerable—'Studies which we have made suggest that they will range from quite low figures in low-density housing to as much as £300 per dwelling, and sometimes more in the very high density estates' (p43, para 199)—and that 'the over-riding concern in designing with the car in mind must be to design for the pedestrian to stay alive' (p44, para 200). It was for this reason that they expressed (p44, para 201) the opinion which we have already noted—that the Radburn system represents 'the right general direction for the future'.

The Parker-Morris Report is an excellent document, but it is excellent within a limited field. Its value is restricted by the committee's interpretation of their terms of reference. They bore in mind the relationship between layout and internal planning, but they did not consider the influences upon layout of building-line legislation, the provision of underground services and the codes of practice of public authorities. They noted the need for coherent landscaping and for an administrative mechanism to ensure its maintenance, but they did not consider the effect of freehold-tenure on landscape-design. They recognised that design should always be the responsibility of qualified people, but they did not consider the effect of the RIBA's code of practice upon the role of architects in the speculative field. They quoted the Road

Research Laboratory's estimate of future car-ownership, but they did not discuss the effect of technological changes, such as improvements in telecommunications, upon man's way of living and hence upon patterns of development.

Complaints such as these are perhaps unreasonable. The committee had to stop somewhere. They concentrated their attention upon the internal planning of people's homes, a task which is complex enough for any group of men. Had they extended their field of enquiry to include such matters as land-tenure systems, professional codes of practice and the social consequences of technological change their job would have been endless. They limited their studies to those parts of the housing-problem which seemed to be the most important and the most difficult. What they did they did well, but some questions were not considered at all, others were not studied in sufficient depth and, despite the title of their report, their investigations were concerned more with the home of today than with those of tomorrow.

6 *'Residential areas, higher densities': Homes for today and tomorrow* was not followed, like the Dudley and Tudor-Walters Reports, by a housing manual containing a number of standard house types. The Parker-Morris Committee had specifically rejected such an approach to design.[12] Instead the Ministry of Housing published a number of bulletins on such matters as the amount of space needed for various domestic activities and the layout of children's play-spaces in relation to blocks of flats. One of these bulletins, *Residential areas, higher densities*, described a new national policy in regard to housing-density and sought to persuade planning-authorities and developers to act in accordance with it.

The authors of the bulletin declared that there were national land-use policies—the prevention of urban sprawl and the preservation of the countryside—all of which pointed 'to the need for compact development, closely integrated with existing development and making the fullest use of available land'. They added (p5, para 10) that thirteen houses to the acre is a very modest density, it still allows up to 3,000 square feet of land for each house and garden. Densities of up to sixty persons to the acre (net) or about twenty dwellings to the acre are perfectly practicable with two-storey terrace-housing and modest gardens. Densities of up to ninety persons per acre (net) allow an average of about thirty dwellings to the acre, and can be used to provide a good variety of housing types—some two- and three-storey houses, and some three- or four-storey flats—in schemes covering several acres.'

The most important item in the bulletin was a curiously half-hidden statement about optimum density from the standpoint of land-consumption. The bulletin included a table giving details of land needed for housing 1,000 people at various densities. This table showed, inter alia, figures of net population densities[13] varying from 24 to 222 persons per acre, together with the total land-requirements for the populations concerned, allowing eight acres per thousand people for other uses (such as open space, primary-schools and local shops). This information was supplied only in tabular form. A graph can, however, be easily drawn to show the relationship between these two sets of figures. Such a graph is shown opposite. It indicates that increase in net residential density is subject to the law of diminishing returns. Considerable savings in land can be made by raising such densities from twenty-four persons per acre to about sixty, but from then onwards the graph flattens out and an increase from sixty persons per acre to two hundred and twenty-two only saves half as much land as an increase from twenty-four to sixty. Thus a net residential density of between sixty and eighty persons per acre appears to be the optimum from the standpoint of land-consumption.

The authors of the bulletin did not draw this conclusion from their own figures, but they did suggest (p6, para 11(4)) that a density of sixty is likely to be the best from the standpoint of building-costs: 'Once density is increased beyond about twenty dwellings (sixty persons) per acre, development above two storeys becomes increasingly necessary and building-costs begin to rise sharply'.

Though it was unstated, the implication was clear: a density of sixty to eighty persons per acre had taken the place in the official mind of the twelve houses to the acre which had been recommended by the Local Government Board in 1918 and confirmed (in a translated form of thirty to fifty persons per acre) in the Dudley Report of 1944. Furthermore, this density should be obtained by means of compact two-storied developments with small (though the bulletin euphemistically called them 'modest') gardens. This arrangement came to be given the clumsy but descriptive title of high-density, low-rise housing.

The authors of the bulletin may not have been as indifferent to the social implications of small gardens as were the designers of the south-western area of Peterlee, but they paid no attention to this aspect of the problem. Indeed, like their predecessors, the authors of the *Density of residential areas manual* of 1952, they totally ignored the social aspect of housing-density. The reason for this omission is obscure. The authors may have regarded these matters as too touchy to be included in a quasi-political document like an official bulletin, or they may have felt that such discussions should not be included in a paper which proposed a new, and so far untested, idea. There is in any case no doubt that at the time that the bulletin was published, high-density, low-rise housing was still a theoretical concept. Schemes of this kind had been produced on paper, but little or nothing had been built, and it was therefore hardly possible for the authors of the bulletin to discuss the detailed implications of their advice.

It was some time before an appraisal of the new idea could be made. Developers were chary of putting the theory into practice, and it was not until 1968 that enough estates had been built in accordance with the new canon for a study of this kind to be published. In that year the Ministry of Housing and Local Government's Urban Planning Directorate issued for limited circulation a technical study entitled *Land-use and densities in*

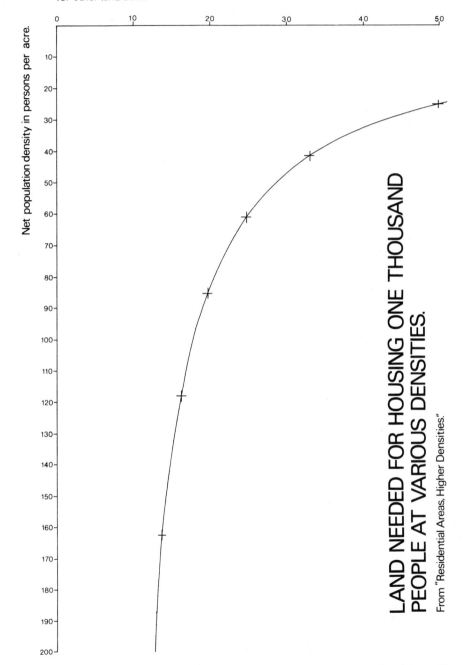

Total land requirement, assuming ten acres per thousand people for other land uses.

Net population density in persons per acre.

LAND NEEDED FOR HOUSING ONE THOUSAND PEOPLE AT VARIOUS DENSITIES.

From "Residential Areas, Higher Densities."

Figure 3: Land needed for housing one thousand people at various densities. (From 'Residential areas, higher densities')

traffic-separated housing-layouts. This essay included analyses of twelve different schemes, nine of which took the form of two-storey development at an average net residential density of eighty 'bed-spaces' (or we might say 'persons') per acre. The schemes illustrated were all densely-textured systems, usually with alleyway-access to the houses in the manner of Cumbernauld, and often including a continuous landscaped belt containing walk-ways to shops and schools and linking such things as infants' play-spaces, blocks of flats with their communal gardens, playgrounds for older children and small public parks. The average area of private garden was 680 square feet—the figure given (p104) is 75.5 square yards—a size which is, of course, substantially less than that of the gardens in the outer-ring development scheme illustrated in the *Housing manual* of 1949.

7 *Garden-size and usage:* The Parker-Morris Committee had warned against serious reduction in garden size, but their study of garden-usage was brief, and very little had been written on the subject since 1959, when Professor G P Wibberley published an account of several surveys of land-uses in private gardens which had been carried out during the war and the ten years which followed it.[14]

These studies showed that at that time the private garden was an important source of food, and Wibberley suggested a density of twelve houses to the acre as the optimum from the standpoint of food-production. Such a density provided gardens which were large enough for the householder to grow a supply of vegetables, while at the same time avoiding wastage of the farmer's acres. Circumstances changed, however, during the succeeding years. Food-rationing became a distant memory, the deep-freeze in the corner-shop provided a ready supply of virtually fresh vegetables, and many men preferred to spend their weekends tinkering with their cars rather than digging their vegetable plots. But despite these changes, no comprehensive studies of garden-usage have been made since the early 1950s.

The lack of information on garden-usage made it very difficult for the Urban Planning Directorate's study to include an assessment of the social implications of the small gardens which it illustrated. Furthermore, the study was, like the bulletin on density, an official document published under the imprint of the Ministry of Housing and Local Government. In the same year, however, an essay on 'Gardens on housing-estates' appeared in the politically uncontentious pages of the *Town planning review* (vol 39, 1968). Its author, J A Cook, was a member of the Building Research Station's technical staff. Cook studied seven recently-built medium-density residential layouts of which five were in new towns and two were in Sheffield. He found (p224, table 1) that 49% of householders with gardens of less than 800 square feet considered them to be too small, but that this figure fell to 21% of those with gardens between 800 and 1399 square feet in area. 800 square feet was also the effective minimum so far as children's play is concerned: 'Few respondents with gardens up to 800 ft^2 can find room for the play generated by three or more children, and many smaller families feel a lack of space. Thus the extent of any reduction in garden-size would probably be limited by the desire to ensure a reasonable level of satisfaction on this score.' He added, however, that 'if other means were available of satisfying the demand for play-space near homes, such as semi-private enclosed areas associated with small groups of dwellings, the small private garden might well be adequate for most current needs' (p232).

Cook went on to consider, but not to discuss, the space-problems which seemed likely to result from increased affluence. He pointed out that 'with more leisure and affluence, people will require more space for the often bulky equipment associated with sports of various kinds, such as caravans, boats, racing-cars, trailers, etc. The storage and maintenance of these items however raise problems of access, noise and visual amenity which it would be very difficult to resolve satisfactorily in the context of the private garden in most housing-schemes. These matters are perhaps best considered as part of the general problem of housing-layouts, rather than the specific one of garden-design' (p233).

Cook's essay is a valuable but limited study in a field which has been largely ignored by planning-theorists. His sample was both small and restricted. He only discussed recently-built new-town and municipal estates with their characteristic social and economic structure and their inevitable preponderance of young married couples and small children. If his investigation had included speculative as well as municipal development, and had been extended to cover the long-established as well as the recently-built estate, his conclusions might have been different. He did, however, raise issues which are fundamental to any proper study of housing, but which were not considered in the somewhat facile recommendations of the Ministry's bulletin.

8 *Leisure and affluence:* Cook's recognition of the need to consider the impact of affluence and of leisure activities on the pattern of housing-development was part of a trend in planning-studies which had been in existence for several years previously.

This trend was launched in 1965 when the *Architect's journal* published a survey, 'The fourth wave, the challenge of leisure,[15] which had been prepared by Michael Dower under the aegis of the Civic Trust. Dower quoted an American report which declared (p123) 'that their population would double, but the demand for outdoor recreation would *treble* by the year 2000. Our own population is expected not to double but to increase by almost half again . . . The flood-gates which have opened in America are beginning to open here, and it seems likely that our own surge of leisure will be more dramatic than the Americans' in proportion to population. Until the vital study of leisure-growth had been made we must assume that demand for active leisure in Britain may well treble within this century.'

Most of Dower's essay was concerned with such things as parks, water-ways and sports-centres, but he did include a section on housing. He declared (p140) that adequate space for leisure both inside and outside the home must push down densities. To explain this opinion he illustrated his essay with a layout plan of the Oakridge 1 estate at Basingstoke, a project to which we have already referred. Dower declared (p141) that the designer's assumptions included the principles 'that 90% of the houses should have gardens, each of 850 square feet, that each house should have a garage, and each two houses a further space for a visiting car, that space should be found for one caravan to be parked for each fifty houses, and one boat for each 200 houses, that one acre of toddlers' or children's play-space and one of allotments should be provided for each 300 houses, and that the estate be threaded by footpaths and small open spaces so that people need not walk on trafficked roads. The result is not only an unconventional layout, but a firm conclusion that these standards can be satisfied only at densities of 55 persons to the acre or less.'

This conclusion was echoed by the authors of *The plan for Milton Keynes* (Messrs Llewellyn-Davies, Weeks, Forestier-Walker and Bor) in 1970. They had conducted a household survey which showed that ninety percent of those interviewed either had a garden and considered it important to have one or did not have a garden and would have liked one. Furthermore, they estimated that sixty percent of the families who were expected to move to Milton Keynes would have children. On this evidence they suggested (p186, para 752) that 50% of Milton Keynes new households should have over 1000 square feet of private open space, that 25% should have 750 to 1000 square feet, that 20% should have small gardens of under 750 square feet and that only 10% should have no private open space at all.

They went on to say (p187, para 759) that 'almost all economic fore-casters estimate that incomes will rise at a faster rate than costs, and the indications are that as incomes rise a large part of the extra money which people are prepared to pay for housing will be directed to securing extra space and paying the relatively small additional costs of the services this requires. In short, present behaviour and preferences, together with costs and income-considerations, suggest that there will be an increasing demand for lower densities.' For these reasons they suggested that densities in Milton Keynes must be determined very largely by consumer-preferences, market-trends and a longer-term view of the quality and adaptability of the housing stock (p187, para 761). They considered that this implied net residential densities of 10 to 12 dwellings to the acre for the early years of the development when most of the houses were to be built for rent, and six to the acre at a later stage when houses for sale were expected to predominate —figures which would provide an average density of eight to the acre for the city as a whole (p31, para 116). They considered that within this average, 'it would be possible to provide a wide range of dwelling-types and environ-ments, by need and preferences, from the close-knit highly-urban quality of flats, terraces and patio-houses to the more open, suburban character of

242

detached houses in large gardens (p187, para 764).

The plan for Milton Keynes was published in 1970, four years before the sharp increase in fuel-costs which followed the Arab-Israeli war of 1974. Today's economic forecasters are less certain of future affluence than those of the 1960s, but if energy-shortages make wealth less likely, the silicon-chip makes increased leisure more probable than ever. It seems that we shall not be short of spare time; and the combination of low incomes and expensive petrol could well lead us to occupy ourselves in growing lettuces rather than in cruising around the country-side in the family car. It is at least possible that the garden will become, as in the early 1940s an important source of food. If that occurs, government could once more regard twelve houses to the acre as the optimum residential density.

9 *Market trends and consumer preferences:* The consultant's conclusion that densities at Milton Keynes must be determined very largely by consumer-preferences, market-trends and a longer-term view of the quality and adaptability of the housing stock was affected by a preliminary decision that 50% of the housing in the city should be built for owner-occupation.

Consumer-preferences were however, seldom explicitly expressed, and the speculative builder whose business required him to provide houses in accordance with these preferences had, for many years, no market-research on which to base his management decisions. In 1968, however, such a study was published. It was carried out by National Opinion Polls on behalf of the National Housebuilders Registration Council, and was entitled 'The new homes people buy and what they think of them'. It included (p13) two questions about consumer-preference. The first was concerned with the type of house which people wanted. It indicated that 85% of respondents would choose a detached or semi-detached house rather than a somewhat larger one in a terrace. The second, which was concerned with gardens, showed that 88% of respondents preferred a private garden of some 900 square feet in size to one of about 20 x 30 feet plus a landscape-garden to be shared with neighbours on the basis of a small annual payment for common upkeep.

Such reports should, of course, be interpreted with care. This one was based upon questions to people who were already living in new houses, 84% of which were found to be either detached or semi-detached. It is at least possible that the respondents bought such houses in the first place because that was the kind of house they liked. Thus the sample upon which the questionnaire was based may well have contained an inherent bias in favour of this type of dwelling. Furthermore, the small private garden combined with a communal open space is a rarity, and it is a safe bet that very few of the respondents had ever lived in such an estate. Mankind is naturally conservative, and one would expect the survey to return a preference in favour of what was known, rather than of what was strange. Nevertheless, so far as the speculative builder was concerned, the report was a conclusive confirmation of the correctness of his established policy. Following its publication, few speculators catering for the mass market would care to risk their company's financial success on projects which either emulated the admirable suburban environments of the Span estates, or sought to achieve the economy of land-use proposed by the Ministry of Housing and Local Government's bulletin on density.

This attitude was expressed clearly in an article in the *Housebuilder* magazine, April 1969, which discussed the work of a firm of developers in Wolverhampton, J S McLean and Sons. It defined their philosophy in the following terms: 'We must always begin with the customer, not with our ideas of what he ought to want'. The author added that whatever terraces were called, and however well they may be designed, 'it seems to be a fact that the majority of people do not want them and will not buy them if there is a choice of alternatives. In certain special locations and individual circumstances they may appeal to a minority market, but throughout the main span of building-demand McLean believe that the private buyer wants: (a) privacy; (b) the definite separation of his house from the others; and (c) the car next to the house.'[16]

One might have expected that the rising land-costs of the 1960s and 70s would have forced speculators to build more densely than before, despite their convictions about their customers' dislike of terrace-housing. This, however, only occurred to a limited extent. We have already noted the National Opinion Poll's finding that 84% of new dwellings sold were detached or semi-detached. This unexpected circumstance arose from the fact that density-increase puts up the cost of land to the developer, but produces a small though discernible reduction in its sale-value per dwelling. Dr P A Stone, our leading authority in this field, declared in an article in the *Estates' gazette*, published in 1964 that an increase in density of five dwellings per acre generally results in a rise in price-per-acre to the landowner, (and by implication in cost-per-acre to the builder) of £2000 to £3000. On the other hand, except in the high-price areas, 'an increase in density from ten to fifteen dwellings per acre might reduce the cost of land per dwelling . . . by £50 to £100 and the corresponding reduction for land per dwelling for an increase from fifteen to twenty dwellings per acre would be about half these amounts.'[17] In these circumstances, the speculator's reluctance to build at the densities recommended in the Ministry's bulletin is easier to understand. He built detached and semi-detached houses not only because he was convinced that the public did not want terraces, but also because the operation of the land-market discouraged development at densities higher than those of suburbia.

We can, I think, conclude that until a comprehensive study of garden-usage has been carried out, any opinion about the advantages or disadvantages of suburban densities as against those of high-density, low-rise housing must be somewhat tentative. Nevertheless, the existing evidence does not support the advice given in the Ministry of Housing's bulletin. Their essay was concerned with the means by which urban-sprawl might be avoided, the countryside preserved, and the cost of building kept low. Had the bulletin's authors paid attention to questions of garden-size in relation to children's play, of the need to allow for changes in the shape and size of dwellings, or of the demands of the speculative market, they would surely have recommended a lower density than that which they proposed.

10 *Social and medical researches:* It must be realised, however, that if the authors of the bulletin had recommended development at suburban densities they would have had to face the belief current in the early 1960s that suburbia was 'socially' sterile.

There was more evidence for this view than appeared in those journals in which opinion was most frequently expressed. Young and Willmott had shown that the inhabitants of 'Greenleigh' lived a life which was less active and vital than that of the inhabitants of Bethnal Green. Dr Stephen Taylor, senior medical officer at the Royal Free Hospital, had discovered in the 1930s that the housewives of suburbia were prone to a disease which he christened 'Suburban Neurosis',[18] and a team of investigators, Drs Martin, Brotherston and Chave, had studied the mental ill-health of the population of a new housing-estate in north London and had found that the proportion of the estate's population which suffered from nervous symptoms was nearly twice that found in a nationwide survey. The team drew the general conclusion that this high rate could be attributed partly to the shock of rehousing and partly to the poor social facilities on the estate, which led to 'a degree of loneliness and social isolation incompatible with positive mental health'.[19]

Later researches suggested, however, that these conclusions were premature. First Willmott went on to study Dagenham and found that as it became established its inhabitants came to possess much the same attitudes, feelings and loyalties that he and Young had found and admired at Bethnal Green. Secondly Drs Hare and Shaw, of the Maudsley Hospital London, questioned the findings of Martin and his associates. They pointed out that statistics of nervous illness are always higher in urban areas than in the country at large, and suggested that the high incidence of nervous symptoms which had been found in the north London estate might have been due to the fact that it was an urban area rather than to any inadequacy in the estate's social facilities. To test this hypothesis, they compared the mental health of the inhabitants of a new estate in Croydon with that of persons living in an older area of the same town. They not only found that there was no difference in the prevalence of mental ill-health in the two sample populations, but also that the proportion of persons expressing a general dissatisfaction with their neighbourhood was about the same in each.

Thirdly, Dr (now Lord) Taylor (the discoverer of suburban neurosis) joined forces with Dr Sidney Chave (one of the team that had investigated the north London estate) in a comprehensive study of mental health in one of the new towns near London, *Mental health and environment*, published in 1964. They found (p174) that 'about nine-tenths of the new population are satisfied with their environment, and the one-tenth who are dissatisfied are for the most part constitutionally dissatisfied—that is to say they would be dissatisfied wherever they were. Full satisfaction with the environment is a matter of time. It takes time to establish strong roots as well as the branches of social intercourse. The longer one lives in any community, the greater the degree of satisfaction.'

Taylor and Chave compared the population of the new town ('Newton') both with that of 'Outlands', a pseudonym for the north London estate which Chave had studied previously, and with that of 'Oldfield', the name given to the London borough from which most of the new town's inhabitants had come. They found (p156) that the incidence of 'nerves', depression, irritability and sleeplessness in a degree serious enough to be trying to the patient, but not serious enough for him to consult a doctor, was virtually the same in all three places; that there was no lack of opportunities for friend-ship in the new town; that there was a much greater degree of visiting each other's homes than had been anticipated; that loneliness and boredom were found much more among those subject to minor psychiatric ill-health than among the remainder; and that these troubles seemed to be due to an inherent lack of capacity on the part of those afflicted to make friends easily (p158). 'We found', they wrote (p175), 'no real evidence of what one of us (Taylor) twenty-five years ago described as " the suburban neurosis" nor of what has more recently been described as "new town blues" (Ministry of Housing and Local Government, 1961). Some people do indeed show loneliness, boredom, discontent with environment and worries, particularly over money. It is easy enough for enterprising enquirers to find such people and to attribute these symptoms to the new town. But a similar group of similar size can be found in any community if it is sought.'

A new town is not suburbia, but most of the housing of Harlow, which seems to have been the 'Newton' of Taylor and Chave's study, is suburban in character, a fact which makes it fair to include their evidence in this discus-sion of the suburban ideal.

Their researches, together with those of Hare and Shaw at Croydon, of Willmott at Dagenham, of Willmott and Young at Woodford[20] and of Pahl at Tewin[21] suggest that the thesis of suburbia's social sterility has little basis in fact. People may take time to settle down in a new estate, and during this period they will probably feel lonely now and then, but man is an adaptable creature and he soon establishes himself in new surroundings. The social vigour of a housing-estate is, indeed, more a factor of its age than of its density, though the designer of such a place can help its inhabitants to settle down, partly by arranging his layout so that people are brought together naturally in culs-de-sac, walk-ways and communal open spaces, and partly by providing easy access to the primary-school, the pubs, the social-centre and the local shops.

It should be realized, however, that facilities such as these need a fairly small catchment area if they are to thrive, and that the higher the housing

246

density, the smaller the area required. It is not easy to provide a good range of such facilities at the densities of suburbia, and this fact seems to contribute the strongest social argument against the suburban ideal. Much research is, however, needed before we can reach any firm conclusion about the complex inter-relationships which must exist between leisure facilities (including the garden and the television-set as well as the pub and the social-centre) and such matters as housing-density, layout-patterns and the social well-being of an estate's inhabitants. Meanwhile, however, we can declare with some confidence that once they have settled down, people seem to be as happy or as miserable in suburbia as they would be anywhere else.

11 *Commuting:* The reader will remember that the cost, discomfort, and waste of time which results from a long commuting journey provided one of the strongest arguments of those who were opposed to the suburban ideal. We are well aware that for most of us the journey to work is a hateful experience, whether it be by means of the crowded bus-service of a provincial town, the black hole of London's Underground, or the mad scramble of a drive along an arterial road. Life would be far more agreeable if we could all come back for lunch. And yet, despite this obvious fact, many men continue to seek houses at ever greater distances from their places of work. They choose to endure the daily discomfort and expense of a long commuting journey rather than to live at a higher density, closer to the factory or the city centre.

Why do they do it?

At a superficial level we can suggest that they do it partly in order to provide as much space as they can afford for their wives and children, and partly in order to give themselves a garden in which they can potter at week-ends. The ethologist may be able to suggest more profound reasons why they make this choice, but it is surely evident that no one would accept such a situation except under very strong pressure. Perhaps the suburban commuter is affected by a human version of the nesting-instinct. In any case he seems to want a little box of his own, and this desire is fortified by the developing technology of communications and the peculiar character of England's housing tradition.

However this may be, the suburban ideal can be regarded as the theoretical principle which seeks to resolve this combination of forces: man's desire for a house of his own and a patch of ground to go with it, the opportunity which the car and the railway provide to achieve this desire in the context of an affluent, technologically-developed society, the accidents of geography which have led to the Englishman's traditional preference for a house rather than a flat, and the influence of the romantic movement on townscape. The ideal cannot, however, be considered on its own; it is a part of a general theory of urban-structure—the theory of the dispersed urban region, a concept which is itself generated by the forces which we have described. Some commuting is inherent in this theory, and any consideration of the validity of the suburban ideal from the standpoint of commuting must bring the theory into question.

In this book, however, we are concerned with tactics rather than with strategy, with the shape and character of suburbia itself, rather than with general theories of urban-structure. From this it follows that the question whether the cost, waste of time, and discomfort of commuting invalidates the suburban ideal, is a matter which lies outside our terms of reference, though we may fairly draw attention to the strength of the forces leading to that urban dispersal which H G Wells anticipated, and the consequential difficulties of devising effective barriers against them.

12 *Aesthetic concepts:* The other objection to the suburban ideal, its alleged aesthetic impurity, constituted a repudiation of its fundamental principle, namely that the architect of a housing-estate should design it in such a way as to establish a fusion of town and country. Thomas Sharp, and those who thought with him, held that these two constituents of our landscape should be kept apart. In *Town and countryside* he wrote as follows (p162): 'Is it not a thousand times more sensible to maintain these two entities of beauty in their full purity, in all their dramatic contrast, setting them off one against the other, than to neutralize them into one thing where they compete and clash in an exhausting disunity?'

The question which Sharp raised is fundamental to the aesthetics of townscape. We should, however, remember that he posed it in 1932, at a time when the countryside of Britain was being despoiled by the grotesque semi-detached villas of inter-war speculative suburbia and the dreary terraces of its municipal counterpart. Today we can, perhaps, be less dogmatic in our approach to the theory of urban-design. The town-and-country-planning legislation of the post-war era has done much to limit the depredations of the developer, and we can consider the problem in a less frenetic mood than was possible to the possessor of a sensitive mind surveying the England of the late 1920s.

In our consideration of Sharp's demand for the separation of country and town we should realize that the corollary of this demand is rejection of the romantic approach to townscape; for the essence of romanticism in the visual arts lies in its idealization of the picturesque, and any picturesque theory of townscape must surely include the opportunity to fuse town and country into a new amalgam.

The battle against romanticism in the arts was lost in the early nineteenth century, and it would be absurd to reopen the struggle. The designers of our cities and countryside ought certainly to provide occasions for the purity and contrast which Sharp demanded, but it hardly seems reasonable to pro-pound a theory of urban-design which cannot accommodate such places as Park Village West, the Span estates, or Kenwood Park, Sheffield. Indeed their very existence shows that an attractive environment can be achieved without that separation of town and country which Sharp demanded.

Sharp spoilt his case by over-emphasis, but there is nevertheless much truth in what he wrote. The tragedy of suburbia lies in the fact that in most suburban developments country and town do 'compete and clash in an exhausting disunity'. Much of suburbia's ugliness is due to factors which we have discussed—its fragmented floorscape, poor spatial-design and futile attempts at landscaping—but behind these matters there lies a more fundamental weakness. Except at arcadian densities, suburbia, like the pair of semi-detached houses which is its most potent symbol, is an example of duality, that 'uneasy balance between two competing parts' to which we referred in the first chapter. The duality of the semi-detached pair is a duality of form; the two halves are mirrored about the party-wall. The duality of suburbia is a duality of content, where neither building nor planting is dominant. This combination of duality, the weaknesses which we have described and the restrictions under which suburbia's designers usually have to work, makes the creation of an attractive environment from the material of an ordinary suburban estate a task of exceptional difficulty.

13 *The Essex design-guide:* A recognition of suburbia's duality, and a rejection, on that account, of the suburban ideal constituted the central theme of a well-produced, richly-illustrated volume entitled *A design-guide for residential areas*, a manual which was published by the Essex County Council in 1973. This document included formal statements of the county council's policies on planning and design, as well as detailed interpretations of these policies and of their implications.

The Essex design-guide was a comprehensive study of the problems of medium-density housing-layouts. It discussed such widely differing topics as ground-cover plants suitable for planting on the verges of arcadia, and an analysis of the statistics included in the bulletin on *Residential areas, higher densities*. Its central theme was a rejection of the suburban ideal. Its authors, Melville Dunbar and his associates,[22] followed the lead given by Richards twenty years previously in his article, 'Failure of the new towns'. They held that spaces and buildings should be designed either according to the 'low-density or rural approach' in which the landscape dominates the buildings, or in accordance with the 'higher-density urban approach' in which the buildings contain the space. They went on to declare (p62) that recent housing development 'has failed to recognize these two basic principles. This has resulted in "suburbia" where there are too many buildings for the landscape to dominate and yet buildings are too loosely grouped and of insufficient height to enclose space. THIS IS THE FIRST AND MOST IMPORTANT REASON FOR THE VISUAL FAILURE OF PRESENT HOUSING DEVELOPMENT.'

The conclusion from this analysis of the suburban problem was that Essex should have no more suburbia. The County Planning Committee accepted this view and their minute of January 26 1973 records the decision (p15) that 'New housing areas shall create a visually satisfactory environment,

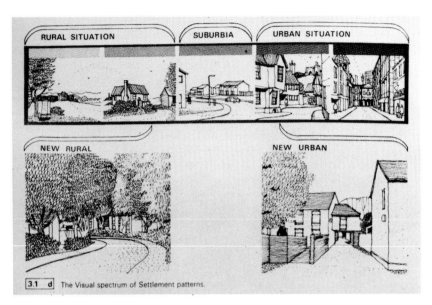

126: The duality of suburbia—a diagram from the Essex design-guide.

achieved by employing either the principles of: i) buildings set within a dominant landscape of a character indigenous to Essex; or ii) buildings set to satisfactorily enclose spaces of individual identity.'

In suggesting ways by which this policy might be implemented, the guide's authors had not only to work within a net density range of 13-15 houses to the acre, a figure which had already been determined by the Country Development Plan's written statement (p22), but also to follow another ruling of the county council—that except in certain special circumstances no back gardens should be less than 100 square metres, or about 1080 square feet, in extent (pp13, 35). They could hardly have managed it had they prepared their essay at the time of Richards' article in the *Architectural review*, but by 1973 circumstances had changed. The Department of the Environment had issued a manual on sunlight and daylight which superseded the seventy-foot rule, and the repeal of building-line legislation had made it possible for the architect to set his houses beside the footway, using the space so saved to enlarge the back garden.

Thus liberated, Dunbar and his colleagues were able to propose that front gardens be omitted and that the space between the house-fronts be reduced in suitable circumstances to as little as twenty-one feet (p84, diagram 4.11d).

Having covered such matters as garden-size, roads and services and the organization of space, the county council's statement of policy went on to deal with the less tangible topic of house-design. It declared (p15), under the heading of 'Regional character', that in order to perpetuate the unique building character of the county and to re-establish local identity, 'development shall generally employ external materials which are sympathetic in

250

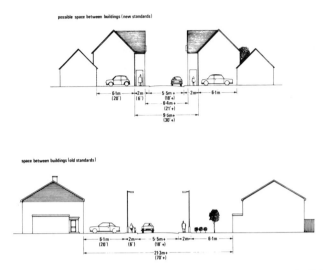

possible space between buildings (new standards)

space between buildings (old standards)

127: Drawings from the Essex design-guide illustrating space between buildings.

colour and texture to the vernacular range of Essex materials', and it also established a set of 'building-design principles' which included such requirements as 'the volumes making up the block form of the building (should be) proportioned and related to form a satisfactory composition', and that 'architectural detailing (should be) used to reinforce the character required by the building and its location' (p15).

To interpret these imprecise phrases Dunbar and his associates had perforce to enter the jargon-encumbered realm of architectural theory. They declared that the statement of building-design principles was 'based on the assumption that the aim in the design process must be to achieve a sense of harmony and repose', and in an appendix they included some notes and diagrams which sought to describe how these objectives might be achieved. They discussed the somewhat arcane concepts of visual ambiguity, unity and duality, root-2 rectangles and additive and subtractive forms, topics which were until recently part of the stock-in-trade of second-year architectural students.

As for facing materials, the guide's authors considered that the re-establishment of local identity should not prove to be too onerous a task for the designer. They pointed out (p72) that most new housing in the county uses traditional forms of construction—brick or rendered walls, tiled roofs, timber windows; 'it is really a question of which brick, which tile, which detail. Within the constraints of the Essex discipline the good architect should be able to produce elegant 20th-century architecture.'

Then, having expounded these theoretical propositions, they showed, in pattern-book form, a set of plans, elevations and housing-layouts which provided case-studies in the practical implications of their concepts.

The schemes illustrated took the form either of arcadian estates or of

251

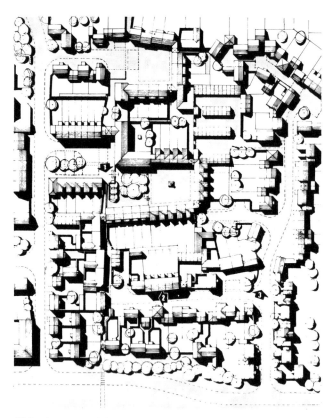

128: A suggested layout-plan from the Essex design-guide.

gardenless roads and paved mews-courts. These were laid out in an irregular, village-like fashion with houses whose steep plain tile roofs, brick or rendered walls and horizontal weatherboards sought to re-create the Essex vernacular. The notes which accompanied the illustration of one of the mews-courts declared that because the buildings would be seen at close range, the quality of materials and detailing must be high. 'The concept of the mews-court is to make possible the creation of high quality, intimate scale, urban places, NOT SUBURBIA WITH THE FOOTWAYS LEFT OUT' (p96).

There can be no doubt that the Essex developers' need to adhere to the guide's canon has greatly improved the appearance of that county's speculative developments. One need only compare the fragmented floorscape, wide indeterminate spaces, and tedious sequence of semi-detached houses at Rylstone Way, Saffron Walden (illustrations 106 and 107), with the unified floorscape, intimate controlled spaces and varied street-pictures of the Chelmer Village estate at Chelmsford to see what a difference the guide has made.

Comments, however, have not been wholly favourable. Lydia Robinson, reporting in the *Architect's journal* on the operation of the Essex guide,

129: *A view in the scheme proposed in the Essex design-guide.*

130: *Part of Chelmer Village.*

253

declared that many local architects dislike its 'mock mediaeval' image and that some regard it as a 'passport to Noddyland'.[23] These remarks are hardly fair. A revived Essex vernacular may not be a suitable symbol of late twentieth-century technology, but it is surely no less appropriate for this purpose than the (presumably acceptable) anglo-scandinavian style, and it may well express society's current disenchantment with Corbusian functionalism. As for Noddyland, any small, two-storied, narrow-fronted, detached dwelling possesses something of the proportions of a dolls' house. A treeless assembly of such buildings can hardly avoid a flavour of Toytown, and if the guide had suggested such estates, the Essex architects' accusation might perhaps have been justified. In fact, however, the guide made no such recommendation. On the contrary, half of its pattern-book designs are for terrace-houses, and the schemes illustrated in its case-studies include a large proportion, perhaps over one-third, of terraces.

Terraces, however, have disadvantages for a developer. If they are included among the closely-packed houses of an Essex design-guide estate, the place will lack the semblance of privacy which is provided by the front gardens and wide spaces of traditional speculative suburbia. In order to compete in the market, speculators have to do something to compensate for this loss. To this end (and perhaps also to provide each home with an individual identity) the estates built by Countryside Properties Ltd, the developers of Chelmer Village, include few of the terraces which appear in the guide's case-studies. Instead their schemes consist almost entirely of detached houses. In consequence, a Countryside Properties estate, though often attractive in detail, appears restless when considered as a whole. The company's interpretation of the guide's canon is a valiant attempt to solve an exceedingly difficult problem, but their estates would be more varied, more

131: Part of Chelmer Village.

254

restful and less Noddyland-like in appearance if they would soften some of their houses' hard surfaces with climbing plants, and include a substantial proportion of terraces in their projects.

14 *The design-guide controversy:* If the Essex County Council's statement of policy had been limited to matters of garden-size and the organization of external space, their guide would probably have created little stir among architects (though speculative builders might have complained that the county council's insistence on a garden-size of a hundred square metres made it difficult for them to build houses which would sell at the lower end of the market). But its discussion of the aesthetics of house-design touched the profession at its most sensitive point. Light-angles, sight-splays and the diameters of turning-circles might well affect the appearance of a street, but they were issues which had long been the subject of bureaucratic intervention. Aesthetics was another matter. Design-control was bad enough, but for bureaucracy to issue general directives about the appearance of houses—that was too much.

The complaint might not have been too serious if Essex had been the only authority to act in this way, but it was not; others followed. In a year or two the production of design-guides had almost become an industry, and by 1976 the professions had become alarmed. In these circumstances the Department of the Environment decided that some facts were required. They commissioned the firm of Llewellyn-Davies, Weeks, Forestier-Walker and Bor to conduct a survey of design-guides.[24]

The consultants circulated all local authorites and a representative sample of house-builders. They found that while about two-thirds of the responding authorities had published standards or policies for roads and car-parking, only a few had gone on to advise on other matters of design—67 percent on roads and parking, 18 percent on general site-planning and 13 percent on detailed design and landscape (p11). The situation, however, was changing. 41 percent of the authorities without design-guides were preparing them at the time of the survey (p20). The consultants also discovered that some authorities had simply taken over parts of the Essex guide (regardless of whether the Essex vernacular was appropriate to their areas), while others had adopted its advice on density while remaining loyal to orthodox highway-standards (p50), a circumstance which must have set some tricky problems for any housebuilder in the areas concerned.

As to the developers, the consultants pointed out that the guides' advices were not based on market-research. Indeed, it seemed at least possible that suburbia provided the nearest practical approach to the ideal image of the developer's customer: 'Do house-purchasers really want a higher-density urban townscape with its inevitable terraced house and garage-courts, or would they prefer "suburban" development, which, although it could be considered visually unattractive, is the nearest to the arcadian idyll which they can afford?' (p51).

The architects' fear that design-guides might stifle creativity led the RIBA to declare, in its evidence to the Environment Sub-Committee of the House of Commons (p442, para 26), that the Institute did not believe 'that detailed design-guides, whether exhortatory or, which is more likely, requiring powers of control over enforcement, are likely to serve a nationally useful purpose', and in July of the same year Eric Lyons, at that time President of the Institute, published a leading article in the RIBA *Journal* in which he declared that he was very positively against design-guides. They were, in his view, a well-meaning attempt, 'and if there were no architects, they would be the right thing to have. But the difficulty is that they establish a set of aesthetic constraints which then have to be administered. No matter how broad-minded the originator of the guide, in the end it has to be administered by "someone behind a counter". All design-guides are like guides to conduct. Either they have to be consulted and agreed, or they will constrain in an unnatural, detrimental way, preventing new ideas.'[25]

It was a natural comment—the opinion of a right-minded libertarian in conflict with the unthinking mechanism of bureaucracy—but it was written by a busy professional man with little time to consider either the philosophy of the guides or their historical precedents.

We have discussed pattern-books earlier, and we should perhaps distinguish the pattern-book from the design-guide. A pattern-book provides the reader with one or more ready-made sets of plans and elevations; a design-guide is a document which defines a discipline of design. There is nothing new in either. Pattern-books existed long before the 1850s, when they began to be published in a form appropriate to the requirements of the suburban speculator; and we have seen how, in the century which followed, sets of plans and elevations were published in the *Illustrated carpenter and builder*, and the housing manuals of 1919, 1944 (which showed plans but no elevations) and 1949. As for design-guides, they have an even more respectable ancestry. From the late fifteenth to the twentieth century, the books of Vitruvius provided every architect in the West with a discipline of design based on the classical orders.[26]

In these circumstances it may seem perverse to complain that design-guides 'constrain in an unnatural, detrimental way'. There have always been regulatory systems in the fine arts, and the adherence to the Vitruvian canon did not inhibit the creativity of Alberti, Inigo Jones, or François Mansart. The problem, however, is not as easy as that. In assessing the validity of Lyons' argument we have to realise first that, following the onset of the romantic movement, many architects rejected the Vitruvian canon; secondly, that even such a formally respectable designer as Palladio was ready, when occasion demanded, to produce an exuberant piece of mannerism (as, for example, the garden pavilion at the Villa Maser); thirdly, that adherence to the canon was hardly ever a requirement of bureaucratic control, though it must often have been a demand of the client or patron;[27] fourthly, that the guides are aimed, not at the creative designer, but at that substantial number

256

of developers who build without benefit of architect; and finally, and most important of all, that the central concern of the guides' discipline is less a matter of architectural form than of the environment as a whole.

Lyons complained that the guides 'constrain in an unnatural, detrimental way', but he did not say to whom, or to what they were detrimental. A constraint which appears detrimental to the architect, thinking in terms of his own particular site, may well be necessary if seen in the context of the street. The street, however, does not consist only of buildings. It is an amalgam of many things, including spaces, buildings, floorscape, vehicles, planting, street-furniture and people. There would be no problem about leaving the job to the architect if every architect possessed Lyons' skill in the manipulation of this amalgam; but it is a sad fact (as anyone knows who has worked in this field) that few of them possess this ability. The RIBA may consider that the 'more responsible use of the nation's expensively-trained designers . . . is likely to be much more effective and much less costly to administer' than the production and administration of design-guides, but the expensive training which an architect undergoes is too often concerned to develop the student's ability to devise an original design on the site 'shown outlined in pink on the attached plan', rather than to provide him with an understanding of how to combine creativity of conception with respect for the confusing mass of objects and activities which together constitute the local urban or suburban environment. The RIBA should have remembered this when they prepared their evidence to the House of Commons' Environment Sub-Committee.

Lyons' other point, that design-guides have to be administered by 'someone behind the counter', is better justified than his complaint that they constrain in an unnatural, detrimental way. The controls which they apply would not chafe so much if they were administered by a wise and enlightened patron, or even by a broadminded architect-planner in the service of the local authority. This, however, seldom happens. Lydia Robinson, in the article on the Essex guide in the *Architect' journal* to which we have referred, reported that while officers at county level, where many of the planners are also architects, are willing to consider new suggestions, 'officers at district level . . . do not have the professional qualifications to use discretion . . . Of the fourteen districts in Essex, only Colchester has an architect working in its development-control department.'

Design-guides and planning-briefs are both attempts to provide positive, rather than negative, systems of design-control. As such they are surely to be welcomed, but welcomed with certain provisos; in particular, that they be well-conceived and administered by people who not only possess the ability and the professional background to interpret them with finesse, but are also able to judge when the guide's canon may properly be ignored. In practice, however, they are not always well-conceived, finesse is not always a characteristic of the bureaucrat, and the officer whose task it is to administer the guide's policies is not often appropriately qualified for the job.

Perhaps for these reasons, the present government has adopted a cool attitude to design-guides and planning-briefs. The draft circular *Development control-policy and practice*, to which we have already referred, does not go so far as to condemn these devices as undesirable, but it does declare (para 18) that authorities 'should not attempt to control such details as shapes of windows or doors or the colour of bricks', and adds (annexe B, para 15) that 'functional requirements within a development are probably a matter for the developers and their customers. For example local authorities should not lay down requirements on the mix of house-types, provision of garages, internal standards, sizes of private gardens, location of houses or plots and in relation to each other provision of private open space.' I am not the one to interpret these phrases in the context of a possible Section 52 agreement on the conditions applying to the approval of a new suburban estate, but it would certainly be difficult to devise an effective agreement of this kind without including at least some of these items. Furthermore, it is hardly possible to envisage a design guide which does not contain such material. It seems indeed that if the draft circular is confirmed (and, if confirmed, is then strictly applied), any positive control of suburbia's design will be denied us. This would be a sad consequence of the secretary-of-state's very proper desire to disentangle the bureaucracy of planning.

15   *The problem of suburbia:* The secretary-of-state will certainly have confirmed or varied the draft circular before this appears in print. We must hope that his decision will not involve jettisonning the two pieces of administrative machinery which offer the best hope of improvement in suburbia's design. In addition we must hope—though not with much expectancy—that during the next few years our urban-design courses will have been modified and expanded in such a way as to provide us with skilled design staffs in our district council offices, and that the council of the RIBA will not only have revised its code of practice to allow architects to operate as speculative builders, but will also have adopted a more constructive attitude to design-control and (should they survive) to design-guides. We should realize, however, that such changes, however desirable they may be, will not dispose of that complex of social, political, professional, economic and technological issues which together make the design of suburbia such an intractable problem.

Some of these matters are likely to be very difficult to dispel. Class-consciousness is the Englishman's most persistent vice, and so long as the municipalities continue to provide subsidized housing, the speculators will find it necessary to build estates which are visibly different from the municipal product; public taste (and with it the taste of planning-committees and building-society managers) will take many years to improve; large areas of similar building do not easily avoid monotony, and the semi-detached house to the universal plan provides what is for many the ideal dwelling—it is cheap to build, it avoids the social stigma of living in a terrace, and it supplies all the requirements of rear-access and a conveniently-situated garage.

Indeed, the evidence here assembled suggests that suburbia offers the most convenient and most practical solution to the problem of family housing. It provides the kind of home which most people seem to want (certainly that which most people say they want to buy). It is not, after all, socially sterile, and on present evidence (which may be negated when we know more about leisure activities and garden usage) its densities seem to offer the best compromise between economy of land-consumption, a manageable walk to shops, pub and school, and the need to provide sufficient outdoor space for children to play, teenagers to dismember their motor-bikes, mothers to hang out their washing, elderly people to potter in their gardens, and families to keep a car and perhaps a caravan or a boat. Furthermore, the changes in accommodation which must accompany increased leisure can be fitted more easily into the loose texture of suburbia than into the tight, rigid layouts of high-density, low-rise housing.

Nevertheless, even if these technical, and social impediments are removed, the central problems of suburbia's design will remain. There are five such problems: suburbia's duality of content, which is an inevitable aspect of the suburban ideal except at arcadian densities; its monotony, caused by the need to provide large estates of virtually identical dwellings; its weakness of scale, caused by the fact that economy and convenience set a limit of two stories to the height of these dwellings, while the cost of land, the need to avoid overshadowing, and the householder's preference for private, rather than communal gardens, deny suburbia the space for tall forest trees; its restless silhouette and formless spaces, which result from a multiplicity of detached or semi-detached houses, and its fragmented floorscape which is caused by man's desire for a garage beside his home, together with the drives and carriageways that are a necessary concomitant of a garage.

These problems have been circumvented in various ways. The architects of Peterlee's south-western area overcame the problem of duality by reducing garden-size, devising a classical layout of houses, and separating their buildings from their planting. At Cumbernauld, Sir Hugh Wilson created a pleasing assembly of spaces by raising the density to some eighty persons per acre, incorporating a fairly large proportion of flats, and ignoring man's desire for a garage beside his house. At Tewin Wood, an attractive arcadian landscape has resulted from well-treed gardens and sparsely scattered houses; in the Span estates Eric Lyons created an admirable suburban environment, achieved by a combination of communal gardens, skilful landscaping and well-designed buildings; while Countryside Properties have shown that an agreeable if restless environment can be created in accordance with the canon of the Essex design-guide.

We should realize, however, that these are all, in their different ways, special cases. The design-guide firmly rejects the suburban ideal, Lyons designed for a limited clientele, Tewin Wood has an uneconomic density of two or three houses to the acre, the high density and large proportion of flats at Cumbernauld make it unacceptable as a model for more than a small proportion of developers, and the architects of Peterlee ignored the social aspects of their problem when they devised their estate.

None of these projects attempts to solve the central problem of speculative suburbia: that of creating a pleasing, restful, well-planted, varied environment of saleable houses at the density of about six houses to the acre which was recommended for the later developments at Milton Keynes. The design of such estates is perhaps the most difficult, as well as the least studied problem in the whole field of environmental choreography. It should provide a worthy challenge to the research departments of those universities and polytechnics which offer courses in urban-design.

REFERENCES

1 *The architect*, vol XVI, 1876, p33.

2 Raymond Unwin: 'On the building of houses in the garden city'. Paper read at the Garden City Conference at Bournville, *Report of proceedings*, London 1901, p70. Quoted by Mervyn Miller in 'Garden city influence on the evolution of housing policy', *Local government studies*, November/December 1979.

3 A T Edwards: 'A criticism of the Garden City Movement', *Town planning review*, vol IV, July 1913, p154.

4 Thomas Sharp: *Town and countryside*, Oxford University Press, 1932.

5 J M Richards: 'Failure of the new towns', *Architectural review*, vol 114, 1953.

6 Lionel Brett: 'The environmentalists', *Architectural review*, vol 125, 1959, p304.

7 *Architectural Association journal*, vol 77-78, 1961-63, p7.

8 The scheme is illustrated in the *Architectural review*, 'High-density, low-rise housing experiments at Harlow', vol 140, July-December 1966, pp36-41 and vol 142, July-December 1967, p367.

9 Ministry of Housing & Local Government: *Homes for today & tomorrow* (Parker-Morris Report), HMSO, 1961.

10 In paragraph 159 (p36) they declared that the pressure on land, and the need to rebuild in city centres is compelling the building of a large proportion of flats; in paragraph 117 (p27) they declared that a higher proportion of the homes to be built in the future were likely to be flats; and in paragraph 118 (p27) they noted that 'The human problem for the future in the design of flats and maisonettes is to provide for people who live in them an environment which is as workable and satisfactory as for people who live in houses'.

11 'We found it to be the universal feeling among the tenants of local-authority houses now being built that if the store contains the dustbin and/or the fuel, the accommodation is insufficient for the kinds of things that the tenant wishes to keep in it. If the store also serves as a passage it is even more inadequate.' Page 23, paragraph 96.

12 'There is no substitute for skilled design and this is obtainable only if qualified people are employed to undertake it. The belief that the design of homes is a job that anyone can tackle with success is entirely without foundation—it is one of the most difficult tasks in the whole field of architecture. Our recommendations are made on the basis that architects must be employed as the designers of houses.' Page 7, paragraph 21. 'There are many standard plans of houses and flats, but to employ one or other of them in ordering the building is to lose half the advantage of employing an architect; for not only does it do half his work for him—it also restricts his scope and makes new and worthwhile

developments in house-design all the less likely. We therefore do not advocate particular forms of plan or revised minimum dimensions of rooms' (p4, para 14).

13 The bulletin used the phrase 'net population density'. In this book I use 'net residential density'. They mean the same thing.

14 G P Wibberley: *Agriculture and urban growth*, Michael Joseph, 1959, pp118-134.

15 Michael Dower: 'The fourth wave: the challenge of leisure', *Architect's journal*, vol 141, Jan-June 1965.

16 L W Madden: 'No more terraces for McLean', *Housebuilder and estate developer*, vol 30, no 4, April 1969, p220.

17 P A Stone: 'The price of sites for residential building', *Estates gazette*, January 1964.

18 Stephen Taylor: 'The suburban neurosis', *Lancet*, vol ccxxxiv, Jan-June, 1938, p759.

19 Quoted by E H Hare and G K Shaw: *Mental health on a new housing estate*, Maudsley monograph no 3, 1965, p2.

20 Peter Willmott and Michael Young: *Family and class in a London suburb*, Routledge and Kegan Paul, 1960.

21 Pahl, *The two-class village*.

22 In an acknowledgement paragraph at the end of the book, Mr D Jennings Smith, the County Planner, declared that the work on the guide was a team job, but added that the 'leader of the team and prime-mover from my department' was Melville Dunbar.

23 Lydia Robinson: 'The Essex Design-Guide: a first-time report', *Architect's journal*, vol 164, 1976, p534.

24 Llewellyn-Davies, Weeks, Forestier-Walker and Bor: *Design-guidance survey*, HMSO, 1976.

25 Eric Lyons: 'Aesthetic control, user involvement in housing', RIBA *Journal*, vol 83, 1976, p266.

26 'Classical architecture needs to be understood in a large and general way, as the most comprehensive and stable manner of design the world has ever seen. It needs to be understood also in detail, as a language with something very like declensions, conjugations and moods, with rules which can sometimes be broken, but only after they have been mastered.' Summerson: *The classical language of architecture*, BBC, 1963.

27 I have encountered only one British example of bureaucracy requiring adherence to the Vitruvian canon and it has already been mentioned (p182).

BIBLIOGRAPHY

ABERCROMBIE, Sir Patrick: *The Greater London Plan 1944*, HMSO, 1945.

ACTS, LOCAL AND PERSONAL: *Russell Square Act*, 38 & 40, Geo 3, 1800, vol 1, chapter 50.

ACTS, PUBLIC GENERAL: *Building Societies Act 1874*, 37 & 38, Vict, vol 42, chapter 42; *The Community Land Act 1975*, chapter 77; *The Finance Act 1974*, chapter 30; *The Highways Act 1952*, 7 & 8 , Eliz 2, chapter 25; *Housing (Additional Powers) Act 1919*, 9 & 10, Geo 5, chapter 99; *The Leasehold Reform Act 1967*, chapter 88; *The Local Government Act 1972*, chapter 70; *Public Health Act 1875*, 38 & 39, Vict, vol 42, chapter 55; *The Public Health (Building in Streets) Act 1888*, 51 & 52, Vict, chapter 52; *Roads Improvement Act 1925*, 15 & 16, Geo 5, vol 94, chapter 68; *The Town and Country Planning Act 1932*, 22, Geo 5, chapter 48; *The Town and Country Planning Act 1947*, 10 & 11, Geo 6, chapter 61; *The Town and Country Planning Act 1968*, chapter 72; *The Town and Country Planning Act 1971*, chapter 78.

ALDRIDGE, Henry R: *The national housing manual*, National Housing and Town Planning Council, 1923.

THE ARCHITECT: vol 16, 1876, p33, *My house 'in' London*, no author credited; vol 104, 1920, p93, *Professional conduct and practice*, leading article, no author credited; vol 104, 1920, p123, *Illicit commissions and fair considerations*, leading article, no author credited.

THE ARCHITECTS' JOURNAL: vol 52, 1920, p152, *Professional conduct and practice of architects*, no author credited; vol 172, 1980, p245, *RIBA poll stalemate*, no author credited.

ARCHITECTURAL MAGAZINE: vol 1, 1834, p116, Comment by the editor in reply to an article on London street-houses and shop-fronts by 'R'.

THE ARCHITECTURAL REVIEW: vol 95, 1944, p3, *Exterior furnishing*, by the editor (who was at this time J M (Sir James) Richards); vol 140, 1966, p87, *High density, low rise*, no author credited; vol 142, 1967, p367, *Private and new towns: Harlow (Bishops-field)*, no author credited.

ASHWORTH, W: *The genesis of modern British town planning*, Routledge & Kegan Paul, 1954.

BAKER, Robert: *On the state and condition of the Town of Leeds (in the West Riding of the County of York)*, see British Parliamentary Papers, The Chadwick Report, p997.

BANFIELD, Frank: *The great landlords of London*, Spencer Blackett, 1890.

THE BARLOW REPORT: see Ministry of Labour.

BARNES, D W: *The Leasehold Reform Act 1967*, Butterworth, 1968.

BARR, A W Cleeve: *Public authority housing*, Batsford, 1958.

BEARD, Geoffrey: *The work of Robert Adam*,

BERESFORD, M W: *The back-to-back house in Leeds 1787-1937*, see Chapman, Stanley D (editor), *The history of working class housing*.

BILLS, PUBLIC: *Leasehold Enfranchisement (by purchase or rent charge) Bill*, 1887, vol 3; *Leaseholder's (Purchase of Fee Simple) Bill*, 1888, vol 3.

BOARDMAN, Philip: *Patrick Geddes, maker of the future*, Carolina University Press, 1944.

BOURNVILLE VILLAGE TRUST: *The Bournville Village Trust*, Publications Department, Bournville, undated (probably about 1939); *Landscape and housing development*, Batsford, 1949; *Sixty years of planning: the Bournville experiment*, Bournville, 1948; *When we build again*, Allen and Unwin, 1941.

BOWLEY, Marian: *Housing and the state (1919-1944)*, Allen and Unwin, 1945.

BRETT, Lionel, (Lord Esher): 'The environmentalists', *Architectural review*, vol 125, 1959, p303. See also Esher, Lord and Llewellyn Davies, Lord.

THE BRICK BULLETIN: *New Ash Green, self-contained and self-controlled community*, vol 8, no 4, p10.

BRITISH PARLIAMENTARY PAPERS: *The Chadwick report on the sanitary condition of the labouring population with local reports for England and Wales and other related papers 1837-42*, Irish University Press, 1971.

BRITTON, J and Pugin, A: *Illustrations of the public buildings of London*, 1825.

BUCHANAN, C D: *Mixed blessing, the motor in Britain*, Leonard Hill, 1958. See also Ministry of Transport.

THE BUILDER: vol 2, 1844, pp370, 371, 385, 386, *London as it was in 1800 and as it is in 1844*, no author credited; vol 7, 1849, p572, *Extension of London*, by Londoniensis; vol 14, 1856, p145, *Paris and London houses*, by JPW; vol 16, 1858, pp629-630, *Concerning architecture and London housebuilding*, no author credited; vol 21, 1863, p98, *Dwellings for the industrial classes, Finsbury*, no author credited; vol 22, 1864, p67, *The Peabody building in East London*, by 'One who knows'; vol 30, 1872, pp623-4, *A workmen's city*, no author credited; vol 44, 1883, pp880, 883, 885, *The artisan's estate at Hornsey*, no author credited; vol 119, 1920, p143, *Professional conduct and practice*, no author credited.

BUILDING NEWS: vol 3, 1857, p1, *A Parthian glance at '56*, leading article, no author credited; vol 3, 1857, pp380-384, *Building progress*, no author credited; vol 31, 1876, p357, *Architecture at the West End*, no author credited; vol 31, 1876, p409, *Building at Hampstead*, no author credited; vol 31, 1876, p621, *The Bedford Park Estate, Turnham Green*, no author credited; vol 32, 1877, p134, *Bedford Park Estate, comical criticism*, letter signed 'the Freeholder' but evidently from Jonathan Carr.

BUILDING NEWS: vol 45, 1883, p398, *Houses and house-hunters*, no author credited.

THE BUILDERS PRACTICAL DIRECTOR 1855-58: published anonymously but generally attributed to Edward L Tarbuck, Leipzig and Dresden, A H Payne; London, J Hagger.

BURNETT, John: *A social history of housing 1815-1970*, David and Charles, 1978.

CAIRNCROSS, A K: *Home and foreign investment 1870-1913*, Cambridge University Press, 1953.

CENTRAL HOUSING ADVISORY COMMITTEE: Report of the Design of Dwellings sub-committee, *The design of dwellings*, (the Dudley Report), HMSO, 1944; Report of sub-committee, *Homes for today and tomorrow*, (the Parker Morris Report), HMSO, 1961.

CHALKIN, C W: *The provincial towns of georgian England*, Edward Arnold, 1974.

CHANCELLOR, E Beresford: *The history of the squares of London*, Kegan Paul, 1907.

CHAPMAN, Stanley D (editor): *The history of working class housing, a symposium*, David and Charles, 1971; with Bartlett, N: *The contribution of building clubs and freehold land soceites to working class housing in Birmingham*, see in *The history of working class housing*.

CHERRY, Gordon E: *Urban change and planning*, G T Foulis, 1972.

CHESHIRE COUNTY COUNCIL Department of Highways and Transportation and Planning Department: *Design aid, housing: roads*, 1976.

CLARK, Kenneth (Lord Clark): *The gothic revival*, Constable, 1928.

COLLISON, Peter: 'The Cutteslowe Saga', *New society*, vol 1, 25th April 1963.

COOK, J A: 'Gardens on housing estates', *Town planning review*, vol 39, 1968.

COUNTY COUNCIL OF ESSEX: *A design guide for residential areas*, 1973.

CRAWFORD, David, in discussion with Melville Dunbar: 'Straitjacket', *Architectural review*, vol 154, 1973, p228.

CREESE, W L: *The search for environment, the garden city before and after*, Yale University Press, 1966.

CROSBY, Theo: 'Notes on a domestic style', *Architect's yearbook*, no 8, 1957.

CULLEN, Gordon: *Townscape*, Architectural Press, 1965.

CULPIN, E G: *The garden city movement up to date*, The Garden Cities and Town Planning Association, 1913.

DARLEY, Gillian: *Villages of vision*, Architectural Press, 1975.

DAVISON, Ian (seminar introduced by): 'Design guidance, a critical review' Town and Country Planning Summer School, *Report of proceedings*, 1979.

DAVISON, T Raffles: *Port Sunlight, a record of its artistic and pictorial aspect*, Batsford, 1916.

DE SOISSONS, Louis, with Kenyon, A W: *Site planning in practice at Welwyn Garden City*, 1927.

DEPARTMENT OF THE ENVIRONMENT: *Sunlight and daylight, planning criteria for the design of buildings*, HMSO, 1971; with Scottish Development Department and the Welsh Office, *Roads in urban areas*, HMSO, 1966; Circular 26/76, *Community Land*; Circular 6, *Land for private development, acquisition, management and disposal*, HMSO, 1976; *Development advice note 1. The development brief: private residential development*, HMSO, 1976; *Development control — policy and practice*, published for limited circulation 1980; *Planning procedures*, HMSO 1978.

DEPARTMENT OF THE ENVIRONMENT, DEPARTMENT OF TRANSPORT: *Design bulletin 32, residential roads and footpaths*, HMSO, undated (about 1977).

DEPARTMENT OF THE ENVIRONMENT, SCOTTISH OFFICE, WELSH OFFICE: *Land*, HMSO, 1974.

DOWER, Michael: 'The fourth wave — the challenge of leisure', *Architects' journal*, vol 141, 1965, pp140-141.

DREW, Edward: 'Plan and elevation for cottage', *Illustrated carpenter and builder*, vol 19, 1886, p280.

DUDLEY REPORT: see Central Housing Advisory Committee.

DUNBAR, Melville: see County Council of Essex; see also Crawford, David.

DYOS, H J: 'Railways and housing in victorian London', *Journal of transport history*, 1955; 'The speculative builders and developers of victorian London', *Victorian studies* (Indiana University), vol 11, Summer 1968; *The suburban development of Greater London south of the Thames*, PhD thesis in the University of London Library, 1952; *Victorian suburb — a sudy of the growth of Camberwell*, Leicester, 1961.

EDWARDS, A T: 'A criticism of the garden city movement', *Town planning review*, vol 4, 1913, p154.

EDWARDS, K C: see Simpson, M A and Lloyed, T H, editors.

ENCYCLOPEDIA OF HIGHWAY LAW AND PRACTICE: Sweet and Maxwell, first issued 1965, added to thereafter at thrice-yearly intervals.

ENCYCLOPEDIA OF HOUSING LAW AND PRACTICE: Sweet and Maxwell, first issued 1958, added to thereafter at thrice-yearly intervals.

ENCYCLOPEDIA OF THE LAW OF TOWN AND COUNTRY PLANNING: Sweet and Maxwell, first published 1947, added to thrice-yearly from 1960 onwards.

ESHER, LORD, and Llewellyn Davies, Lord: 'The architect in 1968', *Journal of RIBA*, vol 75, Oct 1968.

EVANS, C P: *Raymond Unwin and the municipalisation of the garden city*, Transactions of the Martin Centre, Cambridge, 1976.

FERRIDAY, Peter (editor): *Victorian architecture*, Cape, 1963.

FLETCHER, Bannister (Sir): *Model houses for the industrial classes*, Longmans, 1871.

FRANKLIN, Norman: 'Housing from estates to environment', *Architects' journal*, vol 147, 1968, p119.

GATES, B R: *The planner and communal management of open space in new housing estates*, unpublished thesis, the School of the Environment, The Polytechnic of Central London, 1972.

GAZZARD, Roy, with Victor Pasmore and Peter Daniel: 'Housing experiment at Peterlee', *Architectural Association journal*, vols 77-78, 1961-63, p6.

GEDDES, Patrick: *Cities in evolution*, Williams & Norgate, 1915.

GIBBERD, Frederick (Sir): *Town design*, Architectural Press, 1967; see Ministry of Housing and Local Government, *Design in town and village*.

GIBSON, H (estate agent and surveyor): Advertisement in *Ideal home*, vol 11 no 4, 1925, plxix.

GILL, Roger: *Till we have built Jerusalem*, University of Sheffield PhD thesis, 1960.

GINSBURG, Leslie B: 'Summing up', *Architectural review*, vol 154, 1973, p264.

GIROUARD, Marc: *Sweetness and light, the 'Queen Anne' movement 1800-1900*, Clrendon Press, 1977.

GLADSTONE, Florence M: *Notting Hill in bygone days*, Anne Bingley, 1969.

GOODHART-RENDEL, H S: 'The English home in the 19th century', *Architects' journal*, vol 108, 1948, p470.

GRAY, George Hubert: *Housing and citizenship; a study of low cost housing*, Reinhold, 1946.

GREEVES, T Affleck: *Bedford Park, the first garden suburb*, Anne Bingley, 1975; 'London's first garden suburb, Bedford Park, Chiswick 1', and 'The making of a community, Bedford Park, Chiswick 2', *Country life*, vol 142, 1967, pp1524 & 1600.

GROSSMITH, George and Weedon: *The diary of a nobody*, Penguin, 1967.

HARE, E H, and Shaw, G K M: *Mental health on a new housing estate*, Maudsley Monographs no 12, Oxford University Press, 1965.

HAWKES, D: 'The architectural practice of Barry Parker and Raymond Unwin', *Architectural review*, vol 163, 1978, p327.

HAZAN, Joe: *The treatment of aesthetics in urban planning, a comparative study of development control practice*, Polytechnic of Central London, School of Environment Planning Unit, 1979.

HEMMING, Samuel: *Designs for villas, parsonages and other houses*, Thompson, 1859.

HILL, H A: *The complete law of town and country planning and the restriction of ribbon development*, Butterworth, 1953.

HINTON, David: 'An early garden suburb, North Oxford in the 19th century', *Country Life*, vol 156, 1974, p845.

HITCHCOCK, Henry Russell: *Early victorian architecture in Great Britain*, Yale University Press, 1954.

HOSKINS, W G: *The making of the English landscape*, Penguin, 1970.

HOUSE OF COMMONS: *Sessional Papers no 395 1-2 eighth report from the Expenditure Committee Session 1976-77*, vol 1.

HOWARD, Ebenezer: Letter to the *Times*, March 26 1919; *Tomorrow — a peaceful path to real reform*, 1898, republished 1902 as *Garden cities of tomorrow* with preface by Sir Frederick Osborn, Faber, 1946.

HYAMS, Edward: *Capability Brown and Humphry Repton*, Dent, 1971.

IDEAL HOME: vol 6, 1922, p194, *A small country house*, no author credited.

ILLUSTRATED CARPENTER AND BUILDER: *Enquiry by 'Alpha'*, vol 8, 1881, p103; *Notes and queries* columns, passim.

INSTITUTION OF CIVIL ENGINEERS and the Institution of Municipal and County Engineers: *Report of the joint committee on the location of underground services*, Institution of Civil Engineers, 1946.

JACKSON, Alan A: *Semi-detached London: suburban development, life and transport 1900-39*, Allen and Unwin, 1973.

JAMES, Hurford: Letter to *Chelsea news*, May 6 1966.

JAY, G M: 'Terrace of cottages', *Illustrated carpenter and builder*, vol 8, 1881, p249.

JENKINS, Eddie: 'Revisit part one', *Architects' journal*, vol 169, 1979, p586; 'Revisit part two', ibid, p593.

JENKINS, Lord Justice: see Reports of Committees, Leasehold Committee, final report.

KELLET, John R: *The impact of railways on victorian cities*, Routledge and Kegan Paul, 1969.

KLAPPER, Charles: *The golden age of tramways*, Routledge and Kegan Paul, 1961.

KNIGHT AND CO: *Knight's Annotated Model Byelaws of the Local Government Board*, 1883.

KRETCHMER, W: 'The architect in planning', *RIBA journal*, vol 74, third series, 1967, p373.

LADY'S PICTORIAL: vol 3, 1882, p314, *Bedford Park*, no author credited.

LEASEHOLD COMMITTEE: see Reports of Committees.

LEASEHOLD ENFRANCHISEMENT ASSOCIATION: *First annual report*, 1843.

LEASEHOLD REFORM IN ENGLAND AND WALES: HMSO, 1966, Command 2916.

LEE, Charles E: *The horse bus as a vehicle*, British Transport Commission, 1962.

LEFEVRE, G Shaw: see National Association for the Promotion of Social Science, Birmingham meeting 1884.

LIPMAN, Alan: 'Social aims: bureaucratic structure', *Journal of RIBA*, vol 75, 1968, p494.

LLEWELLYN DAVIES, WEEKS, FORESTIER WALKER AND BOR: *Design guidance survey*, HMSO, 1976; *The plan for Milton Keynes*, 1970.

LLOYD, T H, with Simpson, M A (editors): *Middle class housing in Britain*, David and Charles, 1977.

LOCAL GOVERNMENT BOARD: *Housing manual on the preparation of state-aided housing schemes*, HMSO, 1919; *Report of the Committee on Building Construction and Dwellings for the working class* (the Tudor Walters Report) 1918.

LONDON COUNTY COUNCIL: *The planning of a new town*, Tiranti, 1961.

LOUDON, J C: *Encyclopedia of gardening*, 1850; *The landscape gardening and landscape architecture of the late Humphry Repton Esq*, Longman, 1840.

LYONS, Eric: 'Aesthetic control, user-involvement in housing', *RIBA journal*, vol 83, 1976, p266; 'Urban housing', Town and Country Planning Summer School proceedings, 1961, pp62-73.

MADDEN, L W: 'No more terraces for McLean', *House builder and estate developer*, vol 29, 1969, p220.

MANSER, Michael: 'Barriers to design', *RIBA journal*, vol 86, 1979, p401.

MASLEN, T J: *Suggestions for the improvement of our towns and houses*, Smith Elder, 1843.

MATTHEWS, Victor: 'Homes fit for first gentlemen', *Housebuilder and estate developer*, 1969, p224.

MILLER, Mervyn: *Garden city influence on the evolution of housing policy*, Local Government Studies, 1979, pp5-21.

MINISTRY OF HEALTH: *Housing manual 1944*, HMSO, 1944; *Housing manual 1949*, HMSO, 1949; *Type plans and elevations of designs for state-aided housing schemes*, HMSO, 1920.

MINISTRY OF HOUSING AND LOCAL GOVERNMENT: Circular 64/52, *Housing Acts, sale of houses*, HMSO, 1952; Circular 54/70, *Sale of local authority houses*, HMSO, 1970; *The density of residential areas*, HMSO, 1952; Design Bulletin 7, *Housing cost yardstick for medium and high densities*, HMSO, 1963; Design Bulletin 10, *Cars in housing, some medium density housing layouts*, HMSO, 1966; *Design in town and village*, HMSO, 1953; *Land use and densities in traffic separated housing layouts*, Urban Planning Directorate Technical Study, 1968; Planning Bulletin 2, *Residential areas: higher densities*, HMSO, 1962.

MINISTRY OF HOUSING AND LOCAL GOVERNMENT AND THE WELSH OFFICE: *Development plans, a manual on form and content*, HMSO, 1970.

MINISTRY OF LABOUR: *Report of the Royal Commission on the Distribution of the Industrial Population* (the Barlow Report), HMSO, 1940, Command 6153.

MINISTRY OF RECONSTRUCTION: *Reconstruction problems 2: housing in England and Wales*, HMSO, 1918.

MINISTRY OF TOWN AND COUNTRY PLANNING STUDY GROUP: *Site planning and layout in relation to housing*. Addendum to the Report of the Design of Dwellings sub-committee of the Central Housing Advisory Committee (the Dudley Report), HMSO, 1944.

MINISTRY OF TRANSPORT: *Roads in urban areas*, HMSO, 1966; *Traffic in towns*, (the Buchanan Report), HMSO, 1963.

MINISTRY OF WORKS AND PLANNING: *Expert Committee on Compensation and Betterment. Final report* (the Uthwatt Report), HMSO, 1942, Command 6386; *Report of the Committee on Land Utilisation in Rural Areas* (the Scott Report), HMSO, 1942, Command 6378.

MOGEY, J M: *Family and neighbourhood*, Oxford University Press, 1956.

MOTTRAM, R· H and Coote, Colin: *Through five generations, the history of the Butterley Company*, Faber, 1950.

MUMFORD, Lewis: *The city in history*, Secker and Warburg, 1961.

MUTHESIUS, Hermann: *Das Englische Haus*, (3 vols), Berlin, 1905/5.

NATIONAL ASSOCIATION FOR THE PROMOTION OF SOCIAL SCIENCE: *Transactions, Birmingham meeting 1884, Sheffield meeting 1865, Cheltenham meeting 1878*.

NATIONAL OPINION POLLS: *The new homes people buy and what they think of them*, National Housebuilders Registration Council, 1968.

NATIONAL UNIONIST ASSOCIATION OF CONSERVATIVE AND LIBERAL UNIONIST ORGANIZATIONS: *History of housing reforms* 1913.

NOBLE, James: *The professional practice of architects*, John Weale, 1836; with Evans, Keith and Whitaker, Ron, see Ministry of Housing Design Bulletin 32, *Residential roads and footpaths*, HMSO, 1977.

OLSEN, Donald J: *The growth of victorian London*, Penguin, 1979; *Town planning in London: the eighteenth and nineteenth centuries*, Yale University Press, 1964.

OSBORN, Sir Frederick: see Howard, Ebenezer, *Tomorrow — a peaceful path to real reform*; and Whittick, Arnold: *The new towns — the answer to megalopolis*, Leonard Hill, 1963.

PAHL, R E: 'The two-class village' *New society*, vol 3, February 27th 1964; *Urbs in rure, the metropolitan fringe in Hertfordshire*, LSE Geographical Papers no 2, 1964.

PAPWORTH, John B: see Britton, J and Pugin, A: *Illustrations of the public buildings of London*.

PARKER, Barry: article on Raymond Unwin in the *Dictionary of national biography*, 1931-1940, p877.

PARKER-MORRIS REPORT: see Central Housing Advisory Committee.

PEPPER, Simon: 'The garden city legacy', *Architectural review*, vol 163, 1978, p321; with Swenarton, Mark: 'Garden suburbs for munition workers 1915-18', *Architectural review*, vol 163, 1978, p366.

PEVSNER, Nikolaus (Sir): 'Model houses for the labouring classes', *Architectural review*, vol 93, 1943, p119; see also Ferriday, Peter (editor), *Victorian architecture*.

PLANNING ADVISORY GROUP: *The future of development plans*, HMSO, 1965.

POOLE, Melville: *The Portman Estate 1952*, unpublished thesis in Westminster City Library Archives Department.

POTTER, Margaret and Alexander: *Houses*, John Murray, 1973.

PRICE, Seymour J: *Building societies, their origin and history*, Franey & Co, 1958.

PURDOM, C B: *The garden city*, Dent, 1913.

RASMUSSEN, Steen Eiler: *London: the unique city*, Cape, 1937.

REISS, Richard: *The Hampstead Garden Suburb, its achievements and significance*, Hampstead Garden Suburb Trust, 1937; *The home I want*, Hodder and Stoughton, undated (probably about 1919); *Municipal and private enterprise housing*, Dent, 1945.

REPORTS OF COMMITTEES: *Design and layout of roads in built up areas*, Ministry of War Transport, HMSO, 1946; *The design of dwellings*, see Central Housing Advisory Committee; *Eighth report from the Expenditure Committee Session 1976-77*, Sessional Papers, no 395 1-2, 1976-77; *Expert Committee on Compensation and Betterment final report* (the Uthwatt Report); see Ministry of Works and Planning; *Homes for today and tomorrow* (the Parker Morris Report), see Central Housing Advisory Committee; *Leasehold Committee final report*, HMSO, 1950; *Report of the Committee on Building Construction and Dwellings for the Working Class* (the Tudor-Walters Report), Reports from Commissioners 1918, vol 7; *Report of the Committee on Land Utilization in Rural Areas* (the Scott Report), see Ministry of Works and Planning; *Report of the Royal Commission of the Distribution of the Industrial Population* (the Barlow Report), see Ministry of Labour; *Report of the Select Committee Appointed to Consider the Housing of the Working Classes Amendment Bill 1906*, vol 9; *Report of the Select Committee on Town Holdings*, Reports from Committees 1887, vol 13.

RICHARDS, J M (Sir James): see *Architectural review*, 'Exterior furnishing'; *The castles on the ground, the anatomy of suburbia*, John Murray, 1973; 'Failure of the new towns', *Architectural review*, vol 114, 1953, p29.

RITTER, Paul: *Planning for man and motor*, Pergamon, 1964.

ROBERTS, Henry: *The model houses for families built in connection with the Great Exhibition of 1851 by command of His Royal Highness Prince Albert, KG*, Society for Improving the Condition of the Labouring Classes, 1851.

ROBERTS, Neal Alison: *The reform of planning law*, Macmillan, 1976.

ROBINSON, Lydia: 'The Essex Design Guide, a first time report', *Architect's journal*, vol 164, 1976, p534.

ROSSI, Hugh: *Shaw's Guide to the Community Land Act 1975*, Shaw and Sons, 1976.

ROWAN, Alistair: 'After the Adelphi, forgotten years in the Adams brothers' practice', *Royal Society of Arts journal*, vol 122, 1974, p659.

ROYAL ACADEMY OF ARTS: *Lord Leverhulme*, 1980.

ROYAL INSTITUTE OF BRITISH ARCHITECTS: *Design pays*, report of symposium, 1958; 'Draft of amended code of professional conduct', *RIBA journal*, vol 87, 1980. pp83-84; 'Professional conduct and practice', *RIBA journal*, vol 27, 1920, p423; *The resource costs of planning*, evidence submitted to the Environmental sub-committee of the House of Commons Expenditure Committee, House of Commons Sessional Papers no 395 1-2, 1976-77, p449; 'The case for professionalism' (the institute's evidence to the Monopolies Commission), *RIBA journal*, vol 76, 1969, p57.

ROYAL TOWN PLANNING INSTITUTE: 'Current trends of the Town Planning Institute's member and associate classes', *Journal of the Town Planning Institute*, vol 53, 1967, p245.

RUSKIN, John: Letter to *Pall Mall Gazette*, March 16th 1872.

SACHS, H: *A study of New Ash Green*, Social Research Unit, Centre for Environmental Studies, unpublished, undated (about 1970).

SAINT, Andrew: *Richard Norman Shaw*, Yale University Press, 1976.

SAUNDERS, G L: see National Association for the Promotion of Social Science, Sheffield meeting, 1865.

SEGAL, Walter: 'Frontage and privacy in terrace housing', *Architectural design and construction*, vol 13, 1943, p202.

SEYMOUR PRICE, J: *Building societies, their origin and history*, Franey & Co, 1958.

SHANKLAND, COX & Associates: *Private housing in London; people and environment in three Wates' housing schemes*, undated (about 1969).

SHARP, Thomas: *The anatomy of the Village*, Penguin, 1946; see Ministry of Housing and Local Government, *Design in town and village*; *English panorama*, Dent, 1936; *Town and countryside*, Oxford University Press, 1932.

SHAW, G K: see Hare, E H.

SIMMONS, Jack: *Transport: a visual history of modern Britain*, Vista Books, 1962.

SIMPSON, M A and Lloyd, T H (editors); *Middle class housing in Britain*, David and Charles, 1977.

SITTE, Camillo: *The art of building cities*, translated by Charles T Stewart, Reinhold Publishing Corporation, 1945.

SNELL, Charles: *Modern suburban homes*, Batsford, 1903.

SOUTH COAST LAND AND RESORT COMPANY LTD: Advertisement in *Ideal home*, vol 6, July 1922, pix.

SPENCE, Sir Basil: 'Inaugural address as President of the RIBA', *RIBA journal*, third series vol 66, 1958/59, p48.

STATHAM, Heathcote: see National Association for the Promotion of Social Science, Cheltenham meeting, 1878.

STEIN, Clarence: *Toward new towns for America*, Liverpool University Press, 1958.

STONE, P A: 'The price of sites for residential building', *Estates gazette*, Jan-March 1964, p85.

STREET, J: 'How to succeed in gardening', *New society*, vol 2, 1963, p9.

SUMMERSON, John (Sir): *Architecture in Britain 1530-1830*, Penguin, 1953; 'The beginnings of Regent's Park', *Architectural history*, (Journal of the Society of Architectural Historians of Great Britain), vol 20, 1977, p56; *The classical language of architecture*, BBC, 1963; *Georgian London*, Penguin, 1962; *John Nash, architect to King George IV*, Allen and Unwin, 1935; 'The London suburban villa', *Architectural review*, vol 104, 1948, pp63-72.

SURVEY OF LONDON (vol 36): *The Parish of St Paul Covent Garden*, Athlone Press, 1970.

SUTCLIFFE, Anthony (Editor): *Multi-storey living*, Croom Helm, 1974.

TARN, John Nelson: *Five per cent philanthropy*, Cambridge University Press, 1973; 'Some pioneer suburban housing estates', *Architectural review*, vol 143, 1968, p367; *Working class housing in 19th-century Britain*, Lund Humphreys for the Architectural Association, 1971.

TAYLOR, Stephen (Lord Taylor): 'The suburban neurosis', *Lancet*, vol 234, 1968, p759; and Chave, Sidney: *Mental health and environment*, Longmans, 1964.

THOMPSON, F M L: *Hampstead, building a borough*, Routledge and Kegan Paul, 1974.

THOMPSON, Morris: 'Professional conduct and practice', letter to the *RIBA journal*, vol 27, third series, 1920, p450.

THORNS, David C: *Suburbia*, Paladin, 1973.

THE TIMES: Article on history of housing reform, December 4th 1913, no author credited.

TOWN PLANNING REVIEW: 'Government housing scheme, Woolwich', vol 6, 1915-16, p147, no author credited.

TREBLE, J H: *Liverpool working-class housing 1801-51*, see Chapman, Stanley D (editor). *The history of working class housing*.

THE TUDOR WALTERS REPORT: see Local Government Board.

UNWIN, Raymond: *Cottage plans and common sense*, Fabian Tract no 109, Fabian Society, 1902; *Nothing gained by overcrowding*, Garden Cities and Town Planning Association, 1912; *Town planning in practice*, T Fisher Unwin, 1909; and Parker, Barry: *The art of building a home*, Longmans, 1901.

THE UTHWATT REPORT: see Ministry of Works and Planning.

VINCENT, John: *Country cottages*, 1860.

WELLS, H G: *Anticipations of the reaction of mechanical and scientific progress upon human life and thought*, Chapman & Hall, 1902.

WHITE, H P: *A regional history of the railways of Great Britain; volume II Southern England*, David & Charles, 1964.

WIBBERLEY, G P: *Agriculture and urban growth, a study of the competition for rural land*, Michael Joseph, 1959.

WILLMOTT, Peter: *The evolution of a community, a study of Dagenham after 40 years*, Routledge & Kegan Paul, 1963; and Young, Michael (Lord Young): *Family and class in a London suburb*, Routledge & Kegan Paul, 1960.

WINSER, J K: 'Varieties and manufacture', *Architectural review* (special issue about bricks) vol 79, 1936, p229.

WOHL, A S: *The housing of the working classes in London 1815-1914*, see Chapman, S D (editor), *The history of working class housing*.

WYRARDSBURY, Hieronimo: 'Squares and villas', letter to *Building news*, vol 4, 1858, p606.

YORKE, F R S: *The modern house in England*, Architectural Press, 1937.

YOUNG, Michael (Lord Young) and Willmott, Peter: *Family and kinship in East London*, Penguin, 1962.

INDEX

White, H P, 121-2
Wibberley, Professor G P, 240
Width of streets, 159
Wilkinson, William, 132, 138, 189
Willmott, Peter, 225-6, 245, 246
Wilson, Sir Hugh, and Cumbernauld, 227-9, 259
Wistaston, Cheshire, ribbon development, 117
Wohl, A S, 76
Woking, 122, 123, 136
Wollaton Park Estate, Nottingham, 113-14, 116, 159
Wood, Edgar, 18
Wood, John, Senior and Junior, 9-11, 133, 138, 176, 214

Wood Green, 78; Noel Park Estate, 71, 72, 85
Woodford, 246
Woodland estates, 139-40
Working-class speculative housing, 47-50; London 'rookeries', 47, 51
Workmen's fares, 77-8
Wormwood Scrubs, Old Oak Estate, 91-2
Wright, Henry, 167
Wythenshawe Estate, Manchester, 2, 110

Yorkshire: South, 197; West, 197
Young, Michael (Lord Young), 225-6, 245, 246